OPENING THE DRAWER

In memory of my parents

OPENING THE DRAWER
The Hidden Identities of Polish Jews

BARRY COHEN
Photographs by Witold Krassowski

VALLENTINE MITCHELL
LONDON • CHICAGO, IL

First published in 2018 by Vallentine Mitchell

Catalyst House,
720 Centennial Court,
Centennial Park, Elstree WD6 3SY, UK

IPG, 814 N. Franklin Street,
Chicago, IL 60610

www.vmbooks.com

Copyright for this edition © 2018 Vallentine Mitchell
Text Copyright © 2018 Barry Cohen
Photographs Copyright © 2018 Witold Krassowski

British Library Cataloguing in Publication Data:
An entry can be found on request

ISBN 978 1 910383 81 0 (Paper)
ISBN 978 1 910383 82 7 (Ebook)

Library of Congress Cataloging in Publication Data:
An entry can be found on request

All rights reserved. No part of this publication may be reproduced in any form or by any means, electronic, mechanical, photocopying, reading or otherwise, without the prior permission of Vallentine Mitchell & Co. Ltd.

Printed by IPG, Chicago, IL

CONTENTS

Foreword by Antony Polonsky   x

Introduction   1

PART 1
Children of the Holocaust

Aleksandra (Ola) Leliwa-Kopystyńska	11
Helena Tos	17
Romuald Jakub Weksler-Waszkinel	23
Maria Rochowicz-Lewandowska	33
Joanna Sobolewska-Pyz	39
Róża Górska	45
Tomasz Prot	53
Jadwiga Gałązka	59
Jerzy Bander	65
Janina 'Nina' Griebel	71
Maciej Czarniecki	77
Anna Szpanowska	80

PART 2
Second Generation

Jarosław Górnicki	85
Agnieszka Markowska	91
Piotr Kowalik	97
Barbara Czachowska	105
Danuta Celińska-Cedro	111
Monika Rakusa	117
Piotr Stasiak	123

Ewa Wolańczyk	127
Jacek Młynarski	135
Zygmunt Stępiński	141
Robert Chmielewski	147
Ania Boros	153
Leszek (Lesław) Piszewski	159
Joanna Tarasiewicz	169
Artur Davidson	175
Barbara Rogowska	179
Jacek Jurkowski	183
Piotr Kadlčik	187
Viktoria Korb	193
Zbyszek Sokulski	197

PART 3
Third Generation

Jan Kirschenbaum	203
Jakub Wasilewicz	209
Karolina Wańtuch-Gazda	215
Magda Gudzińska	223
Marta Ansilewska	227
Emil Jeżowski	233
Krzysztof Gutkowski	239
Gosia Szymańska-Weiss	247
Paweł Bramson	253
Katka Reszke	258
Jakub Gruszczyński	267
Hanna Olszewska	273
Łukasz Godlewski	279
Kamil Marczak	283
Olga Lewińska	289
Izabela (Iza) Wojnarowicz	293

Justyna Szpanowska	297
Andrzej Jankowski	301
Paula Tonder	309
Esther Fuerster	312
Eryk Kowalski	315
Acknowledgements	321

FOREWORD

We are the third generation that is shaking off the trauma of the Holocaust that our grandparents – and even our parents – carried with them. We are far more comfortable than previous generations in expressing our Jewish identity. At the same time I don't believe in the Orthodox or Conservative approach, which insists that you must find a Jewish partner to maintain a Jewish life in Poland. We have a young community of people who have some kind of Jewish identity, as well as a lot of energy to develop something positive. We expect our community to grow.

Kamil Marczak

This important and moving book is an account, through the words of those involved in it, of the revival of Jewish life in Poland since the negotiated end of communism in 1989. During the period of communist rule, which began in 1944, it proved impossible to establish a viable Jewish community. Only 400,000 of the estimated pre-war Jewish population in 1939 of 3,330,000 were still alive at the end of the war, of whom perhaps 50,000 had survived in Poland. Not all of them returned to Poland from the Soviet Union, where the largest proportion had survived. As a result, in the immediate post-war period the Jewish population of the country numbered perhaps 250,000. They were, for the most part, resettled in the western territories acquired from Germany as was the case with many of those who contributed to this volume. Łódź, the largest undestroyed city in the country, also became a major Jewish centre. Many of the Jews who had survived were unwilling to remain in a country where most of their relatives and friends had perished, while their experience of the Soviet Union made them unwilling to live under a communist dictatorship. They were, moreover, threatened by a wave of anti-Jewish violence, in which between 650 and 2,000 Jews lost their lives.

The violence was the result of a number of factors. The war had not brought an end to anti-semitism or seriously compromised the anti-semitic ideology, since the Nazis had persecuted the Polish radical Right, the main supporters of anti-semitism in Poland, as fiercely as they did all other manifestations of Polish resistance to their rule. In addition, anti-semitism had been deliberately encouraged by the Nazis and intensified by the long-standing identification of Jews with communism. This was reinforced by the belief in extensive Jewish collaboration with the Soviet occupying authorities in eastern Poland between 1939 and 1941 and by the presence of a number of people of Jewish origin in prominent positions in the post-war government. In these circumstances, old superstitions could take on a new incarnation. The worst outbreak of anti-Jewish violence took place in Kielce in July 1946, when the 200 survivors of the pre-war community of around 18,000 were attacked by an angry mob, incited by rumours that a Christian boy had been abducted by the Jews, who needed his blood because their wartime experiences had left them anaemic. In the ensuing mayhem 42 Jews were murdered and another 30 were murdered in the vicinity of the town.

In all, by 1950, more than 180,000 Jews had left the country, most of them going to Israel, leaving an estimated number in Poland in 1955 of between 72,000 and 80,000. Some have questioned whether this remnant could be described as a functioning community. Certainly only a small proportion declared themselves Jewish in their personal documents, or belonged to one of the two Jewish communal organizations. In effect, what made them Jewish was that they were so regarded by the surrounding society and the authorities.

The years 1956–1958 saw a further emigration of Jews from Poland, which continued into the early 1960s. This was caused, at least in part, by a sense of insecurity arising out of the open expression of anti-Jewish sentiments, which accompanied the crisis that brought Gomułka to power. In addition, migration had been halted in 1951, and many of those who had wanted to leave then now took the opportunity to do so. So too did many of the 18,000 Jews who were able to return to Poland (along with another 249,000 Poles) under the new repatriation agreement with the Soviet Union signed in November 1956. By the early 1960s, the Jewish population had stabilized at somewhere between 22,000 and 35,000, most of whom had no affiliation with the organized Jewish institutions.

A further exodus took place as a consequence of the 'anti-Zionist' campaign of 1968 in which some 9,000 people lost their jobs, the great majority of them Jews. At this time, more than 15,000 Jews and non-Jewish family members left Poland for Israel, Western Europe, and North America. Those who left were given a travel document stating that the bearer was 'not a Polish citizen' and were required to declare that their destination was Israel, where only approximately a quarter of them settled. Many of those who contributed to this volume allude to this stressful and troubling period.

The historian Jan Tomasz Gross has characterized fear as the main emotion felt by those Jews in Poland in the immediate post-war years who had survived the Holocaust. It is certainly true that the anti-Jewish violence and the problems inherent in regaining property taken during the war created serious difficulties for Jewish survivors. At the same time, there was also hope, shared by many Poles, that the new Poland would prove democratic and pluralistic and that it would be possible to find a place in it for the surviving Jews. The key factor in the revival of Jewish life was the Central Committee of Jews in Poland (Centralny Komitet Żydów w Polsce; CKŻP), which had the support of a number of international Jewish organizations, above all the American Jewish Joint Distribution Committee. One of the main preoccupations of the Jewish leadership in Poland and its foreign supporters was to create a stable economic base for the surviving Jews. A significant proportion of the funds from outside also went to support the Jewish school system. A major concern of the Jewish organizations in post-war Poland was to provide for those children who had survived and also to reclaim children who had been adopted by non-Jewish families or were being sheltered in convents. An umbrella Zionist organization, Koordynacja, was established to find such children, and until April 1948 more than 1,000 lived at some stage in its homes. There was also strong competition between the Zionists and the communists for control of orphaned children.

Apart from the Orthodox, all the main Jewish political groupings were represented on the CKŻP, the Zionists, the Bundists, and the communists and this became the main arena for the political conflicts on the Jewish street. When it was formed in Lublin late in 1944, it had a clear Zionist majority. In 1946, as a result of negotiations between the various Jewish groupings, its presidium was made up of thirteen Zionists, four Bundists, six communists, and two representatives of the Union of Jewish Partisans (Związek Partyzantów Żydowskich) (the Orthodox Agudah and Mizrahi parties refused to participate because of the failure of the CKŻP to observe the Sabbath). In addition, the needs of religious Jews were catered for by the Organizational Committee of Jewish Religious Associations (Komitet Organizacyjny Żydowskich Zrzeszeń Religijnych), which was soon renamed the Jewish Religious Congregation (Kongregacja Wyznania Mojżeszowego) and which, in August 1949, became the Religious Union of the Jewish Faith (Związek Religijny Wyznania Mojżeszowego).

Attempts were also made to revive Jewish culture. The most successful was the project to document the tragic fate of the Jews during the war. On 29 August 1944, barely a month after the liberation of Lublin, a group of five Polish Jews established the Historical Commission (Komisja Historyczna), affiliated to the Jewish Committee, which four months later was reorganized as the Central Jewish Historical Commission in Poland. It sought to collect testimonies from the survivors, calling on them to assist by 'immediately delivering [to the members of the Commission] any materials at present in private hands' and providing accounts of their wartime experiences, since 'each and every Jew that has remained alive is a part of history'. The importance of these testimonies is highlighted by a number of the contributions to this volume. Subsequently, many memorial books (*yizker-bukher*) were produced, almost all outside Poland, which both allowed the expression of collective trauma and provided valuable information to historians.

The history of Polish Jewry, like the history of Poland itself, took a radical new turn with the communist establishment of a monopoly of power in 1947. The authorities now proceeded, under the close supervision of the Kremlin, to impose their own 'solution' to the 'Jewish question,' which involved the suppression of all groups not under direct communist control. In February 1949, the CKŻP was taken over by the communists, and its chairman, Emil Sommerstein, and a number of other non-communist members, including Adolf Berman, the brother of Jakub Berman, the *eminence grise* of the regime, responsible for propaganda, ideology and the security services. Like the Polish Socialist Party, the Bund was forced to unite with the Polish Workers' Party (Polska Partia Robotnicza; PPR), and all independent Jewish newspapers were suppressed. From the second half of 1948 the Jewish faction of the PZPR, like the party as a whole, began to attack Zionism much more aggressively and in July 1949, the Ministry of Public Administration prohibited the organization of Zionist summer camps. In the autumn, all Zionist parties were banned. In April 1949, the various Jewish school networks, which now had around 3,000 Jewish pupils (60 per cent of the Jewish age cohort) in 18 schools, were taken over by the government. In October 1950, the CKŻP merged with the Jewish Art and Cultural Society (Żydowskie Towarzystwo Kultur; ŻTK) , which had been set up in autumn 1947 to form the Jewish Social and Cultural Organization (Towarzystwo

Społeczno-Kulturalne Żydów; TSKŻ), firmly under communist control and with no political role. Already in the previous year the Joint Distribution Committee had been compelled to halt its activities in Poland.

One of the most disputed issues in the historiography of this period is the role played by communists of Jewish origin in the new regime, a subject which comes up in a number of the contributions to this volume. The war had certainly strengthened the perceived identification of Jews with communism. In their hope that the new regime would remedy the defects of the Second Republic, Jewish supporters of the new order were at one with a significant part of the Polish intelligentsia. In addition, in the near civil war conditions of post-war Poland the Jewish community could expect protection only from the new communist-dominated authorities.

Communists of Jewish origin played a significant, though not dominant, role in the new regime. In the political apparatus, they included Jakub Berman, Roman Zambrowski, who had been one of the principal creators of the communist-dominated Polish army in the USSR, and Hilary Minc, a key economic planner. Jews also played a key role in the cultural policy of the new regime, among them Jerzy Borejsza, the founder of the journal *Odrodzenie* and chief executive of the Czytelnik publishing house, until he was dismissed from all his positions in 1949.

However, anti-semitism was also not absent from the PPR itself. Official government policy was to defend the Jews and foster their economic rehabilitation, but within the party some factions were much less sympathetic to the difficult plight of the Jews. This was also the case in the local administration. In the country as a whole, Jews were widely viewed as playing a key role in the security apparatus of the new regime. Certainly there were a number of Jews in leading positions in the security apparatus, including Anatol Fejgin, the head of the notorious Tenth Department of the Ministry of Public Security (Ministerstwo Bezpieczeństwa Publicznego; MBP), which was responsible for the surveillance of all members of the PZPR, and his deputy Józef Światło. At the same time, there was a strong tendency to categorize as Jews anyone of whom one disapproved. Thus, in his account of his tenure as American ambassador in Poland, Arthur Bliss Lane, writing presumably under the influence of his Polish contacts, described Stanisław Radkiewicz the (non-Jewish) minister of public security, as 'a good-looking man, apparently of Russian Semitic origin, with carefully combed oily black hair, a keen mobile aesthetic face'.

Our understanding of the situation in Poland (as of that in the Soviet Union) has been transformed by the opening of archives, which give a much fuller picture both of the role of Jews in the Polish security apparatus in the immediate post-war years and of the process by which they were purged from it after the death of Stalin. They have revealed that Jews made up a significant proportion of the workforce of the Ministry of Public Security, though never a majority, and that Soviet 'advisors' played a key role. The percentage of Jews in the head office fluctuated between 30 and 40 per cent, with the exception of the years 1944 and 1945, when it was somewhat lower. In the local administration, the percentage of people of Jewish origin was much smaller. Of course, these were communists and internationalists far from any involvement in Jewish life. They entered the security service at a time in which the struggle to impose communism was particularly intense and when loyalty to the system was the overriding criterion both of the Polish communist leadership and their Soviet overlords.

After 1956, Jews were to be largely purged from the security apparatus. Even in the period between 1944 and 1955, their role had aroused opposition among 'native' communists who felt that the significant number of people of Jewish origin in important governmental positions increased their own unpopularity in Polish society and barred their path to high office. Why was it that Jews were allowed to hold a considerable number of important posts in the security apparatus in Poland when they had already been removed from such positions in the Soviet Union, at a time when Stalin was engaged in the destruction of the Soviet Yiddish cultural establishment and in a full-scale purge of 'Jewish cosmopolitans'?

At root, the presence of communists of Jewish origin in significant positions in the security apparatus has to be seen as a consequence of Stalin's deep distrust of the Poles. It took place at the same time as the purge of Yiddish cultural activists in the Soviet Union and the wider campaign against 'cosmopolitanism,' which was essentially an attack on Russified Jews within the new Soviet intelligentsia. The retention of Jews in these positions in Poland was clearly intended by Stalin to be a temporary expedient until a larger group of reliable local communists could be trained. Indeed, the history of Polish communism can be seen as the unsuccessful attempt to create such a group.

The thaw period from 1954 and, in particular, the early 1960s, saw the final removal of Jews from the security apparatus. A series of defections by intelligence officers of Jewish origin in the Polish Military Intelligence Service, which started with that of Paweł Monat in September 1959, had already set in motion a succession of countermeasures that aroused intense suspicion and paranoia, as well as anti-semitism, throughout the military as well as in the state security organs. Investigations accused Jews collectively of disloyalty and undermined the position of those among them who remained inside the party state apparatus. One result was that the most senior Polish Jew in the party, Politburo member Roman Zambrowski, was forced to resign in 1963.

At the same time, among those who remained in Poland, the processes of acculturation and Polonization proceeded rapidly – another major theme in post-war Jewish history in Poland. This made the revival of Yiddish cultural life difficult to achieve. A number of major Yiddish writers, including Chaim Grade and Avrom Sutzkever, spent short periods in Poland after the war, but soon moved on to the United States and Israel. Some other surviving Yiddish writers, like Itsik Manger, Sholem Asch, and Isaac Bashevis Singer, remained in the West. A small number did re-establish themselves in Poland, including Binem Heller, Leib Olitski, Hadasah Rubin, Lili Berger, Moshe Szkliar, Shlomo Beilis-Legis, and Daniel Kac, but most subsequently emigrated in 1956 and 1968.

One index of Jewish acculturation was the large role played in Polish literary life by people of Jewish origin and the emergence of what has been called 'the Jewish School of Polish Literature' – a group of writers including Julian Stryjkowski, Stanisław Wygodzki, Henryk Grynberg, Bohdan Wojdowski and Hanna Krall – who have explored the main dilemmas faced by Polish Jewry, above all, how to record and memorialize the Holocaust and how to go on living in the country where it took place and where the attitude of the majority of the population left a great deal to be desired.

Since 1989, as this book shows, there has been a slow and incomplete revival of Jewish life in Poland which had been dealt a devastating blow by the events of 1968. In 1971, a publication of the New York-based Committee for Jews in Poland described the 'recent exodus of the Jews from Poland' as 'the end of a thousand years'. Yet, from the late 1970s, Jewish life began to revive. People of Jewish origin, including Stanisław Krajewski, Konstanty Gebert and Adam Michnik, who came from the Polonized Warsaw Jewish milieu, played a large role in the political unrest that ultimately gave rise to Solidarity in the summer of 1980. Already in the summer of 1979, the American sociologist Carl Rogers had conducted a workshop in Poland.

Approximately ten of those attending discovered that they shared a similar Jewish background, which became apparent during a special smaller session devoted to the subject of Jews in Poland. Discussion of their Jewish background continued in Warsaw and involved members of the liberal Club of the Catholic Intelligentsia (Klub Inteligencji Katolickiej). As early as 1971, members of the club organized the first annual Week of Jewish Culture, intended to provide a better 'understanding of the rich and yet poorly known culture' of a people that 'lived among us for centuries' and whose 'gigantic tragedy in the last war we witnessed'. The discussions took place in different private apartments in order to circumvent restrictions on meeting. The group called itself the Jewish Flying University (Żydowski Uniwersytet Latający, ŻUL), modelling itself on the Flying University organized by the democratic opposition, itself drawing on experiences of the similar movement that had functioned under Russian rule before 1914.

The group, which numbered nearly one hundred, met periodically until the imposition of martial law in December 1981. According to one of its founders, Konstanty Gebert, they regarded themselves as the 'last Jews' of Poland, although the nature of their Jewish identity was still undefined. Essentially, their interest in their Jewish background was driven not so much by a desire for Jewish continuity or religious belief as by their opposition to the communist regime and the desire to shape a Polish identity with which they could identify.

As martial law was relaxed, the group resumed its activities and, in April 1983, it took part in an alternative, oppositional celebration of the fortieth anniversary of the Warsaw ghetto uprising. Their activities continued on a larger scale after the negotiated end of communism in 1989. It is difficult to give an accurate estimate of the number of Jews who remained in Poland. According to the Polish census of 2002, some 1,100 people gave their ethnicity as Jewish. The survey of the American Jewish Committee of 2005 estimates the core Jewish population as 3,300. In the Polish census of 2011, 2,000 people gave their ethnicity as Jewish and 7,000 gave their ethnicity as Polish, with Jewish as a second ethnicity. These figures clearly underestimate the number of people with some connection to Jewish life; according to Michael Schudrich, chief rabbi of Poland, there are at least 30,000-40,000 Jews in Poland. The number of people with some connection to the Jewish world is even larger.

With the end of communism and the decline in hostility to Jews, more people have been willing to acknowledge their Jewish identity, while significant numbers of 'hidden children' were told of their Jewish roots by their Christian foster parents. Although the community is small, it has shown remarkable dynamism since 1989, partly as a result of a new generation of leaders, above all the journalist Konstanty Gebert and the philosopher Stanisław Krajewski. The two principal Jewish organizations remain the Union of Jewish Religious Communities, which was reorganized in 1993, and the Social and Cultural Association of Jews, which existed throughout the communist period but which has been transformed since 1989. Each has around 2,000 members. In addition, there are a number of reform synagogues, most notably Beit Warszawa and Beit Kraków, as well as a conservative secession, Eitz Chaim. Jewish Community Centres (JCCs) have been established in Warsaw and Kraków.

Other smaller Jewish organizations are the Polish Union of Jewish Students, reorganized in March 2007 as the All-Poland Jewish Youth Organization (Żydowska Ogólnopolska Organizacja Młodzieżowa, known by its acronym ZOOM) and the Association of Children of the Holocaust (Stowarzyszenie Dzieci Holokaustu), which is made up of child survivors, many of whose members tell their story in this volume. Linked with it are the groups 'Second Generation' and 'Third Generation' whose members are also well-represented here. In addition, a Jewish sports club, Makabi, modelled on the pre-war organization with the same name has been created. The Ronald S. Lauder Foundation funds the Lauder-Morasha School, the only Jewish school in Warsaw, as well as summer and winter camps. Additional funding for the community is provided by the Ted Taube Foundation and from proceeds of the restitution of communal property under a law passed in 1997. The Lauder Foundation has also sponsored the publication of a high-quality monthly, *Midrasz*, originally edited by Konstanty Gebert and now by Piotr Paziński, which is devoted to past and present Polish Jewry. The American Jewish Joint Distribution Committee and the American Jewish Committee both have offices in Poland. In 2004, the late Chris Schwarz, a British photographer, and Professor Jonathan Webber of the University of Birmingham, founded the Galicia Jewish Museum in Kazimierz, dedicated to the celebration of Jewish culture in Galicia and the commemoration of victims of the Holocaust. In Oświęcim, under the influence of the New York-based philanthropist Fred Schwarz, the Auschwitz Jewish Centre has been established with a prayer hall and museum, located in the premises of a pre-war *beit midrash*.

Some aspects of the revival of Jewish life in Poland have only been possible because of the participation of non-Jewish enthusiasts. The Kraków Festival of Jewish Culture, first held in 1988 and organized by Janusz Makuch, has become an annual event, drawing more than 20,000 people for eight days of music, theatre, art exhibitions and workshops, led mostly by Jewish performers and educators from Europe, Israel and North America. The Centre for Jewish Culture, established in 1993 by the Judaica Foundation and headed by Joachim Russek, runs programmes of Jewish and civic interest in a restored *beit midrash* in Kazimierz. Finally, the Pogranicze (Borderland) Foundation was established in 1990 by Krzysztof Czyżewski in Sejny, near the Polish border with Lithuania, Belarus and the Kaliningradskaya oblast. Its goal is to examine and commemorate the multi-cultural and multi-ethnic heritage of this region.

Jewish studies have also thrived. The Jewish Historical Institute, established in 1947, has had a new lease of life since 1989 and has reorganized its archives and undertaken an extensive programme of publication under its former director Feliks Tych, which was extended by his successors Eleonora Bergman and Paweł Śpiewak. Its journal, *Kwartalnik Historii Żydów* (formerly *Biuletyn Żydowskiego Instytutu Historycznego*), is one of the best in the field. Impressive Jewish studies programmes have also been established at the universities of Warsaw, Lublin, Poznań, Wrocław, Gdańsk and Łódź and at the Jagiellonian University in Kraków. In 1995, the Polskie TowarzystwoStudiów Żydowskich (Polish Association for Jewish Studies) was formed with its headquarters in the Department of Jewish Studies at the Jagiellonian University. Today it has around ninety members.

One of the most difficult tasks facing the community is the preservation of Jewish heritage in Poland. Poland has more than 400 synagogues still standing, which are used for various purposes, some appropriate, others not. In addition, there are at least 1,400 Jewish cemeteries, a few well preserved, many in a parlous state. Some of the synagogues have been returned to the community under the communal restitution law, but resources for large-scale preservation are not available.

Certainly the efforts of all those involved in the re-creation of Jewish life in Poland have been little short of Herculean. Yet, at the same time, a note of caution should be added. It may be possible for a Jewish community as small as that in Poland to survive on the basis of pride in its past, rather than upon the existence of a critical mass of Jews prepared to commit themselves to sustaining the collective Jewish existence. It remains an open question, which is posed by several contributors, as to whether this community can again become self-sustaining and a significant cultural centre, even on a much smaller scale than in its heyday.

The years since 1989 have also seen the slow posthumous integration of the Jews into Polish history and the attempts to come to terms with the painful legacy of the past. A major factor in this has been the opening of the POLIN Museum of the History of Polish Jews in October 2014. It is located on a highly symbolic square, site of the imposing monument of Natan Rapoport to the 'Jewish People, its Martyrs and Fighters' and also of monuments to Jan Karski and Willy Brandt and a passageway named after Irena Sendler, who was responsible for rescuing a large number of Jewish children from the Warsaw ghetto and is a stones-throw away from 18 Miła street, the site of the bunker where at the end of the Warsaw ghetto uprising, its leaders, including Mordekhai Anielewicz, died rather than be taken prisoner by the Germans. In spite of the problems caused by the attempts of the present government in Poland, which came to power in 2015 to foster a more apologetic view of the Polish past, something which is referred to by a number of those who contributed to this volume, it does seem that in the discussion of problems in Polish-Jewish relations, we are now beginning to enter a new stage, in which apologies and apologetics will increasingly be replaced by careful and detailed research and reliable first-hand testimony. The goal should be to move beyond strongly held, competing and incompatible narratives of the past and reach some consensus that will be acceptable to all people of goodwill and will bring about a degree of normalization both in Poles' attitudes to the past and in Polish-Jewish relations.

This is a development to which this book will certainly contribute. Made up of contributions by the three generations of Polish Jews, those who survived the war, those who grew up under communism and the third generation which has emerged since 1989, it gives a multi-sided and nuanced picture not only of Jewish identity in Poland but of the complex history of Poland and its Jews from the Second World War to the present. It is an essential source for a proper understanding of these developments and deserves the widest possible circulation.

Antony Polonsky
Chief Historian, POLIN Museum of Polish Jews
Emeritus Professor of Holocaust Studies, Brandeis University

INTRODUCTION

My journey toward acquiring a Jewish identity was long. It wasn't spontaneous, but more like opening the drawer in my brain.

Karolina Szykier-Koszucka

For a millennium Jews populated the Polish lands where they found refuge from less hospitable societies. By the twentieth century Polish Jewry was the beating heart of European Jewry. With a population of 3.3 million on the eve of the Second World War, Poland's Jews were renowned for their varied and multi-layered religious, cultural and political life. Virtually all religious strands and political parties thrived to one degree or another, while Jewish writers, musicians and artists created a vibrant cultural scene. The extensive use of Yiddish in daily life constituted a veritable Yiddishland.

Yet despite widespread anti-semitism and occasional hostility, many also chose to integrate into mainstream Polish society – whenever opportunities arose. These Polonised Jews played a major role in fashioning the country's modern commercial, intellectual and creative industries. Indeed Polish history is difficult to grasp without acknowledging the Jewish contribution.

By the end of the war three million Polish Jews had perished in the Holocaust. For the survivors, their former world disappeared beneath a landscape of apocalyptic devastation. Ongoing and often murderous anti-semitic incidents, combined with an increasingly repressive Communist regime, convinced many survivors their future lay outside Poland. Successive waves of post-war emigration throughout the 1940s and 1950s to Israel and western countries significantly reduced the Jewish population. In 1968, the Communist government unleashed an anti-semitic campaign which stripped most Jews of their jobs and prominent positions, forcing many thousands (often Communist Party members) into exile.

By the 1970s Poland appeared, to the outside world, a country empty of Jews. Polish behaviour towards its remaining Jewish citizens gave the impression the country was relentlessly anti-semitic. Jews in the Diaspora concluded that Jewish life in Poland would never recover; therefore, their main interest was confined to the history of the Holocaust and the Nazi death camps. Overall Jewish attitudes towards Poland generally tended to be quite negative. But the relationship is complex: approximately 70 per cent of Ashkenazi Jews can trace their lineage back to Poland. This connection increasingly draws overseas Jews to the country to explore their family origins, particularly since the fall of Communism in 1989.

Several years ago I was one of them. I was on the road to north-eastern Poland, to my mother's *shtetl* of Narewka, bordering on the magnificent Białowieża forest; one of the last primeval forests remaining in Europe. While I couldn't avoid the sombre realisation that the region we travelled through had once been thickly populated with bustling *shtetls*, I had already begun to sense that Poland was not as empty of Jews as I had thought. Over the course of my visit I saw evidence of a Jewish cultural revival, and heard many anecdotes about a post-Communist phenomenon whereby growing numbers of Poles were discovering and exploring their Jewish ancestry. This struck me as very positive and hopeful, yet these developments were largely unknown outside Poland. Soon the idea gripped me that this story needed to be told to interested readers abroad. Moreover, as a form of oral history, it had to be related in the words of the individuals involved in the phenomenon.

Initially I feared my project was impractical. I am a writer and journalist and have some knowledge of Polish Jewish history. But I don't speak Polish, and live in London – not Warsaw or Kraków. Could I overcome the language barrier, and find a diverse spectrum of Poles who would be ready to speak about a subject which explored deep emotional issues and scars?

It seemed the best step was to approach experts for their opinion. Conversations followed with scholars of Polish-Jewish studies, as well as public intellectuals and rabbis in Poland. In each case, I was encouraged to go ahead – despite the difficulties I might face.

Through the websites of various Jewish publications and organisations, such as the Jewish Community Centres in Warsaw and Kraków and the chief rabbi's office, notices went out describing my project and requesting volunteers for interviews. Word of mouth also played a helpful role.

During my early trips to Poland, diffidence and uncertainty lingered. The feeling diminished once I started to build a relationship with the outstanding Polin Museum of the History of Polish Jews in Warsaw, which opened in 2014. The museum provided me with private space to hold interviews, along with suggestions for potential interviewees.

From the outset it was clear my book would be designed for a general audience. The specialised field of Polish-Jewish studies is flourishing and I had no intention of engaging in that area of expertise. Instead I wanted the profiles to be accessible: to involve members of three generations who were prepared to recount their experiences, the impact of the discovery on their relationships and lives.

Each generation grew up in a specific period of Polish history. Clearly the experience of a child survivor of the Holocaust differed sharply to that of a third generation interviewee who grew up in a democratic, post-Communist society. Their individual stories also reflect the milieu in which they live, and shed some light on the broader trends taking place in Polish life.

Holocaust survivors usually emerged from the war as orphans, lacking the structure and psychological support of a family. The creation of the Association of Children of the Holocaust in 1993 proved to be a seminal event. Many members of the association were inevitably traumatised by the wartime experience of being separated from their parents, and hidden by Catholic families or religious institutions. As survivor Helena Tos, says: 'Those who survived were afraid of their own shadow, and carried an ever present fear that terrible times might return to Poland.'

The organisation provided a crucial sense of belonging and, in many ways, serves as a therapeutic forum. At the same time, some members continue to maintain their Catholicism as a key component of their identity, leading the Polish writer, Konstanty Gebert, to wryly observe: 'The Association of Children of the Holocaust is unique. It's the only Jewish organisation in which most members are Catholics.'

A good deal of the credit for the recent revival of Jewish life needs to be attributed to members of the second generation. A large number are the offspring of Communist Party or leftist parents who were deeply committed, in the post-war period, to building a socialist society. Their ideology was also militantly internationalist, which tended to exclude any form of Jewish consciousness. This was reinforced by pressure within the Communist regime for Jewish party members to Polonise their names and outward identities. 'My father decided to pass as a Pole because it would be easier to persuade people about the merits of Communism if he promoted the ideology as a Pole and not as a Jew', recalls Jarosław Górnicki.

The pre-war conception that Jews were a nation, rather than an ethnic or religious entity, lingered over the decades. This perception also reinforced the idea that Poles and Jews are separate nationalities, contributing to the complexity of Polish-Jewish relations and identity.

Many second generation Jews also experienced a traumatic period during the anti-semitic campaign of 1968. As the purge spread, individuals were suddenly informed of their Jewish origins for the first time in their lives. This resulted in the loss of jobs, government positions and university places, even leading up to the revocation of citizenship and, ultimately, exile. Those who managed to remain in Poland felt compelled to adopt an underground identity.

The rise of the Solidarity movement in the 1970s, in which Jewish activists played a key role, triggered questions about identity that had been repressed, particularly since the events of the late 1960s. A Flying Jewish University served as an umbrella where these issues could be addressed and shared. As the Communist regime weakened and lost any credibility, the Second Generation organisation was created to bring together the post-war Jews who were prepared to emerge from the shadows and connect with their suppressed Jewish roots.

Second Generation can now boast hundreds of members. There have been ironical encounters when new members discover old friends in the group they never knew were Jewish. Like the Association for Child Survivors of the Holocaust, the Second Generation offers members not only a Jewish cultural milieu, but also a psychological refuge. As Danuta Celińska-Cedro points out: 'When I talk to my friends from Second Generation, we all feel we found a family we did not possess for many years.'

After the horrors of the Holocaust and the oppression of the Communist regime, the third generation can be regarded as comparatively fortunate. Emerging into a civil society that is also a member of the European Union, this generation discovered their Jewish origins in a far more conducive environment. Emil Jezowski, an activist in the Jewish community, says: 'In terms of the challenge of seeking out family roots, it's often the third generation that pursues the story.'

Yet it has not always been plain sailing for the younger Polish Jews. Often the discovery of their Jewish identity initially triggers a negative reaction. Growing up in a society where anti-semitism is still prevalent, they sometimes need to confront the negative stereotypes of Jews that they internalised as Polish children. Fortunately, in some families, there are parents and grandparents they can turn to for support. And since the fall of communism, a network of Jewish institutions – including community centres, schools, summer camps, Makabi sports clubs, new religious congregations, cultural festivals, Limmud, Taglit (Birthright) trips to Israel – offers the third generation the resources to construct a more viable community. It is also notable that the Israeli connection is a crucial element in shaping this generation's identity to a far greater degree than in the older generations.

The varied profiles reveal how the three generations share similar experiences in terms of discovering hidden aspects of their identity. Interviewees often recount how there was always something different about their families. They recall certain kinds of jokes told or food eaten in the household; the absence of an extended family; numerous references to Israel; the discovery of old identity documents; an inexplicable tendency to be drawn towards Jews.

Until recently, it was rare to have a Jewish upbringing in Poland, or even two Jewish parents. Most Jews, including those from a secular background, were routinely baptised as an insurance policy against potential threats, as well as expressing a desire to belong to Polish society. Those who lived as Catholics are often confused by new knowledge of their Jewish background. Unsurprisingly, when hidden Jews embrace their new identity, the majority don't choose the religious option, possibly due to a secular upbringing, but also because adopting Judaism appears too demanding and complicated.

The profiles reveal the range of responses precipitated when individuals emerge into the light of their new identity. Non-Jewish partners, relatives and friends react in sharply different ways, ranging from enthusiastic support to disappointing hostility. In some cases hidden Jews were raised in anti-semitic households, a cruel irony they needed to address. Yet it is often reported that Poles have a greater respect for self-declared Jews, rather than those they suspect of hiding their identity.

In 2013, the Polish film *Ida* controversially tackled the theme of hidden Jewish identity. It portrays the experience of a young woman in 1962 who was left as an orphan in a convent and is about to take her vows. Her encounter with her aunt, a Communist zealot and her one surviving Jewish relative, sends both on an odyssey in which the nun and the aunt have to consider their place in Polish society. The film, which was highly successful and won an Academy Award, reflects the ongoing attraction to Jewish themes among Polish artists.

An encouraging trend in Polish society has been the widespread interest in the renewal of Jewish communities and the underlying themes of Polish-Jewish history. For many Poles it has become fashionable to frequent Jewish cultural events, and even to reflect whether there is a Jewish link in their own family histories. This interest is partly nourished by a nostalgia for the pre-war past when Poland was a less monochrome and more multi-national society. In recent years, graffiti appeared in Polish cities announcing 'Jews We Miss You'. To redeem the past, non-Jewish volunteers have been restoring Jewish cemeteries and dilapidated synagogues while others help run Jewish Community Centres in Warsaw and Kraków.

The Polin Museum of Warsaw is the most prominent symbol of the renewal of Jewish life in Poland. It is widely regarded as one of the most beautiful and impressive Jewish museums in the world. Depicting the continuation of a Jewish presence over the past millennium, and the consequently deep symbiosis of Polish-Jewish relations, it chronicles the saga and accomplishments of Polish Jewry throughout the centuries. The museum has made a big impact on Polish perceptions of the country's Jewish legacy, and has rapidly become one of the main tourist attractions in Warsaw. Other Jewish museums in Kraków and Lublin offer a more focused account of Jewish history in Galicia.

While Polish Jews welcome the increasing public interest in their history and culture, there is a gnawing concern about the rightward shift in the country's politics. The electoral victory of the authoritarian, populist Law & Justice party in 2015 has raised concerns that civil liberties and minority rights are threatened. After all, anti-semitism has traditionally been part of the core nationalist identity in Poland. The changing atmosphere compelled a couple of interviewees to withdraw their participation in this book, citing their fears of going public. At the same time, many Jews are quick to point out that their institutions still do not require the tight security measures that have become the 'new normal' for other Jewish communities in Europe.

Polish Jews are divided on whether they can build a sustainable community in the coming years. A thriving community will depend on Jewish partners coming together to create Jewish families. There are also differing views on whether most Poles with a hidden Jewish identity have already come forward, or whether thousands remain below the radar.

However, there are positive signs that the foundations are more secure. For many years the Jewish community was very dependent on U.S. philanthropists such as Ronald Lauder, Tad Taube and Sigmund Rolat, as well as aid organisations like the American Jewish Joint Distribution Committee. But gradually Jewish organisations are becoming more self-sustaining, and trends like the 'cold war' among Jewish religious groups can be taken as a sign of a typical Jewish community. Perhaps Polish Jews are on course to create a new Jewish culture and communal life that will owe less to the pre-Holocaust past than has so far been imagined.

In an era marked by relentless globalisation, identities are more fluid. But people still need to know their origins and where they belong. A genuine identity remains a basic human need. For those who have discovered their Jewishness, they are compelled to revisit their self-image and family narrative.

Throughout the profiles, self-definitions appear in a variety of designations. Readers will encounter, for example, Jewish Pole, Polish Jew or Pole of Jewish origins. For Olga Lewińska, there is no dilemma. As she forthrightly says: 'It's natural to feel both Polish and Jewish. After all, my family has lived in Poland for centuries.'

Barry Cohen
London, 2018

PART 1

Children of the Holocaust

ALEKSANDRA (OLA) LELIWA-KOPYSTYŃSKA

I knew nothing about my mother's family origins until much later in life. Everything that happened before the war is a black hole.

My mother was Jewish and my father was Polish, a military man. In order to marry, he required the permission of the higher officers and so my mother changed her religion. As a result of her Catholic marriage her father threw her out of the family, which was probably observant.

When the war started my father went to the front. During the bombing of Warsaw my mother taught me the address of our home, which I still remember, because it was drummed into my head to ensure I wouldn't get lost. Suddenly my father returned from the front and probably realised how dangerous the situation had become. There was a German order that all Jews had to move to the ghetto. Although my mother had converted we were all required to go, including my father, as he was the husband of a Jewish woman. However, my father went to a village 100 kilometres from Warsaw, where he organised a hiding place for us. In the spring of 1940 we departed from our apartment, leaving everything behind. We didn't tell anyone our destination. At the time, German control wasn't so well established; it was still possible to escape from Warsaw without so-called Aryan documents. Nevertheless, my grandmother and other members of the family wound up in the ghetto.

It was a small isolated village without electricity, surrounded by forests. We were introduced to the local population as the family of the rich owner of the water mill, Mr Pac. We were helped by Madame Pac, who was a distant cousin of my father's, while my father became a director of the water mill.

The Germans forbade the use of this mill and they sealed it off. But, during the night, the Germans didn't dare come to the village; they were afraid of the partisans operating in the forest. And almost each night the partisans came to the farmers in the village for food.

A young worker at the mill called Pietrzak was cheating the farmers and my father told him to stop being dishonest or he would lose his job. People in the village must have suspected our Jewish origins because Pietrzak sent a letter to the Gestapo. His sister intercepted the letter and made sure it never reached the Gestapo. But Pietrzak no doubt became angry that his letter yielded no results. On 24 February 1942 someone knocked on our window at night. My father was asked to go to the mill because farmers were waiting there. This was the last time we saw him. The following day my mother was informed that my father was dead. Later, as a result of Pietrzak's post-war trial, we learned from his sister that he had killed my father. He escaped immediately after to avoid the vengeance of the partisans for my father's death.

I was four years old at that time. I was sent to the village convent because my mother was unable to look after me. My father's family came from Warsaw to attend his funeral. His brother and sister declared that my father's tragedy was my mother's fault because (due to her) we had been compelled to escape. They left us without offering to help us.

Meanwhile, we could no longer remain in the village once the news became public. We returned to Warsaw to stay with Madame Pac's brother, who was a priest in a parish church called Na Kamionku, located in Praga. My brother couldn't stay with us and was sent to another place where he was badly treated. My mother could remain in the parish as a cleaning lady with a small daughter. With the help of the priest she got desperately needed birth certificates for herself and her children, which allowed her to live and move around on the Aryan side.

I couldn't understand what was happening around me. Even when I went to the kindergarten on the same street as the church, I would access it by simply going through a gate which avoided the street. In recent years, I discovered other people in our Association of Children of the Holocaust who were also in the same kindergarten. So it's very likely that the people running the kindergarten knew about our origins and helped us survive.

On one occasion, a German car passed along our street announcing that everyone should go into hiding because a bombing was imminent. The car stopped in front of me and my friend and a German in uniform advised us to go home. Unfortunately, he decided to accompany us. As the church was involved in underground activity, everyone there became paralysed with fear. Subsequently, the priests living there decided that our presence constituted a danger and we were sent back to the village, probably in the summer of 1943.

I remember several occasions when the Wehrmacht entered villages where we were staying. Once my mother managed to deal with them, probably because she knew Yiddish which is very similar to German and a simple German soldier could not distinguish between the two. By the end of the war, our final hiding place was in a village near Lublin, which was the first area to be liberated by the Soviet army.

After our wartime experience I was convinced that the Pac family in the village were truly my family and I would often go and spend vacations there. My mother and brother decided not to reveal anything to me about my true origins in order to protect me.

We lived outside Warsaw due to the severe lack of housing in the city. I went to church with my friends in the evening and on Sundays, and became a very good Catholic. However, my older brother would laugh at me because he knew about our background. Over time he influenced me in such a way that I eventually stopped going to church.

When I married, I had to have a church wedding. Although my son was baptised, he never practised Catholicism – probably due to my influence. Today, no one in our family practises religion. My brother married a woman from an Eastern Orthodox background. My son's wife is philo-semitic. She sent their daughter to the Lauder kindergarten. My grand-daughter went to Israel with Taglit and returned so happy that she declared she was Jewish. Finally, she became more Jewish than me, who knows nothing about the Jewish religion.

In the post-war years, I studied hard and joined the physics faculty at Warsaw University where I earned my Ph.D and became a professor of physics. I was not interested in examining my origins because there was nothing to spark my curiosity.

I was not directly affected by the events of 1968. At the time, my son was three years old; I had recently married and had my position at the university. Furthermore, I had the 'Polish looks', probably inherited from my father, so no one suspected I was Jewish.

I noticed that when I told my mother I planned to marry a man from a noble Polish family, with the name of Leliwa-Kopystyński, she was not happy at all. I realise now that she was afraid that my mother-in-law, who was a snob, might not be very pleased if she were to learn that I was Jewish.

My brother, however, was directly affected by the anti-semitic campaign in 1968. He had studied in a military faculty of medicine in Łódź and became a very good surgeon, He was invited to work in a military hospital in Warsaw with the rank of major. Suddenly, in 1968, he was thrown out of his job. But he rationalised it to me by saying he had decided to leave after so many years in the military. I was quite surprised; it wasn't normal to suddenly leave one's career. He knew everything about our family's Jewish background, but he and my mother had an agreement not to reveal anything to me.

Because of 1968, I saw many people leave Poland. In my physics faculty, many were forced out of their positions and disappeared. During this period, I often felt a deep revulsion because every manifestation of anti-semitic behaviour made me aggressive toward the person behaving in this way.

When I entered the physics faculty in 1954, my mother told me that my uncle had been a professor of chemistry in Warsaw University before the war. So I asked her for his name but she quickly brushed off my question. I later learned that his name was Centnerszwer and that he had escaped from the Warsaw ghetto, only to be betrayed to the Gestapo and murdered.

For a long time before I realised that I was Jewish, I felt there was something mysterious in my family's life. My mother's younger brother lived in Kalisz and although I didn't see him often, I noticed around the late 1980s that his face increasingly took on a Jewish appearance. It was a clue I filed away in the back of my mind. Today I have to admit that I probably understood, but didn't want to speak about this discovery.

In December 1990, my mother was terminally ill and died on 24 December. Before she passed away I told her I knew about our origins and had also told my son, her beloved grandson. She took my hand and said: 'I beg you not to tell this to anybody.' I will never forget those words nor the fear in her eyes.

After my mother's death, I decided to search for documents to discover the history of my family. The first step was to go to Kalisz and ask my uncle about family names. At first, he didn't want to tell me. He seemed so afraid, even in his own apartment, and looked around to make sure no one was listening. I learned for the first time that his name, and my mother's maiden name, was Waksenbaum. He also told me that the maiden name of my grandmother was Matylda Centnerszwer. This proved to be very important because, while I didn't find any information about the Waksenbaum family, I did discover a lot about the Centnerszwer family. This enabled me to locate my Centnerszwer relatives currently living in Scotland and Australia. Today we are in constant contact. In fact, among my mother's documents I found correspondence from the 1950s and 1960s between my mother and these relatives.

Many years after the death of my mother and uncle I went to the Jewish Historical Institute where I found information left by my mother immediately after the war, confirming that we had survived. Within that document were all the original family names. I was shocked. Why did I not know anything about my background when the truth was written and available for everybody to see in the Institute?

Two years before I retired in 2007, when I was 70, I started to go to the Association of Children of the Holocaust. I felt very attracted to this organisation because I found people there who were in a similar situation to myself and they have become almost like family. Otherwise I couldn't openly say I am Jewish. I was never a real Catholic and the transition to becoming Jewish was extremely powerful in my old age.

I have twice been to Israel to visit friends. When I went for the first time I took along a photo of my grandparents and told the photo: 'Look. I finally came here.'

HELENA TOS

My entire family was taken to the Lwów ghetto, but I was smuggled out when I was about six months old. I don't know the details; I was saved through the efforts of Mrs Krompf and Mr Denenfeld, who were friends of my parents. Tragically my parents and everyone else in the family perished. I was the only survivor.

I was placed with a Polish family, the Korczyńskis, who had no children of their own. In order to explain my sudden arrival, they claimed I was a child of Mrs Korczyński's sister, who had given birth out of wedlock. After Mr Korczyński was drafted into the army, my foster mother and sister moved westwards to the former German territories in Poland. They settled in the village of Czarnowąsy, near Opole, at around 1945-46. There I began primary school.

My foster mother kept in touch with the people responsible for placing me in her care. This included Mr Denenfeld, who was now living in Wrocław, but his origins are unclear. There is speculation that he may have had Jewish roots.

I always referred to Mrs Korczyński by her surname, and never called her anything other than foster mother. I cannot utter the word 'mother' because she isn't my biological mother. Although she took care of me, we never had a close mother-daughter relationship. There was a lack of emotional ties; we failed to create a strong bond.

After some time my foster mother found her husband, and discovered he was involved with another woman. Officially I was their adopted child; she wanted to claim child support. She took me to Wrocław, where they discussed this matter. That was a rare occasion when I actually saw Mr Korczyński, my foster father.

I left the village to attend high school in Wrocław. As my foster mother had died, I lived in an orphanage there. When I was eighteen, I noticed a man on the street in Wrocław who resembled my foster father. I approached him and asked if he was Mr Korczyński. He gazed at me and asked if my name was 'Nuna', my childhood nickname. I confirmed that it was, which surprised him. He gave me his phone number and urged me to call him. We agreed that I would visit his home. But he also informed me he already had five children with his current wife.

When I went to visit him, he greeted me; but his wife didn't want to let me into their house. She told me I was not really his daughter and, moreover, that I was Jewish. I confronted him as to whether this was true; he confirmed that it was. It was a horrible experience; my foster father behaved in a very cold manner. I said goodbye and never saw him again.

I went to the Denenfelds here in Wrocław and asked them whether this shocking information was genuine. I thought perhaps Mr Korczyński's wife feared I wanted something from my foster father. The Denenfelds confirmed it was true. They explained they had never told me about my Jewish origins because they didn't want to create an identity crisis for me.

As for the Denenfelds, their daughter said they descended from Austrian Jews. At that time, people didn't come out of the closet; they were constantly afraid – even after the war. Those who survived were afraid of their own shadow and carried an ever present fear that terrible times might return to Poland. A friend of mine, a Holocaust survivor, didn't want her daughters to live in Poland. She therefore sent one to Austria, and another to the United States. In my workplace when I was very young, there was a Jewish man and people would joke that he liked me because I looked like a Jew. Yet I never told anyone I was Jewish.

At the time of my discovery, which made such a profound impact on me, I was going out with my future husband. However, this news made no impression on him. He felt it didn't make any difference regarding the person he knew. We married a year later, when I was pregnant; we had two children together. My son is now 56 years old and my daughter is 40, but I am separated from my husband.

Discovering my Jewish background triggered an absolute change in my identity. I immediately thought of getting in touch with the Jewish community and found the local TSKŻ branch. I felt more confident in that secular Jewish environment and became involved in their events. Interestingly, the first time I went to their youth club, I met a classmate who I always suspected was Jewish. Generally, only my Jewish friends knew the truth about me. We supported one another and I cherished my connections with them.

After a long period of time I was obliged to present witnesses to TSKŻ confirming I was Jewish. The Korczyński family backed up my story, and then Denenfeld's daughter came to TSKŻ to say the same. This was the basis for my acceptance and, in due course, I received a membership card of the Jewish Combatants Association.

I began to think of trying to find surviving members of my Jewish family. As people were coming from abroad to TSKŻ, I left my address in the hope that someone would contact me. As a result, rabbis from Israel began writing to me and even paid for a cab to take me to Warsaw for a meeting. They tried to convince me to emigrate to Israel or the U.S., but I told them as I couldn't speak another language, emigration would be too difficult. That is what has kept me in Poland. Besides, I'm a modest person who doesn't have great expectations from life.

When the Association of Children of the Holocaust was launched, I immediately joined it in 1993. This constitutes my main network of friends, who are mostly atheists. Many of us find it impossible to believe in God after the Holocaust, when one thinks of the children who ended up in gas chambers. Despite my atheism, I occasionally go to the synagogue on holidays like Rosh Hashanah, Pesach or Chanukah. I used to go more frequently to Shabbat dinners, but nowadays I prefer not to leave my house after dark.

The political atmosphere in Poland has worsened and it's beginning to resemble the 1930s. Nothing is certain and whenever things turn bad, the Jews are always to blame. Nevertheless, I regard myself as a Jew with Polish roots. It's hard to find the balance because on one hand I am Jewish and on the other hand I was adopted. But I think of myself as Jewish – first and foremost – like my friends in the Association.

Officially I'm 76 years old, but I'm not sure. The authorities would need to fabricate new documents in order to make me older. So I'm as old as they will let me be.

ROMUALD JAKUB
WEKSLER-WASZKINEL

I was 35 years old, and a Catholic priest for twelve years, when I discovered I was a Jew.

I had suspected for some time that something wasn't right. I did not resemble my parents; there were many indications that something was amiss. I provoked my mother to talk about it, she had previously been very reluctant. I prompted her in many ways to tell me. Finally, on what I call the day of my second birth (23 February 1978), I asked her who had lived in Święciany. (Stare Święciany, near Vilnius, is my birthplace.)

She said that Poles did, as well as Russians, Lithuanians, Tatars, Karaites. Then she mentioned Catholics, and members of the Orthodox Church. I interrupted her, and asked directly whether Jews had lived there too. I was afraid she'll stop talking, start crying and leave, which sometimes happened. She began to weep. I took her hands, kissed them and said: 'Mum, this is a beautiful part of your life, but it is also my life. You must finally tell me. I won't love you any less, on the contrary.' That was the first time she admitted I had had wonderful parents who loved me, who were Jews and were murdered.

How did I feel before this disclosure, when I suspected I may have Jewish roots while living in an anti-semitic society? Many bad things happened. I didn't want to be a Jew. At the time, the Christian upbringing was fiercely anti-Jewish. It was said they murdered Jesus Christ, that they are the cursed nation. I didn't want to be part of that. I wanted to be like my friends, to have Polish parents like they did. I was very afraid, and avoided the problem for a long time. At some point, however, I became mature enough. Through reading what Christians call the New Testament independently, during my time at the seminary, I discovered the truth: the Jews didn't kill Jesus. That was a huge discovery for me. It was so important for me to learn that his mother, and all his apostles, were Jewish.

The rector there remarked that there were serious doubts about whether I had been baptized. Who else but a Jew would not be baptized? I said I was very interested in this because as a child I'd been called 'Jew'; there were many unpleasant incidents, so if there were any accusations of this sort, I want to know. It turned out there weren't – it was just I didn't look like my parents; I had 'the face of a hundred Jews'. My godmother came to attest that I had been baptized and the problem was solved.

One day (when I was seventeen) after a religious education class, I told the priest of my decision to go to the seminary. I don't know why I said this. When I heard myself, it frightened me. I thought that when I tell my parents, my father will hug me and say his dream is coming true. Instead my parents were incredulous; my father begged me to change my mind. It was very surprising as they were deeply religious people. But when my father contradicted me so strongly, it was as if he was seeing me differently than I saw myself.

I had wanted to be a priest while in primary school, but later the ambition vanished. In high school I was talented artistically, won contests, and thought about going to drama school. Father thought the arty life wasn't for me, but when the idea of attending the seminary materialised, he tried to discourage me, saying I was unsuited to the priesthood. I said I'd do what I wanted, and went to spite him. He came to visit me one day, and began to weep uncontrollably. A few weeks later he died from a heart attack. I felt very guilty, and considered ending my studies.

I had no idea about the Holocaust before 1968. We weren't taught about it in primary or secondary school, at the seminary or at university. Nobody spoke about the extermination of the Jews. Even in films, where you could see the ghetto on fire, the whole of Warsaw was on fire. In 1968 I learned that, in the Communist Party, Jews were arguing with non-Jews, and that was it. I wasn't interested at all, because I wasn't Jewish. Yet for many years I was very bothered by how dissimilar I was to my parents. In high school, I had a theory that my mother had been raped during the war, which would mean my real father was some thug. But they loved me, so it wasn't too important. I suspected he wasn't my biological father.

In 1968, on All Saints' Day, I went to the cemetery. I was studying in Lublin at the time and none of my family or friends were buried there. I had been taught that, in that case, one should go where nobody goes, so I went to the grave of Soviet soldiers. The monument said '1941-1945'. I was very surprised – every child knew the war started in 1939. I knew nothing about the Molotov-Ribbentrop Pact; I had holes in my education like my whole generation. I visited a friend who studied history and asked why did Soviet soldiers start the war in 1941. He said they didn't; they attacked Poland along with Hitler in 1939. I was stunned. He gave me a book by the Polish historian Oskar Halecki, which I think was the first Polish book that described the truth of those years. I learned about the Holocaust from that book. For the first time it clicked for me that I might have been a Jewish child saved by Polish parents. This was the start of a revolution – I started looking for news about Święciany and learned it once had a large Jewish community. In 1975, when my mother moved into my home in Lublin, I was almost convinced I was Jewish, and started pestering her. When I read her Jewish texts, she forbade me to speak about this. It took a long time and much effort to make her talk.

When the truth was disclosed, my first question was: what is my name? The horrible answer was that she didn't know. She didn't want to remember. I lost control and started shouting: 'What am I supposed to do with this Jewishness?' She said I didn't understand anything about those times: she didn't want to remember my Jewish name because if she had been interrogated, she would have revealed it – she was no hero. Not knowing meant that all she could say was: 'He is my child and I love him'. The most important thing she revealed was that my mother had been in the ghetto; also that I had a brother, Samuel. At the time, my Polish mother was very afraid to take me. They lived in a rented room; she had never been pregnant and was worried about the sudden appearance of a child. My birth mother, who wasn't a religious Jew, said: 'But you said you were a Christian and you believe in Jesus. Please save my Jewish baby in the name of that Jew you believe in. When he grows up he will be a priest.'

My father was aware of her words; I suddenly understood the cause of his death. He wanted to stop me becoming a priest because he knew I was Jewish. But I did it anyway, and he died. That was the most important thing to me; it was like my real mother's will. It felt like I was in the back seat in life. It was terrifying and very painful, but there was also some joy in that my birth mother didn't end up lying about my becoming a priest. I doubt, however, that she really wanted me to do it.

Did Pope John Paul II encourage me to explore my Jewish roots? No, he taught me ethics. He didn't encourage me. I found it very difficult to cope with the knowledge of my Jewishness. I didn't know any Jews, there were none around. But to be Jewish and tell nobody is like being pregnant and not giving birth. After some contemplation I dared to write a letter to John Paul II: from a theological perspective he was the successor of St Peter, a Jew. Another reason was that he was Polish and I owed my life to a wonderful Polish family, so it was a good opportunity to thank him. I asked him to pray for me and told him I really wanted to find at least a trace of my real name. I said if I can't learn what it is, I will show with all my life that I love Jews, but will never tell anyone I'm one of them. I sent it with one of my professors who was going to Rome, because I was worried about censors. I received an answer, which started with the words 'My dear brother'. I always say this is the most beautiful ecclesiastical title I've ever received.

I searched for my name for fourteen years. When I found it, I wanted to preserve it. In 1992, the Jewish world appeared in my life when I met my father's brother in Israel, who said my brother was named Samuel after my paternal grandfather. I couldn't take my brother's name, but I didn't know the name of my maternal grandfather, so I took my father's – Jakub (Jankiel). So I have two names: Romuald first and then Jakub. I don't know what my Jewish parents called me. Then the first surname was Jewish, Weksler, and I combined this with the name Waszkinel. I wrote to the Pope to ask if it's acceptable, and not pretentious. I'm no aristocrat, I'm a poor Jew, but that's my name. I wrote that I know I'm a Jew and want to tell the whole world about it. His answer was addressed to Romuald Jakub Weksler-Waszkinel, so I consider this a blessing from the Pope himself.

I contacted a nun to help me find Jews from my town living in Israel. Sister Klara Jaroszyńska saved many Jews during the war, and was a Righteous Gentile Among the Nations. She asked me what I knew about my family and said she had friends in Israel who could help. I told her the little I knew: I had a brother called Samuel and my father was the best tailor in town. He was still alive in 1943, even though when the Germans came in 1941, they did away with the Jewish community within a few days – or actually, the Lithuanians did that. They would, however, leave Jews that were necessary for work, professionals. That's why the whole family survived. I also knew I had my mother's eyes – that was the only thing my Polish mother recalled. She was afraid to remember any other details from the ghetto.

Sister Klara wrote to people in Israel about my search, but there was no reply. Nobody was interested in some priest; also, after 1967, there were no diplomatic relations. It wasn't until she went to Israel that someone suggested a meeting of the survivors from Święciany. She met them in Tel Aviv and told them about me. They all shouted 'Jankele Weksler! He was the best tailor!'. They opened a book – each community has a book of memory – and showed her my mother, a Zionist leader. Sister Klara returned to Lublin and gave me my name, the names of my parents, and my birth mother's photograph – the first person in my life that I resembled. It was uncanny.

I first went to Israel in July 1992, to meet my father's brother and sister. I kept returning for holidays until 1998, and stayed with my uncle, a very religious man who showd me a lot of love. In 1995, my Polish parents were awarded the Righteous Gentile Among the Nations medal. When I initially asked for this, Yad Vashem said that although they saved a Jewish child, they never returned one – Yad Vashem didn't consider me a Jew. I immediately replied that I wasn't a suitcase that could be placed anywhere after the war. I was a living child who had loved his parents and was loved in return. We lived in a small town where there were no Jews – to whom could they return me? If they had given me away, I think I would have gone crazy or died from longing. I wrote to them: Don't tell me things like this, it's inhumane. In reply they asked whether I'm circumcised. I said yes. So on 1 September 1995 my Polish parents received the medal. At that point I wanted to stay in Israel. I was told: 'There's much more work to do in

Poland, you should go back there. If anyone can repair Polish-Jewish and Christian-Jewish relations, it's you.' But it wasn't true; I could do nothing. I felt lonely, particularly after the Pope's death, and in 2009 I decided to leave for Israel.

It was difficult – they offered a two-year visa. I initially thought this was all right, I was ready to just learn the language and return. But in the end I didn't want to go back. An excellent documentary was made about me, there was quite a buzz about it in the press. After that I received a 'resident's visa' (Toshav Keva). This grants permanent residence, but I said: 'I'm a Jew, I don't want to be a resident, I want citizenship.' In the end I do have that, but as an Israelite, not a Jew. The paradox is that in Poland I am a Polish citizen of Jewish nationality, and in Israel I am an Israeli citizen, but not a Jew. I have an Israeli passport, but I'm not considered a Jew, so the Law of Return does not apply to me. But it's their mistake; all the good Jews tell me I'm a Jew.

My identity today? I mostly feel I'm a Jew, but a Polish one. This cannot be undone. I'm old and I've taken Poland with me, along with the language, which is the one I speak most fluently. I work at Yad Vashem, I read documents, I cry often; those closest to me are my parents. I feel increasingly close to those who were taken away from me. This whole Jewish world is my family. In Poland, I felt increasingly alien as I was discovering my Jewishness – not that I encountered only awful anti-semites there. I met some of those, but I also have friends there, a sister, my Polish mum – a child couldn't be loved more than I was. The Polish landscape is beautiful. All this is in my eyes and my heart, but I'm a Jew. If not for the war, I would have been a Jew also in Poland, or anywhere else. So I'm a Jew most of all, but with all the traditions of a Polish Jew.

I still want to cry over the unhappy fate of a Polish Jew. He would love Poland so much, yet was rarely loved in return. I don't want to say the rejection was absolute: one need only go to the Polin Museum to see beautiful parts of that history. But now, for example, those bad winds are being stirred up again. Why? What for? This makes me, as a Jew, very anxious. As a Pole I'm ashamed. But I appreciate the richness of that dual identity; I love it and never want to lose it.

As for my Catholicism, that's a very difficult question. I definitely haven't rejected Christ, but I'm not sure he's a Catholic Christ. He's definitely a Jewish Christ. I would like everything to connect us, not divide us.

I spent my first year in Israel – 2009 – in a religious kibbutz, on the advice of Rabbi Schudrich (the chief rabbi of Poland). He is my close friend. It was also prompted by John Paul II, who said: 'Who encounters Christ, encounters Judaism.' For a year I was fully immersed in the Jewish world, I celebrated all the holidays, went to the synagogue every day, learned Hebrew. It was one of the most beautiful years of my life. Initially the local people were mistrustful, but there was this wordless emanation of love and we grew to love one another. When I was leaving they told me I must stay and marry. In Judaism a man cannot be single. I said at my age I need a nurse, not a wife. I spent my whole life among books, I never thought of starting a relationship in my old age. I'm wary of complicating another person's life. What right do I have to attach somebody to me when I'm seventy-odd years old? That's madness.

In Jerusalem I found myself in a Catholic community, but was removed from it on account of being too Jewish. Now I live in a sort of seniors' residence. I feel very good. I go to synagogue, not regularly, but I pray almost every morning. I especially love visiting the Great Synagogue, not because I understand everything, but because I love music. I think the melody carries my prayers. I get very emotional and hide my tears. I'm a sentimental Jew. I don't wear the tallith or the tefillin: I think it would be disingenuous if I did. This is something you have to grow into. It's not about putting things on, like being a priest is not about wearing the cassock. I'm a very religious man. I don't know how to qualify this religiousness – it's Jewish, like Christ's.

The one thing I would really like to mention is that I'm waiting for the day when my brother knocks at my door. Most probably he was taken with my mother to Sobibór. But if she saved me, it's possible she also saved him. Whenever I speak I mention my brother and say he should find me. I think about him all the time.

About my biological mother's promise that I would become a priest. Here, in Israel, I'm frequently asked to share my experiences with various groups.

One that I like very much is called Michlala: it's a college for religious Jewish girls. At age 19 or 20 these girls have husbands, they're pregnant or already have two children. I like them because they are mothers – they get very emotional about a son whose mother gave him away. They see it as absolutely horrible. I was telling them my story and a beautiful girl stood up and said: 'All right, we all cried with you, but you never said anything about your wife or children.' I said I don't have any. Looking very sad, she asked if I was ill. I said there were no Jewish women for me to marry in Poland. They were very happy to hear this – it's a sort of argument that is intended to appeal to the audience's benevolence. I couldn't explain celibacy to them: a Jewish girl like that wouldn't understand it, see it as unnatural. Family is the foundation of Jewish life.

On the way home I realised I knew why my Jewish mum told my Polish one I would be a priest. If I hadn't gone to the seminary, I would have had a wife and children – the Jewish world would have been unimportant. I'd have other problems and would have had to provide for my children, love my wife and not think about the war. Because I was single and went to the seminary, the Polish-Jewish issue was always present. I work at Yad Vashem, where I mourn the Jewish world which had gone unmourned. Paradoxically, my priesthood saved my Jewishness and led me to the moment when I mourn not only my dead, but all the dead Jews that nobody mourned for during the war.

As for Poles with hidden Jewish identities, I don't think there are many left who are unaware of their roots. Everyone has the possibility of checking, especially now with the Jewish Museum, the Polish Centre for Holocaust Research, the Jewish Historical Institute. Anyone who wants can search. But I don't think there are thousands of hidden Jews; that's no longer true. Maybe there's a handful still in the closet, still afraid, but not many. I don't see a future for Jews in Poland.

I always spend August in Poland. My book collection is still there, which I'm slowly distributing to second-hand bookshops, and to people. My sister is there, we're very close. I go to the theatre now too – the Jewish Theatre put on a beautiful play entitled 'Mothers'. Now it's shown in the Polish Theatre, run by Andrzej Seweryn, a very open, wonderful man. It's a performance featuring three children of the Holocaust, me among them. My plans: a funeral. I'd love to be buried in a cemetery – I won't say which one because I want to live a bit longer – but definitely in Israel.

MARIA ROCHOWICZ-LEWANDOWSKA

I was born in April 1942 in the ghetto of Tarnopol, near Lwów, which was in Poland but is now in the Ukraine. My entire extended family – grandparents, aunts, cousins – was also there, not by choice, of course. They were all taken to Bełżec and murdered. The only survivors were my mother, my father – but only briefly – and myself.

I was still a baby when my father found a Polish family who provided a hiding place for my mother in a forester's lodge near Tarnopol. He also rescued me by wrapping me in blankets and hiding me under his coat. He had searched out an orphanage run by Greek Catholic nuns on the way to the forced labour site. Passing it, he threw me over the fence. He took a huge risk; had the guards noticed, they would have shot us both. But he had been observing them and fortunately found an opportune moment.

The woman who gave my mother refuge visited me at the orphanage. She later said I was dying, blue all over, immobile. The nuns were sitting around me with candles, praying. She was a country woman and started making a fuss; she said she knew a veterinarian in Tarnopol and he brought me back to life. My father also escaped from the ghetto and hoped to join my mother in her hiding place. On the way he was shot in the forest.

A very strong bond developed between my mother and the Polish family that hid her. After the war she married the son of the household; he was also one of the Righteous, he helped his mother hide a Jew. This woman, whom I always called grandma, got the title of a Righteous Gentile.

I come from an assimilated family. My grandfather was a lawyer. I even have his diploma from Lwów which says 'Doctor of Law'. I will donate it to the

Museum of the History of Polish Jews. My father also studied law in Kraków, but then the war broke out. There was no Orthodox observance. Sometimes they celebrated Shabbat, but in a social sense; they saw it as a good opportunity to meet with friends. There was no religious aspect; they didn't observe Jewish holidays. It was a Polonised family.

The orphanage was Greek Catholic because it was Ukrainian. They knew I was Jewish; the nuns saved many Jewish children like me. They rescued orphans whether they were Russian, Ukrainian or Jewish, whoever found their way there. I think there was some natural selection, like with me; I was barely alive and the nuns were praying, not rescuing me, because it was probably expensive and a lot of fuss.

I was perhaps six months old when I was left there. I don't remember anything. After the liberation families arrived in Poland. My mother fetched me from the orphanage and took me, my 'grandma' and her son to Wrocław. They got married there, so I had a stepfather.

Because my mother and stepfather were working, I was raised by my grandmother. She took me to church; I liked it a lot, the gilded sculptures, beautiful organ music. I was fascinated with it. It was only when I grew up and heard those homilies, finally I understood how much anti-semitism there was that I rejected the church.

I went to a Polish school, so while I had some Jewish friends, the majority were Poles. My mother's friends from Tarnopol arrived after the war, like she did, and they had a very close relationship. They were Jewish couples, unlike my mother's marriage. They weren't Orthodox, but celebrated the major holidays.

My mother didn't reveal our Jewish origins to me. But, as a child in primary school, I observed things and listened. From various oblique statements and signs I knew that there's a lack of uniformity, that to Polish children I was different. Children came to the playground; I played with them and heard sayings such as 'don't run around like a Jew in the synagogue'. Negative things were frequently associated with Jews. 'Wash yourself, you're dirty like a Jew!' I didn't know what it was and why it's bad, this Jew in a synagogue, that dirty

Jew. I knew it was bad and vague, and had nothing to do with me. I even used those expressions towards others when I was angry at someone.

But there was an unspoken bond between me and the Jewish children at school, something connected us. We reached the conclusion that we were different because Polish children boasted that their fathers, grandfathers or uncles fought in the war, were heroes, had victories, risked their lives. We could not brag about our fathers and grandfathers. They lived in times of contempt and hid 'like rats'.

I was probably baptised at the orphanage, but my mother never received a certificate, or lost it. I was baptised again, for money, and I have that certificate; that was after the Kielce pogrom. Jews were scared. To protect me my mother got a certificate stating I was Polish and Christian. I have the baptism certificate in a drawer, and right next to it is my birth certificate from the ghetto, where the midwife is Jewish and my name is Kelber. When I showed it at the archive of the Jewish Historical Institute there was a huge stir, because such documents are extremely rare.

I definitely identify more as a Jew. That's why I'm here, in an almost exclusively Jewish environment. I gravitate towards the Association of Children of the Holocaust, because here I can speak about everything openly. Poles are very touchy, you can't talk openly with everyone; here we're honest.

I'll say that at school, university and work – in a Polish environment, because that was after March 1968, you hardly ever met any Jews – I never felt overt anti-semitism. There were moments, but I didn't hide my origins. Whenever I went to a new place, or changed jobs, I provoked a conversation about this and said I was Jewish. Then it quickly became obvious who is who, who's a friend and who's a foe. There were some unfriendly people, so I stayed away from them, but most respected me for telling the truth.

1968 was a traumatic year, because I had to say goodbye to friends who left. I wanted to leave Poland too, because I felt it like a slap in the face; but my husband was Polish and he didn't want to go. I would have convinced him, but my mother was very ill. I was an only child – there was no other choice, I had to stay. I still regret it.

Why? Because in 1968 the disgraceful anti-semitism of Poland was fully revealed. It wasn't only political, but stemmed from people's hearts. I saw those huge manifestations of thousands of workers who shouted 'Jews to Siam', because they didn't know exactly whether it was Zion or Siam. This is related to the past, but I am distrustful and careful. I would leave social events when hearing tasteless jokes about Jews; I commented on this with my absence.

I have a daughter; unfortunately, she's far away in France. I didn't bring her up Jewish, but told her early on that she was a Jew. She felt very proud and told all her friends, because she felt it made her special and unique.

She circumcised her two sons: there was a ceremony which I attended. At first I was nervous, but also proud that she emphasised her Jewishness this way. I was afraid, such horrible things happened. More men died this way during the war because when they had to take off their trousers, it was obvious who was Jewish. I told her: I don't know what to say, I'm happy, but also worried, because this will mark them.

My second husband, who brought me to Warsaw, was Jewish. He died, regrettably. Together we celebrated holidays, attended Shabbat meetings; we had a Jewish life together. His first wife was also Polish, as was my first husband. I never had any of this at home before, so I have good memories of this marriage. It also allowed me to go deeper into Judaism.

My mother was in the closet, she hid her origins. When she died I had her buried at the Jewish cemetery in Wrocław. Many of her work colleagues were surprised. Did she want a Jewish funeral? It was my decision.

Do I know many Jews who continue to live in the closet? Indeed, even in our Association, among my peers, there are people who admit they have a problem with this. There is a woman whose husband knows nothing, as she's been hiding it for years. There's a man whose son has no idea. His wife was Polish. My husband was his friend and persuaded him to tell his son, saying that someone will eventually tell him anyway, which will be even worse. It is a stigma for many people.

In August 2011, there was an international congress in Warsaw of the Children of the Holocaust Associations. People came from all over the world, a crowd of Jews. There was an interesting programme and many private conversations during breaks. My friends gave various answers to the accusations of 'Why haven't you left Poland? Why do you stay?' Everyone had their own reasons. I said that we're sitting on those cemeteries, because we are their guardians. We are needed here after all. I think we are needed, because neo-Nazism is emerging all over the world and we need to react. Jews get involved in anti-Nazi marches. I took part in those too, with my husband and then alone. Recently, we had whistles and by whistling loudly we tried to bar them from crossing the Krakowskie Przedmieście.

I know from the media that there's a resurgence of neo-Nazism all over the world, but what concerns me most is Poland. I have bad associations, because I know about the war. I could have been murdered.

The Jewish community has been taken over by the Second Generation. I am very happy that while they were shy initially, now they emphasise their presence and want to cooperate. It's a little group that I'm sure will grow, as their friends come along. I think we will slowly vanish, due to illnesses and weakness, but those young ones observe and listen. They will get more and more engaged in Jewishness and will propagate it in the future. I think it will not fade away. Maybe they will create a new model. It won't be the old Judaism, the old customs – that's history, exotic and picturesque images from the past. It will be reborn in a modern, progressive way.

I hear there are many conversions of Poles to Judaism. How they study the Talmud and the Bible! Their knowledge puts me to shame.

JOANNA SOBOLEWSKA-PYZ

When my (foster) mother was dying, she said that I shouldn't count on anyone. I understood that perhaps I was born out of wedlock. I suspected some family scandal. Don't count on anyone; you're only my daughter. That's how I understood it. Some time after her death I quarrelled with my father. He said: 'You have no idea what you owe me, what you owe us.' I replied, 'I know, I am not your daughter.' And he said, 'Neither mine nor hers.' That was the moment I learned the truth.

In the 1960s, through my research, I found out that my (Jewish) father's relatives had survived the war and had been alive, but were buried in the Catholic cemetery of Bródno. Why were they buried in the Catholic cemetery? They managed to escape from the ghetto with Aryan papers and changed their name to Rzepliński. They never admitted they were Jewish because they were too afraid. They weren't alone in this. After their experiences in the war, people were scared and said nothing. That's why they were buried there.

They hid their identity only from the outside world, not within their circle of friends. A family friend told me that after the war they would organise 'assemblies of the dead' and read out names of family members, weeping and mourning them. They howled with sadness when they reached my name: I was the only child in a large family. After the war, I was practically their neighbour: they lived in Piękna Street in Warsaw, and I in nearby Wilcza with my foster family.

Regarding people admitting or publicly revealing their Jewish identity, I have a friend in the Association who lives in a small town, and, during the war, was taken care of by her older brother. He told her: 'If you admit after the war that we're Jewish, we're struggling for nothing; I will kill you.' She was a child and he'd threatened her like this; he was so scared. And today he still doesn't admit it. She belongs to the Association and he doesn't. She and many other people don't talk about their origins in their towns, which is a farce because everybody knows. At times people who have nothing to do with Jewishness are suspected of it. So this explains why my relations were buried in a Christian cemetery – people still live in secret.

It's not only because of Polish anti-semitism. What happened in the Holocaust was such a major trauma that people perceived being Jewish as a stigma. Some managed to work their way through this trauma and return to normal life. But many people are very afraid. There are many people who have similar stories but are afraid of becoming members of the Association.

Has there been a change in the past 20 years? A lot has changed, that's true. People talk about it. When I learned about my roots I had no idea about anything. Now it's incomprehensible, how was it possible that we knew nothing? Me – a Jew? I only heard about Jews in ironic and satiric proverbs.

The biggest or most important change is that people started talking about Jewishness; it stopped being some sort of taboo. Children started to learn about it at school.

We were taught history badly, stupidly.

But that's trauma too. If I were to learn today that I was Jewish, who knows, maybe I'd be boastful about it. Or at least it wouldn't have been a shock. Now I know Jews exist and then it was completely abstract. There's a huge difference between now and then.

There's one other problem; we're talking about people who are ignorant of their origins. I met a friend, a film director, and he told me: 'I know that my mother found a little boy close to the railway tracks. That was in Falenica, near Warsaw. It must have been a child thrown out of a train going to Treblinka. So she took the baby, but as she had many children already, she gave it to her sister. She brought him up, he got married, had children. Should this person be told about this? What for? Why should I complicate his life?' He's never been told and his adoptive parents have died. Occasionally my friend gets an urge to talk to him honestly, especially after he'd had some vodka. It preys on his mind.

(The child is now close to 70.) Nobody wanted to hurt his parents, he had a very close relationship with them. It was beyond everybody to tell him then; only his parents could have done that. So why ruin his life?

Was his life built on an illusion? No, it was real. It's the Jewishness that is the illusion. In my case, for example, it was only in my head. In life, I had nothing to do with Jewishness. In day-to-day life, it's an illusion; it's in the sphere of the abstract. When it comes to identity, the whole of my Jewishness is a tribute to those who died, nothing more. Not the culture, the language, not the religion. Just the homage.

It's a question of honour. My family was killed for no reason other than being Jews. Not admitting your Jewish identity is some sort of dishonour. However, the other question is whether if I had never learned that I was Jewish, what is the indicator of being Jewish? If it's in your blood, then it becomes like a racial theory.

I think Jews in Israel or the U.S. have no idea about such issues. When I went to Israel and met the family, for them I was a close person because I was the daughter of people they had known. But it wasn't like that for me. They were completely strangers in a strange world. And while I am adaptable, I felt it, felt this imbalance between us. I couldn't establish that bond so easily.

I don't feel religious in any sense. The synagogue is an exotic place and when I see people swaying, it seems funny to me. I know the theory but it's hard to understand and connect. And to understand it emotionally. Whereas when I enter a church, everything is familiar because I feel very comfortable. It's a place I have known since childhood. Nevertheless, I don't like Catholicism and don't perceive myself as a Catholic.

Regarding the Jewish revival today, I think there are many people who want to profit from getting involved in this situation. I call them *nouveau Jews*. And because the community leaders want numbers, there are more converts.

So in this way it will develop. But our children, like my son and the children of the Children of the Holocaust, are mostly not interested in Jewishness.

It's hard to say whether I'm optimistic or pessimistic. I don't know what to say. First of all I don't care that much, to be honest. Because we are a special group, we Holocaust Jews; I mean the girls, because fewer boys survived. I am not really concerned with what will happen to the community now. It's a very different group from the group I identify with. So this is not my problem. There are many other problems apart from Jewishness.

RÓŻA GÓRSKA

I was born in Łódź on 5 August 1939. My father was a well-known lawyer; he married my mother in 1938, when she was 21 years old. They met at a charity ball, where she was crowned queen of the ball.

My maternal grandparents were wealthy and owned many printing enterprises in Łódź, which were passed on from one generation to the next. My grandfather was last to own these enterprises.

Three weeks after I was born the Germans invaded Poland and Łódź (Litzmannstadt) became part of Germany. They forced Jews to leave their homes and my father, as a lawyer, tried to negotiate with them – to gain time to pack, because it was getting cold. But they beat him up severely. He realised they couldn't remain and survive – the situation was very serious.

Escape, however, was very difficult as they had a newborn baby, myself. My maternal grandparents suggested that my mother leave for a safer place and they would take care of me. At the same time my father, and his brother, who was an architect, decided to go to Lwów as it was a safer place where they could get organised and bring the family over.

After 17 September, when the Soviet army came into Lwów, the Soviets offered my father and his brother Soviet citizenship. But they refused, and were forced to leave for Kazakhstan and put to work in a labour camp in the forests.

I went with my mother and grandparents to Warsaw. It was occupied by the Germans but had not been absorbed into Germany (Generalna Gubernia). They had some financial means but no connections there, neither friends nor family, as since the beginning of the nineteenth century my entire family had lived in Łódź. By 1940, when the Warsaw ghetto was created, they were compelled to go to the ghetto.

My mother, who was an attractive woman, managed to find a job as a waitress in the famous café where Szpilman played. I was looked after by my grandparents.

My earliest childhood memory is of being in a little bed with a net around it, and a picture of a child in a silver frame. One day I heard my mother was very ill, and I was not allowed to enter her bedroom. But when I woke each day I crawled into her room and climbed into her bed. I cuddled her, and felt secure.

One day when I was a year old I ran to my mother's room but she wasn't there. The bed had been stripped; she had probably died. I burst into tears. Suddenly a man appeared and placed me on his shoulder. He said: 'Don't worry, your mother is in the countryside and we're going to join her there.' Remember, he told me, from now on your name is Marysia Kołakowska. This was probably in the summer or fall of 1942. I later heard from my mother's friend, who lived in the same house in the ghetto and managed to survive, that in July 1942 they forced everyone aged over 60 to leave their homes. That's when my grandparents disappeared as well. The morning after I discovered my mother was gone, I woke up in a different place. I remember a lot of women gathered around me, feeling sorry for me and saying, oh, poor child, everyone is dead – everyone is gone. There was a feeling of hopelessness: there was no point in searching for anyone because they had all died.

The fiction about the countryside was only a ruse intended to calm me down. The following day I found myself in a house where nuns lived, and had a school for seamstresses, older or teenage girls. I was the only child. That day was the name-day of the principal of the convent, Sister Zenobia, and she invited some guests, among them Sister Maria Pietkiewicz. Sister Zenobia told them she had a little girl in the school but it would look suspicious as she was the only child there. She asked if they could move her to another convent. Sister Maria Pietkiewicz therefore took me to another convent, called 'Na Kamionku' on the Praga side of Warsaw. There was a private nursery and school there as well as a student residence.

I was the only orphan in that school. All my classmates went home on Saturdays, Sundays, or any major holidays and I was often left alone. I felt very sad about this. When I shared my feelings with the nuns, they became upset and said: 'How can you say that? We are your family; you haven't been left on your own.'

The Principal, Maria Pietkiewicz, was very strict and emotionally distant, but she loved me very much. Whenever she entered a room where I was present, she smiled and beamed with a nice look in her eyes.

After the war, many visitors came to the convent seeking to adopt children. One day a young couple came and Sister Pietkiewicz introduced me to them. They said: 'Oh, it was such a horrible war and people got lost. We are so happy to find her'. And they offered to take me to the United States.

At first the Principal agreed, but when I was about to depart, she withdrew her permission. She said she would never let me go with anyone – she treated me like a daughter. The Principal really liked to be with me – to take me for walks, and give me nice clothes that were sent from the U.S.

In 1949, the government closed all the convent schools, and I had to go to a regular school. But I was pleased because one of the teachers had been really unpleasant to me – not because of my background. She had a serious argument with the Principal and was taking it out on me.

I boarded in the convent residence for a while and went to a regular school. Although I was happy about this arrangement, I was also afraid that if they closed the residence, I would be forced to go to an orphanage. Fortunately, this didn't happen and I finished high school. Also, because of the persecution of religious life, the Principal, Sister Pietkiewicz, had to give up her position and leave the convent. At same time, a couple appeared at the convent looking to adopt a child. They had two sons but also wanted a girl, and were interested in adopting me.

While I was attending the regular school and could leave the premises of the convent, I went to the Polish Red Cross to find out whether any member of my family was looking for me. But unfortunately no one was.

The Principal, Maria Pietkiewicz, couldn't help me any more because she too had to leave Warsaw. So she agreed I could stay with the family who wanted to adopt me. I was then thirteen years old.

During the weekdays I still lived in the convent, but on weekends and holidays I visited that family. Everything was fine in the beginning. The brothers were very nice. I did not call those people Mother and Father, but rather Aunt and Uncle. I had a pretty good relationship with the Uncle, who was really pleasant toward me. But I noticed that the Aunt was becoming competitive and jealous of all the attention and affection I was receiving from her husband and sons. I soon realised this arrangement was doomed.

I didn't know about my Jewish origins. At that time the Principal of the convent school, Zofia Ossowska, was my godmother. I frequently said to her that I was probably Jewish because there seemed to be no trace of my family. But the Principal said it was such a terrible war, a huge disaster and massacre, and it was not surprising no one survived. The Principal said she was sure I wasn't Jewish. She even maintained she had known my parents before the war, and so there was no possibility that I was Jewish.

I suspected this wasn't true. But the Principal taunted me, saying: 'Come on, you are such a smart girl – how can you even think such silly things?'

Then, in March 1968, during the anti-semitic campaign, she said: 'You see what is going on. It's dangerous to be a Jew.' This was long after my time in the school because I was constantly in touch with my godparents and they wanted to take care of me.

Since I was often denied the possibility of being Jewish, and also seeing the situation in Poland at the time, I despaired of delving deeper into it. The atmosphere was not very conducive to research. Even if I wanted to search for my origins, I decided it was too risky and I wouldn't know where to start. So I gave up.

In 1956, I took entrance exams to study at the Catholic University in Lublin and began to study for a degree in psychology. Like most of the students, I was living in student residences where friendships were created and first loves happened. It was the most beautiful time of my life. Many men were after me and I refused them because I had a convent upbringing. Also, I didn't have any family support, so I felt I had to be very self-reliant.

After university in Lublin I returned to Warsaw to live in the convent, which I regarded as my home. I planned to stay until I felt confident that I was fully independent. All the nuns there wanted to keep me, saying it was my home. Around the same time, Sister Maria Pietkiewicz returned to Warsaw. She was now more lenient and also quite old. When I originally came to the convent she was already in her 60s.

In 1965, I married a man who also didn't have a family and was as lonely as myself. His mother and younger brother were living in Kielce – far away from Warsaw. He was a shy, sensitive person, but also very patient. So he managed to win me away from other men.

In 1981, Sister Pietkiewicz died. A couple of years later I went to visit the nuns. There was a nice young nun there whom I had befriended, and we ended up discussing why Pietkiewicz never allowed me to be adopted. Just before Pietkiewicz died, I went to see her and she was incredibly nice to me. She told me she was so sorry for what she had done; and she was sure God would never forgive her. I tried to console her and asked what she meant. But she did not reply.

The other nun, who was my friend, had asked Sister Pietkiewicz about my origins. She was sworn to secrecy, hand on the cross, that she would never reveal the story – neither to me nor anyone else. Sister Pietkiewicz confessed to her that I was a child from the ghetto and my parents' only child. She said that my father was some sort of intellectual and that my mother was a very beautiful woman. After Sister Pietkiewicz died, the other nun felt the promise to keep the secret was no longer valid and that she could share it with me.

I learned about my identity in the mid-1980s. I needed time to digest it, and reflect on what it meant to me. During this period my husband was very supportive.

Then, at the beginning of the 1990s, when the Association of Children of the Holocaust was created, I went to one of the first meetings. A miracle happened. A woman, a total stranger, approached me. She said her name is Anita, and that she is my cousin on my father's side. It transpired that Anita had asked Inka Sobolewska in the Association if she knew of anyone who was rescued by nuns and continued to live in a convent for many years. Hearing this, Inka had suggested me. When Anita saw me, she was struck by the similarity between me and my mother. At first I didn't believe we were cousins, but was won over as Anita recalled many key facts. So that's how I became acquainted with my family history.

Anita's side of the family remained in Łódź during the war because the German husband was able to protect his wife and their children. They left behind precious family photographs and documents. The photographs, in particular, enabled Anita to identify me.

I learned from my cousin that after the war, in 1946, my father took the first available train to Poland because he knew his sister was still alive. He had managed to survive in Kazakhstan. When he reached Łódź, his sister told him that his wife had died and that his daughter was in some sort of convent. My father posted a very big reward for anyone who could help him find his daughter. Of course, he received many letters because people were keen to get this reward. He believed that if she had been in a convent, it would have only been temporary. He chose the most promising letters and went to many places, but it was all in vain. Unfortunately, he didn't have any knowledge of the new name I had acquired during the war.

While he was travelling around Poland, he met a woman who became his second wife. She had a daughter the same age as me. When he got married, he treated that girl like his own daughter. His wife wasn't Jewish.

I am one of the few from the Association of Children of the Holocaust who has traces of her family. There is also a friend of my mother, who lived close to us in the ghetto, and who was the last person to see my father. She is now living in Paris. I visited her there and continue to keep in touch with her.

I was a religious and practising Catholic and remain a Catholic, but in a different sense. Once I learned about my origins, things have not been the same. It's all very difficult for me and there is no easy answer. I would like to combine Catholicism and Judaism in an ecumenical way because both are very important to me. The synagogue is a strange place for me because I never had any association with it. I was a Catholic without thinking that I might be Jewish. But I have a very deep respect for Judaism because I know it was the religion of my ancestors. But I can't connect to it because it's not really my religion.

TOMASZ PROT

For many years, I was a researcher at the Warsaw University of Technology. I later moved to the University of Technology in Radom, where I worked until retirement. I am a Professor Emeritus of chemistry at the Polytechnic in Radom.

I was born in Warsaw in 1930. My family, on both my father's and mother's side, was assimilated. My parents converted to Catholicism before they married. My father came from a Warsaw family, Berlinerblau. My mother came from Kraków, from an old Jewish family named Deiches.

I always knew I had Jewish roots, but until the war I didn't think it was a problem. I thought we were a genuinely Polish family.

During the German occupation, it didn't matter that my family had converted to Catholicism. The Germans, and even some Poles, regarded us as Jews. Germans treated us the same way as Orthodox Jews.

Before the war, my father served in the army as an officer, initially in the Polish Legions under Piłsudski's command. Later on he became a major in the Polish army. At that time, there were a lot of people with Jewish backgrounds in the Polish army. After Piłsudski's death in 1935, politicians tried to get rid of the Jews in the military.

My father was not affected because, after the war with the Bolsheviks in 1920, he left the army. He graduated in chemistry and, in 1927, became the head of a factory which produced gunpowder. The factory was located in Pionki near Radom.

I was raised like a typical Catholic child: I was baptised and had my first communion. My sister, who was older, was similarly raised. My parents felt connected to the Catholic religion. Also, being a Catholic helped my father's career. Also, undoubtedly, the fact that my sister and I were raised as Catholics helped us to survive the war.

When the war broke out, my parents were already separated. My mother, sister and I were in Warsaw, but my father was in Pionki. In Warsaw, we decided against going to the ghetto. Furthermore, we didn't wear the compulsory Jewish badges. However, we couldn't remain in Warsaw because we appeared as though we were possibly Jews. Our presence provoked the attention of neighbours, who questioned how we managed to remain outside the ghetto. We had to leave Warsaw and, in December 1939, arrived at a convent in Laski, where Franciscan nuns ran an institute for the blind. They were relatively progressive Catholics. Moreover, my mother had friends there from before the war.

My father, meanwhile, was no longer in Pionki. In 1939, the gunpowder factory was relocated to the east, away from the advancing Germans. But then it fell into the hands of the Bolsheviks and was shut down. My father came back to Warsaw.

In January 1940, he crossed the Polish border into Hungary, then moved on to France, where he worked at the Curie Institute in Paris. After France was attacked, he escaped to England where he remained until his death in 1957.

In 1957, when the worst Stalinist period ended, I received my passport and could travel to England. There I met my father, but he was very ill and died two weeks later. He was still preoccupied with teaching chemistry and physics at a college in London, and we delayed talking at length until the academic year ended. But, although he didn't know it, he was already very ill and died soon after.

Coming back to the wartime period, we remained in the convent in Laski for about a year and a half. Then we had to leave because the presence of Jews on the premises came to the notice of the neighbours living in the village. Furthermore, five of the nuns staying in the convent had Jewish backgrounds. They too had to leave because they posed a threat to the whole convent.

My awareness of my Jewish roots came to the fore when I had to go into hiding. Previously, our Jewish origins were not a secret, but we thought we were Poles. There was an incident when I was six or seven years old and was visiting my mother's family in Kraków. I spoke to a cousin, and he said: 'We Jews.' And I replied: 'No, I am a Pole.' So my cousin said: 'How is that possible? If I'm a Jew and you're my cousin, you must be Jewish as well.' Although I knew about our background, because I asked my mother about it, at the same time I felt I was a Pole. In my mind, Jews were the Orthodox Jews with beards and religious clothes.

Many Jews in Poland at that time were Orthodox Jews. They were distinguished from the rest of the population by, for example, how they dressed. Women wore wigs and the men had beards. For me they seemed alien, strange people because among my parents' circles there were no Orthodox Jews.

Neither my mother nor father spoke Yiddish. Perhaps the grandparents did. But they would never use it in my presence. If my parents didn't want the children to understand what they were saying, they would switch to French.

We left the convent at the beginning of 1942. We were hiding separately. My sister was the first to return to Warsaw because she wanted to get an education. There were still schools that were open but they taught, for example, a trade – they were not academic schools. There were also some secret schools. She hid with different people and had to wander from one place to another. This was difficult because, after a period of time, she would be asked to leave since she looked very Jewish and harbouring her was dangerous. She had a close friend at the school who offered a place in her home. Initially, the family was unaware that my sister was Jewish. Even after they found out, they decided to keep her as a third daughter. Thanks to them she survived the war.

My family had good contacts on the Aryan side. I went to my mother's friend's house in Żoliborz. She was a mother of two teenagers. Obviously, this woman knew I was of Jewish origin, yet she allowed me to stay although she was very afraid – for herself, and also her children. They were active in the Home Army and later both teenagers were killed in the Warsaw Uprising.

I stayed there for a few weeks, but always in hiding. I couldn't approach the windows and had to go to another room if visitors arrived.

My mother had the 'good looks' and found work as a housekeeper in Warsaw. After some time, she managed to find a place for me in a house for boys run by the so-called Central Welfare Council (Rada Główna Opiekuńcza) which was one of the few Polish social organisations, not associated with the church, that was allowed to continue functioning during the German occupation. It was established as a social services organisation for military families.

I spent the rest of the war with that group. Because I had dark hair, I told people I came from Hungary. I had false documents which my mother arranged. The house was also in Żoliborz. In the near future, a plaque will be placed on the wall of the building commemorating the fact that Jews were hidden there during the war. The head of the household received a medal from Yad Vashem because I filed a request.

When the war ended, we couldn't stay in Warsaw because it had been destroyed. So we moved to Wrocław. I finished high school there and started college, then we moved to Łódź. My sister finished medical studies in Wrocław. My mother held the position of deputy director in a library at the polytechnic in Wrocław.

We returned to Warsaw at the beginning of the 1950s. I finished my chemistry degree and my sister got her degree as a medical doctor. My mother worked in the library of the Warsaw Polytechnic.

The Jewish theme returned in 1968 with the anti-semitic campaign. As a result, my sister decided to leave Poland and move to the United States, along with her Jewish husband and their children. My sister wasn't forced to emigrate, but said she didn't want to raise her children in a country where, after the Holocaust, there still was so much anti-semitism. She remained in the United States, and worked as a doctor. She died two years ago.

As for myself, in 1968 I was working at the Warsaw Polytechnic and feared I would be forced to emigrate. I didn't want to leave Poland; moreover, my wife is not Jewish. So once more I was compelled to deny my background. I was a member of the Communist Party, which organised a meeting. At the meeting, I told them I do not have a Jewish background but I came from Hungary. Later I was so ashamed that I finally decided to be very open about it, and have been ever since. Now, at work and elsewhere, I make a point of emphasising the Jewish heritage of myself and my entire family – apart from my wife, who doesn't have Jewish roots but wishes she did. I now feel that I am a Polish Jew.

I'm a member of various Jewish organisations: the Gmina, the Organisation of Jewish Combatants, The Association of Children of the Holocaust, Bnai Brith. It is true that this active Jewish involvement began after the fall of Communism. But even when I was working in Radom, I was very open about my Jewishness.

My daughter is a psychiatrist and is active in the Holocaust Association as a doctor of medicine. She is also a member of the Gmina. She is a professor now and wrote her post-doctoral thesis comparing the traumatic experiences of Polish and Romanian Jews. My grandchildren are adults and are active in Jewish organisations. In fact, one of my grandchildren is a member of the board of the Gmina. My grandchildren's names are Jacob and Sarah. Their surname is not Prot, but their father is also of Jewish origin.

Because Polish society since 1968 has considered me as a Jew, I consider myself to be one as well.

JADWIGA GAŁĄZKA

I don't know my date of birth, and my name and surname are not my own. I did not begin to discover the story of my life until I was 55. It was as if my real life started then – my Jewish life. I was probably born in Pińczów, but my search of the town's registry office yielded no trace of my birth there.

Around 1941 I was carried to the village of Bogucice, eight kilometres away from Pińczów, and there I was rescued. My adoptive father worked in Pińczów, so I suppose my real parents probably arranged that he and his wife would 'find' me. All this I learned later in life. I wasn't really a foundling. My adoptive parents knew perfectly well who I was.

My adoptive father was involved in partisan activities and, before the end of the war, he had to escape to England. So the two of us were left alone. After the war, we moved to the so-called 'recovered territories' in western Poland. My adoptive mother was constantly changing our address to cover her tracks. She even changed my name several times. She was an alcoholic and a liar.

She frequently shouted at me that I was a nasty Jew, although I had no knowledge of my Jewish origins. I recall one event when we were living in Wrocław. I cuddled her, but she responded angrily, saying: 'Don't hug me, I'm not your mother.' That moment of rejection weighed upon me forever.

At the age of fourteen or fifteen I ran away from her to Warsaw and resided with a family of one of my adoptive mother's friends. There I lived in poor conditions, having to clean and cook for the household. A neighbour in the same building, who befriended me, knew I was adopted and she probably guessed that I was Jewish. She also knew that my situation was hopeless, so she suggested that I approach the TSKŻ, the Jewish social organisation. Although I didn't have any documents, the TSKŻ gave me a little money and I could rent a shared room. This allowed me to leave the family, which helped me to survive the first months in Warsaw. The fact that my adoptive mother had often called me a horrible Jew made me feel drawn to the Jewish organisations like TSKŻ.

Later I met my husband, who was not Jewish. We had two children. After a few years the marriage ended, and I was left with a four-year-old son and a three-month-old daughter.

It never occurred to me that I could look for information about myself. There was nobody who could help me. Once, after I had retired, during a meeting with friends, someone mentioned that she went back to her birthplace to learn about her own background. It convinced me that I should do the same, visit the place where I was supposedly found. That meeting with friends was a turning point in my life.

With a friend, we went to the village of Bogucice. When we arrived there, my first thought was to go to the church. I was sure that I had been baptised. The church was closed. At the neighbouring house I inquired about the family I had stayed with. A woman said that there were a few families with the same surname and directed me to the home of the nearest one. I was only four when we left the village in 1945, yet I recognised the house. That was a big step in my research.

We entered the courtyard. A man emerged. I told him I had a strange feeling that I lived here during the war. He said: 'Are you little Jadzia?' He invited us inside and began to tell the story. It emerged he was the brother of the man who rescued me. After the war, his brother returned from England to Poland. The man said it was a shame I had come too late as his brother had died a month earlier. Before his death, he was clear-headed and could have told me a great deal.

I learned that my adoptive father's son is still alive, living between Poland and Germany. I got his phone number to check if he has any memorabilia. He replied that he indeed has something, but insisted upon a personal encounter. Our meeting was another turning point in my life. He had an empty envelope, which should have contained a letter that was sent in 1963 from Israel to the address in Bogucice, to my adoptive father's name. It appeared that someone in Israel was looking for me, and knew the precise address where I had been left during the war.

He also had a copy of a letter my adoptive father wrote to the Red Cross in 1985, looking for me. But he didn't know that his wife had changed my name. She had learned that her husband had started a new family after leaving Poland, and, in this way, she took her revenge. Today I have the letter which says that my real name is Klara Gross. My real parents were Regina (Rivka) and Siegbert Gross. I was born in Pińczów and my maternal grandparents' name was Rosenberg.

I had such a feeling of happiness upon learning my real name and the names of my parents. I felt that I exist, that I am alive, that I am somebody. I also learned that after the war, people had come to Bogucice to look for me, but they didn't know where I was. These people were probably relatives of my parents and most likely lived in Israel.

In 1995 I went to ŻIH (Jewish Historical Institute) to do some research. I didn't know whether any family members were still alive. At first I was mistakenly told by a genealogist at ŻIH that nobody was alive in Israel. But something about that envelope wouldn't let me give up. Three years later I returned to the same genealogist who, on the basis of that one letter, opened a file on my behalf and discovered that my aunt and her son were dead, but her daughter was alive. That's how the contact with my surviving family in Israel began.

The daughter – my cousin – wanted to talk to me, of course. The problem was that she couldn't speak Polish. We started writing letters; my neighbour, who speaks English, talked to her and interpreted. My cousin invited me to Israel, thanks to a photograph - I have no idea how the photo of me at around the age of four found its way to Israel. It's possible that it was taken even before my adoptive mother took me to western Poland.

When my adoptive father's son gave me the envelope, he also gave me childhood photos of myself left behind by his father. So I had a photo similar to the one that was found in Israel.

As a matter of fact, my cousin asked whether I had any photos from around the age of four – she wanted to verify it was really me. I sent her that photo, which I recently received, for confirmation and then she invited me to Israel.

I flew to Tel Aviv in 2000 and it was a very emotional reunion, very tearful. There was a journalist at the airport who photographed our meeting for a newspaper. They also published an interview which included the photo of me at the age of four.

My cousin explained that before the war, my aunt (her mother) lived in Gdańsk with the parents. My father lived in the same building. The sister of my aunt came to visit her, met him and they got married. This was the Gross side of the family.

I also learned from my cousin that my parents died in Treblinka. In 1939, they had probably thought that Pińczów would be safer than Gdańsk. Those discoveries about my identity meant a lot to me.

After I found some evidence of my origins, in 1995, I contacted the Association of Children of the Holocaust. As I'm neither Catholic nor a practising Jew, I think I define myself as Polish Jewish. And, of course, I now feel part of the Polish Jewish community.

JERZY BANDER

The revelation about my true identity and family history happened late in life. My existence on 'Aryan documents' lasted 45 years because the family members who survived the Holocaust wanted me to retain this identity. The guardian of the family secret was my father's Catholic second wife, Józefa Urszula Bander, who married my father in 1945 and whom, until a memorable day in 1987, I considered my mother.

I was born in August 1942 in Sambor, a small town in Galicia. Most of my childhood was spent with my foster grandparents, Józefa and Władysław Zakrzewski, in Tarnów. At the time my parents lived in Bytom but, when I was nine, I joined them there. I stopped going to church because my father was the headmaster of a secondary school and a member of the Communist Party. Following graduation from high school, I enrolled in the faculty of Electrics and Automatics at the Silesian University of Technology. After obtaining my degree, I started working in the automatics industry in Kęty.

The anti-semitic campaign of 1968 had no impact on my life since no one in Kęty, including myself, knew I was a Jew. By then I was married to a Catholic woman, with whom I had two children. My grandmother had insisted on a Catholic wedding and baptism for the children. No one, however, could find my baptism certificate for the simple reason that I had never owned one. In the end, the resourceful grandmother persuaded my mother (stepmother) and grandmother's sister to testify I was baptised in Sambor, which allowed us to marry in the church and also to baptise our children. I subsequently became a regular church-goer, particularly after the imposition of martial law.

In October 1987 my aunt, Dr Janina Bander – the wife of my father's brother – died. During her funeral in Kraków, I was approached by a well-dressed elderly woman. She handed me an envelope, saying that my late aunt had requested that she give it to me. Later I opened the envelope and found $50, a card with a name, address and telephone number. There was also a note: 'When you're in Warsaw please make sure to visit me. I have something important to tell you.'

One month later I went to Warsaw and visited this woman, Zuzanna Szydłowska. She explained that my late aunt was her friend from pre-war Tarnów, and after my aunt's husband, Witek, died, she would visit Zuzanna several times a year. She always came for Yom Kippur, and they would go to the Nożyk synagogue on Twarda Street. In 1987, immediately after Kol Nidrei, she felt ill. She refused to go to a hospital, and insisted on returning to Kraków. Zuzanna accompanied her on the train, aware she was dying. In Kraków, she lost consciousness and passed away.

The remarks about synagogue, Yom Kippur, and Kol Nidrei confused me. I must have made a stupid face, because she said: 'Yes, that's why I asked you to come. Now I'm not sure how to tell you this. The last will of Janeczka was that you know you are all Jewish. Your aunt Janeczka, her husband Witek, your father, and you. She wanted you to know that the mother who raised you was not your mother, but Ludwik's second wife. Your real mother, your father's first wife, was a Jew and she was murdered shortly after you were born in a Gestapo prison in Sambor. I had to reveal this to you; it was in Janeczka's will. She suffered so much because she couldn't tell you the truth. But your father and his wife wanted you to have a happy childhood, and not suffer as we all did, thinking every day about murdered relatives.'

I felt as though I had been hit with a bolt of lightning. I was so shocked to learn that for my entire life I had been deceived by my family.

Not long after I returned to Warsaw to meet Stefan Boratyński and his wife, Ewa Rosa-Boratyńska. They were also friends of my aunt and had lived in Tarnów before the war. I was hungry to learn what I could about my mother. My father didn't want to tell me anything, and held a grudge against me because I wanted to discover the truth. With his second wife he had decided to cut himself off from the past, and start a fresh chapter in his life. He also argued that he had to be loyal to his second wife, who had raised me very well.

I contacted the Sambor Association, through which I met Ludwik Stypka, who knew my father and had a photograph of my mother. During one of my many visits to Sambor, he pointed out the house where my father hid in the last four months of the war. The house belonged to the Wachulka family and I learned that the eldest daughter, Maria, rescued my father and me after the liquidation of the Sambor ghetto in June 1943. Although she took me to her home, when I cried the neighbours worried I would be discovered. So Maria took me to an orphanage in Sambor that was run by nuns. Despite illness and hunger I managed to survive until August 1944, when the Soviet army entered the town.

In 2001 in Drohobycz, I met Hania Kretz. She had also been hidden in the same orphanage as myself, and lived in Antwerp after the war. Over dinner Hania asked me how I survived. When I recounted my birth in Sambor's Gestapo prison, she cried: 'You're the baby', and burst into tears. During the Aktion in the ghetto, she was imprisoned with 20 other Jewish women. Later a naked new-born baby boy was put in the cell. Hania remembered that it was a boy. The women wrapped him in Hania's coat. Hania was taken out from prison with the help of a bribed Jewish police officer, but had wondered many times whether the baby survived. Sixty years later she found me; since then we have been like brother and sister.

Hania also helped me find my father's two cousins, who live in Israel. She placed a notice on the internet that I was looking for relatives from Sambor. We located Helena Flajszfarb, who lives near Haifa. Our first phone conversation was almost impossible as we were crying so much. In 2003 we finally met in Israel, where Helena gave me photographs and recounted her memories of my mother.

I have spent many years searching for my family's documents. In 1988 I found in the archives of the Jewish Historical Institute a registration card filled in by my aunt, Janina Bander, after her return with her husband, Wiktor, from the Soviet Union in 1945. The JHI advised me to ask Zuzanna Szydłowska and the Boratyński couple to send their notarised statement about my Jewish origins as well as the conditions I endured in the first two years of my life. I have suffered from recurring depression. The psychiatrist, Dr Maria Orwid of Kraków, issued a statement that this was a result of the conditions I lived in during my infancy.

Yet I needed to learn more about my real mother and her family. After my father's friend told me that my parents had a Jewish wedding in Lwów in 1936, I found their marriage certificate in the archives of Zabużańskie Records in Warsaw. In this way, I discovered my mother's maiden name, Rozalia Thun, and the surnames of other members of the family, witnesses and the officiating rabbi. With this new data I went to Lwów where, in the archives, I established that my grandfather, Józef Lejb Thun, had two shops in the Hausman Passage in the centre of Lwów, and that he and my father were members of the Jewish reform community. Before my mother got married, she had lived with her brother and sister in a flat at the Strzelecki Square in the centre of Lwów.

It was both tragic and comical when my father's Catholic wife revised his mother's name to put on his death certificate in 1991, changing the real name of Salomea Robinsohn to Maria Rolska. On my father's tombstone, she inscribed 'Ludwik Maria Bander' so that no one would ever doubt my father's supposed Aryan background. The old caretaker of the Bytom cemetery, who knew my father, would wink at me and I winked in return. Following the death of the Catholic mother, I changed the inscription on my father's tombstone so it simply reads: Ludwik Bander.

I shared the discovery of my Jewish background with my family and close friends soon after I learned the truth. My relationship with these people did not change; but I made many new friends among members of the Children of the Holocaust Association. By now I was discovering my Jewish heritage by reading books that began to appear in the early 1990s. In 1992 I became a member of the Association of Jewish Veterans as well as the Association of Children of the Holocaust. In order to assimilate my experience, I started to write – first poems and then short stories – about Jewish subjects. The stories were published in Poland in 2011. With my second wife, Danuta nee Frajdman, who is Jewish, we sometimes join Gdańsk or Warsaw congregations to celebrate Jewish holidays.

After my first visit to Israel in 2003, I began an application to make *aliyah*. However, it took so long that I finally went as a tourist in 2005. Eventually my wife and I gained our Israeli citizenship. Several years later we decided to return to Poland because my wife would lose her licence to practice as a nurse if she stayed abroad for more than five years. Furthermore, I found it difficult to adjust to the Israeli climate. In 2009, we moved to the seaside town of Sztutowo. I now joke that when a Jew is unlucky he first lives 17 kilometres from Auschwitz, and later 0.5 kilometres from the former concentration camp of Stutthof.

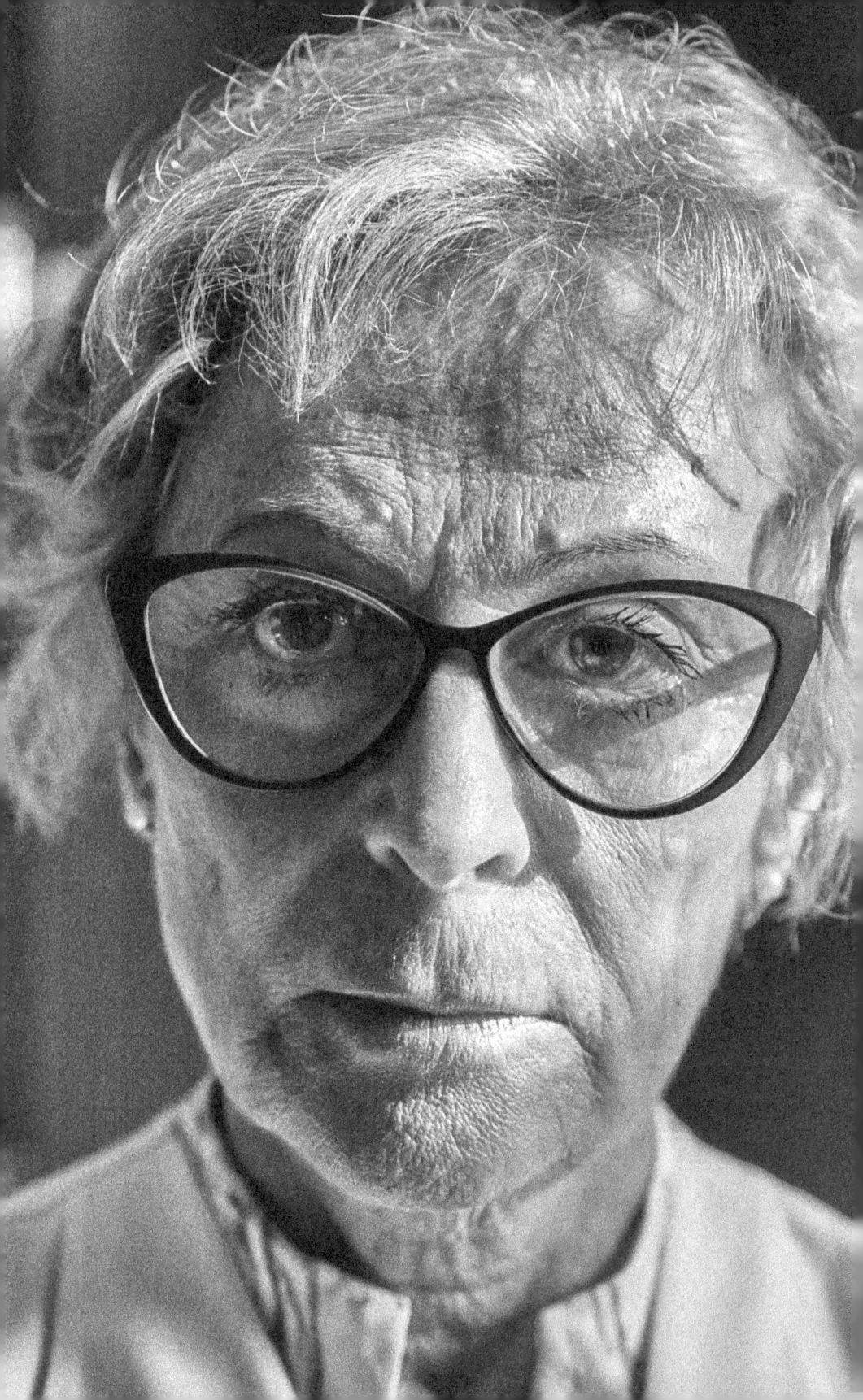

JANINA 'NINA' GRIEBEL

I was born in in the Galician town of Nowy Sącz in 1940, and worked throughout my professional life as a doctor. I specialise as a laryngologist.

My grandfather, whose family originally came from Konigsberg, was a rabbi in Nowy Sącz. My grandmother had seven sets of twins, plus four other children – or a total of eighteen children. All the boys received a good education, and were also trained in practical trades. Unfortunately, only two brothers survived the war.

After the German invasion, my parents were transferred to the Nowy Sącz ghetto. They knew they were destined to die, and arranged for me to be left with my Polish Catholic nanny. I was three years old at the time. I was fortunate not to have semitic features; instead I was blonde and blue-eyed, what people then called 'the good looks'.

My parents gave the nanny enough money to ensure she would be financially secure and capable of looking after me. Nevertheless, she kept me hidden in the shed, in such terrible conditions that I suffered from malnutrition. I don't know how long this dreadful situation lasted, but it might have been one or two years.

Eventually the nanny took me to the people who became my foster parents, and told them she lacked the means to support me. I don't know what year that happened. My foster mother later told me that when they took me in, I didn't know how to eat. I would look at food and didn't know what to do with it. To this day I don't have a robust appetite.

Many years later I learned that my grandmother survived the war. She owned a few general stores before the war; there were many customers still indebted to her. They feared that, following her return, she would want to collect those debts. To avoid repaying her, she was murdered by some Poles. So it's ironical that a Polish family adopted me and gave me all they could, while other Poles killed my grandmother, a survivor of the Holocaust.

In 1946 my foster parents moved back to Krosno, where they came from, and I lived there until I finished high school. When I was eight or nine, I shared a bench with another girl. Someone threw her a piece of paper which said: you shouldn't share a bench with Nina because her parents are not her genuine parents. I went to my father's bakery in tears, but he comforted me and said it wasn't true. This was my first inkling there was something wrong with my family story.

I grew up in a Catholic household. My foster parents were very good, honest people; all their fine values were passed on to me. The best proof of this was their willingness to take in a Jewish child during the war. But throughout this time, as I grew up in Krosno, I didn't have a clue about my Jewish origins.

In 1958 my boyfriend and I left for Wrocław University, where we planned to study medicine. We met at primary school, and got married here in Wrocław. After a few years our marriage ended.

Although the nanny gave me away to my foster parents, she remained in touch with one of my two surviving uncles, who lived in Munich. He was wealthy, and regularly sent her money during the 1950s because she convinced him she was still supporting me. But she didn't maintain contact with my foster parents, of course.

When I was eighteen, and had already begun my medical studies in Wrocław, my uncle wrote to the nanny saying that if he didn't get direct contact with me, he would stop paying her. Consequently, the nanny wrote me a letter, informing me she was in touch with an uncle who lived abroad.

During a vacation in Krosno, the nanny came to visit and gave me a letter. It was from my uncle, who said he was my mother's brother and would love to be in touch with me. This was quite a shock; it was then I learned my foster parents were not my real parents. That was a key moment of discovery. Despite the initial shock I felt quite peaceful, and slowly grew accustomed to this news. However, I didn't tell my foster parents. I certainly didn't blame them for not telling me. As I didn't want to hurt them, I decided not to discuss it for the moment. I needed more time before having this conversation with them.

When I visited my uncle for the first time in Vienna, he urged me to stay and take up my medical studies there. He even held my passport over the Danube River, urging me not to return to Poland, where nothing would ever improve. I explained that I couldn't leave behind the people who had rescued me, risking their lives in doing so. If I left Poland there was no going back. Besides I had my boyfriend and all my friends in Poland.

It was only after visiting my uncle that I talked to my foster parents about my discovery of my biological Jewish family. My foster mother responded by reminding me they had always treated me like their very own child.

After the discovery of my Jewish roots I didn't talk about it, and didn't feel the need to express it publicly, like wearing the star of David. On the other hand, I had good relationships with Jews in Wrocław, some of whom later left for Israel. In 1968 some friends were affected by the anti-semitic purge, but at that time few people knew I was Jewish.

I frequently visit a friend in Israel, and her husband says I'm Jewish in so many ways. Perhaps it's my sense of humour. But there is something instinctive in my connection with other Jews.

I don't go to church but I also don't participate in the religious services at the synagogue. I'm essentially an agnostic. For me, belonging to the Association of Children of the Holocaust is a way of expressing solidarity with the community. I am friendly with most women in the Association; we also meet socially outside the organisation. Occasionally I go to the synagogue for cultural events, such as concerts.

My second husband also has Jewish roots on his grandmother's side. I always knew this was the case because he looks Jewish; his entire family has very strong semitic features. Ironically, when I was a medical student and we were discussing facial features, my professor called me up to the podium to discuss my classic Slavic looks!

My son, Maciej Starzyk, who is also a doctor, discovered my Jewish background during a vacation in Krosno. Distant relatives told him that although he loves his grandparents very much, they are actually his mother's foster parents. When he returned and confronted me, I finally told him the whole story. He responded very positively by taking an interest in religion and learning Hebrew. In fact, he has a greater interest in Jewish traditions than I do and has formally joined the Wrocław community.

I have had many opportunities to leave Poland because of my professional reputation. But I am a Polish Jew and I can't hide that reality As for the future outlook, there is still anti-semitism here even if it's not as blatant as in the past. Still, we have a new political situation in Poland which many people find rather worrying.

MACIEJ CZARNIECKI

I was born in Lwów in 1942 just three months after the death of my father, Adolf Ashkenazy. He was shot in the street by the Gestapo. He had been a professional officer in the Austrian Imperial Royal army and, after the First World War, had served as a Polish army captain in the Polish-Russian war of 1919-1923. My mother, Wiktoria, was a Catholic from Lwów.

My father's younger brother, Marcel Ashkenazy, was also a Polish officer who participated in the Polish-Russian War. He was wounded, and awarded the Virtuti Military Cross. As a member of the secretive Polish Military Organisation, he adopted the name of his close friend, Maciej Czarniecki, who convinced him to convert to Catholicism in 1922 in order to keep his new name. He was very proud of his surname; it's the same as one of Poland's heroes, who is mentioned in the national anthem.

His newly acquired Catholic identity, supported by Aryan papers, proved to be very useful during the German occupation of Lwów; it permitted him to take a job as a driver for a factory making washing powder. In this capacity, he had a pass allowing him to deliver products throughout the General-Government area. It also enabled him to get papers under the surname 'Czarniecki' for my mother, my older brother, and myself. Although my mother was not Jewish, people knew she had been married to my father and, as half-Jewish children, we were in constant danger of recognition by Gestapo agents, Ukrainian police and Polish blackmailers. Marcel therefore organised frequent changes of residence while also sending my mother financial means to support us.

This terrible ordeal ended in May 1944 when Lwów was liberated by the Russians. In April 1945 we were repatriated to Poland, and moved to Wałbrzych in Lower Silesia, which had one of the biggest Jewish communities after the war. We nonetheless regarded ourselves as Catholics, and decided to keep the name, Czarniecki, which had been so useful in saving our lives. At the same time my uncle married my mother, and adopted my older brother, Piotr, and myself. We believed he was our biological father.

In May 1947 he was arrested by the Ministry of Public Security. As a member of the pre-war intelligentsia, he didn't fit in with the new political regime. After a rigged trial, he was sentenced to two and a half years of forced labour in salt mines and quarries. By the time of his release, his health had deteriorated so badly that he died shortly after, in December 1949.

Our mother was a fervent Catholic, and raised us similarly. When she died in 1991, I was 50 years old but knew nothing about my Jewish roots. I recalled, however, that she had corresponded with someone from abroad, and decided to go through her papers. Finding an address in Tulsa, Oklahoma on several envelopes, I sent a letter explaining I was the son of the woman who had corresponded. But my mother, fearing that contact with people abroad would impede my chances of going to university, stopped the correspondence while I was still in high school.

The address was the home of my Jewish father's cousin, who had died, but her daughter found my letter and replied, directing me to another cousin, my father's sister's son. He was a retired U.S. diplomat, who had changed his name to John Gunter Dean (from Dinstfertig). In 1998 he invited me to meet him in Verbier, Switzerland. There, over drinks, he told me the whole family story. That's when I found out my father's real name was Ashkenazy.

I was not surprised to learn about my Jewish roots, partly because I had already distanced myself from religious practise and considered myself an agnostic. I have always been interested in different religions, and never believed Catholicism was superior to any of them. So I was pleased to hear about this Jewish dimension in my background. My wife and sons, who are also agnostics, were surprised by this revelation but didn't react negatively. My sons didn't reveal this news to their wives or children. But neither I nor my brother told our friends about these revelations.

I initiated contacts with the Jewish community in Wrocław in 2015, when I learned about the possibility of receiving compensation from the Conference on Jewish Material Claims Against Germany for victims of Nazism. However, to make a claim, I needed documents to prove my Jewish background, and contacted the Jewish Historical Institute in Warsaw. They informed me they had found reports from the late 1940s from Jewish organisations in France and the U.S. concerning the search for children from Lwów who had survived the Holocaust. These documents confirmed my brother's and my Jewish origins.

I am increasingly more connected to the Jewish community. For example, I recently celebrated my first Rosh Hashanah, and have been involved with the Association of Children of the Holocaust over the past year. Last June I went to the Association's annual gathering for the first time, in Miedzeszyn near Warsaw. It was a jubilee convention attended by over 100 people. The participants were of similar age to mine (I am 74) or even older.

During this event, I attended a psychotherapy session where survivors recounted painful facts remembered from their unhappy childhoods. Many were raised by Catholic families or religious institutions. The great majority remained Catholic, due to their wartime upbringing.

While talking about my childhood, I recalled many 'tiny' facts which had faded from my memory. What became clear was that it was easier to bond with these people, as many of their stories were similar to my own. But I did feel regret that I learned about my Jewish roots so late in my life, especially because there I met a significant number of highly educated people of immense culture.

I now feel more connected to the pre-war family I lost. But I do not feel bitter that my Jewish identity was kept hidden from me. After all, my mother had died, and there are no Jewish family members left alive in Poland to hold a grudge against. Today I regard myself as a Pole with Jewish roots.

ANNA SZPANOWSKA

I have no recollection of my biological parents. So far as I know, I was born in the Warsaw ghetto on 13 October 1942. I was taken from there on the last day of the Ghetto Uprising on 15 May 1943, and given to a Polish family. They were a pre-war officer with the rank of major and his wife.

In order for this family to adopt me, I spent a day at the Baudouin House, a young children's home. It was generally known in Warsaw that the director issued falsified birth certificates confirming that the child was found by a Polish family and taken to the Baudouin House to be given up for adoption. I supposedly arrived there as 'Jane Doe'. The house was in Warsaw, on Nowogrodzka Street. Both the house and its archives still exist today.

Once they received those documents, my parents – the ones who brought me up; I never knew the original ones – found a piece of paper with my birth date, and the name Anna. There was no surname, or I never learned it. My adoptive parents had me baptised and my life began.

The adoption probably came about through the Home Army since my father was an officer in the underground. They had no children and there was a reasonable chance they could protect me and bring me up. I remember my childhood as being full of love.

Raised as a Catholic, I went to church almost every week and had my first communion and confirmation. However, my parents still allowed me to visit our Jewish neighbours whenever I was invited to celebrate one of their holidays.

After the war, my father spent two years in the Polish army with the rank of lieutenant-colonel. However, having suffered a lung wound in 1939, he developed tuberculosis and died in 1952. But my greatest trauma was the death of my mother in 1958. I was only fifteen years old and was left utterly alone. So I lived through two major traumas. One was an unconscious one when I was a baby; according to psychologists this wrought havoc in my life which persists to this day: a syndrome of fear and loneliness. The second trauma occurred when my mother died.

As a child I heard rumours from both Poles and Jews that I was a survivor of the ghetto. But every time I asked my mother about this, she denied it. Nevertheless there were murmurs around me that these were not my real parents, and that I was actually Jewish. Anonymous messages were frequently put through the letterbox; Polish children also told me these were not my real parents.

By the time of my mother's death Jewish associations in Katowice, where we lived, had taken an interest in me. (In the late 1950s, there was a substantial Jewish community in Katowice.) Apparently, just before her death, my mother informed the community of my Jewish origins. So it was no longer a secret that I had been rescued from the ghetto. The Jewish community helped me a great deal, particularly with vital financial support, so I could survive without being sent to an orphanage. They also suggested that I emigrate to Israel but I was afraid I wouldn't be able to finish my education.

I was left without anyone close to me who could provide guidance in my life. I started to live on my own, finished school and graduated in biology from Jagiellonian University in Kraków. Halfway through my university degree, I stopped accepting assistance from the community because I feared it would entail some obligation to change my faith. Later I regretted this decision as my financial situation proved to be very difficult, even after I graduated, when my husband and I had to support two children without any parental help.

I met my husband at university and we started a family in 1966. He was Polish and we had a Catholic church wedding, although he knew everything about my background. I continued to practise my Catholic religion by following two paths: I prayed for my biological parents along with prayers for the ones who raised me. I suppose you could say, in a crude sort of way, that I've been straddling the fence with one foot on either side. Perhaps that's been possible because I never delved deeply into Judaism.

In 1968, I was living in Puławy and working at the well-known veterinary institute. There were other Jews, often in high positions, working at the institute and many were forced to leave because of the prevailing anti-semitic campaign. But I had only been living there for a year and I wasn't affected by it.

I have never felt particularly close to the Catholic church and would describe myself as a nominal Catholic; I only go to church when I feel a particular need to do so. But I was brought up as a Catholic and don't want to change that. My relationship to my Jewish ancestry is much more secular. Maybe if I had known my family's surname at least, my connection to Judaism might not have been so tenuous. So, if I am asked today how I define myself, I reply that I'm a Pole of Jewish origin.

As one grows older, issues regarding identity and family history become more important. In particular, we now have the second and third generations seeking answers, whereas I didn't have parents or grandparents to whom I could ask questions. The support received from parents or grandparents is not only financial, but also psychological, and creates a sense of belonging which our generation never had.

My children are shallowly rooted in Catholicism because in Poland, during the 1950s and 1960s, not being a Catholic carried some kind of stigma and I wanted to protect them. However, when my children were teenagers, I decided they needed to be told the truth about their family origins. They seemed very relaxed to discover this aspect of their background. My daughter, Dr Agnieszka Szpanowska-Wohn, now belongs to the Second Generation, but it's the grandchildren who are the most involved. For example, my son's daughter, who says she does not believe in Catholicism, has gone to a few of the Jewish summer camps run by the Lauder Foundation.

I was one of the co-founders of the Association of Children of the Holocaust. Thanks to the Lauder Foundation I went to the first conference in New York in 1992. On the way back to Poland, ten of us decided we had to do something that would bring us together, and we started the association. Since then, it has developed very successfully and I'm very proud and happy. I would like to continue to help it develop as much as possible but in a secular form, because I cannot do it any other way.

[Anna Szpanowska died in April 2015]

PART 2
Second Generation

JAROSŁAW GÓRNICKI

I am 60 years old and work as a doctor in Warsaw, where I lived for about 50 years.

My parents were Communists but only my father was Jewish. Although he grew up in the heavily Jewish Muranów area of Warsaw, he felt closer to Polish culture and after his Bar Mitzvah decided he was no longer interested in Judaism.

During the family's incarceration in the Warsaw Ghetto, he smuggled in food from the Aryan side. When he was caught, his false papers convinced the Germans that he was a Pole. He had assumed the name of Gornicki although his family name was really Weisbaum. He was deported to concentration camps, including Sachsenhausen, where despite contracting typhus, he survived with the help of other Communist prisoners.

This experience of solidarity won him over to the Communist Party, which he joined when he returned to Kraków immediately after the war. He quickly realised, however, that the majority of Polish people remained anti-semitic, despite the Holocaust. He decided to pass as a Pole because it would be easier to persuade people about the merits of Communism if he promoted the ideology as a Pole and not as a Jew. Of course, he kept the Polish name from his wartime papers and, since he had lost all of his family in the Holocaust, very few people ever knew that his original name was Weisbaum.

My parents met in 1945 at a Communist Party training school in Kraków. They married and were together for nearly 50 years.

My father started to work in the propaganda department and was involved as an activist in many places, mostly working within Communist Party structures. In 1947, he was sent to Warsaw and, in 1968, he was appointed deputy to the mayor of Warsaw, a position he held for many years. Despite the anti-semitic campaign in 1968, my father was not adversely affected because he always hid his Jewish identity. Even though some people knew the truth, he had strong supporters in the party who were prepared to protect him. Years later he told me that he was very upset in 1968 because it reminded him of his time in concentration camps, when he had to hide his circumcision not only from the Germans, but also from Polish inmates.

I started raising questions about my family background when I was twelve. I asked my mother about the absence of my father's family. She replied: 'Your father lost his whole family in the ghetto. It's all very emotional for him and he finds it very difficult to discuss. So please don't ask him about it.' My sister, who is five years older than me, received the same response.

My experience could be compared to that of adopted children whose parents don't divulge their adoption. Sometimes adopted children hear strange stories about their parents but don't want to accept them. I also heard such rumours and rejected them like 'spam'. The process of denying is unconscious but, with time, becomes more conscious. Once my older sister asked me: 'What would you do if somebody told you that your father was a Jew?' I think I replied: 'Nothing. I don't care since it's not about me.' And so the process of denial went on.

As children, we constantly heard how the Poles suffered during the war; this was told at school, on censored television and in the cinema. Moreover, there was no distinction about Jewish suffering, as we were taught that everyone is equal. For example, I spent eight years in a primary school named after Janusz Korczak, and by the time I graduated, I didn't know that Korczak was a Jew. Every year a celebrity came to talk to us and tell us how Korczak was a great children's educator; yet his Jewishness was never mentioned. I learned decades later that he was a Jew originally called Henryk Goldszmit.

Due to a serious illness, my father decided to leave his job as deputy mayor of Warsaw and was sent to the Polish Embassy in Belgrade as the Economic Secretary in 1971. I joined my parents at the age of sixteen and lived there for four years. During that period, I stopped questioning his background because I didn't feel it was a problem.

My sister stayed in Poland to continue her studies and, in 1973, she married a socialist activist, Andrzej Zozula, who also happened to be Jewish. Andrzej was very open about his background and always acknowledged that he was Jewish – even when he became the mayor of a small town near Warsaw. Unfortunately, my sister and Andrzej divorced ten years ago. Since then, he has taken on official roles in the *kehilla* of the Warsaw Jewish community. My sister is also involved in the *kehilla* although, like me, she is a non-believer. It confirms Jean-Paul Sartre's theory that anti-semitism creates Jews.

When I returned with my parents from Belgrade in 1975, the situation in Poland had changed a lot. There was a great deal of social unrest, including widespread strikes. Particularly during the Solidarity period of the 1980s, we began to discuss our family origins; it was easier for my father as he no longer held a high office. But he still could not escape from the need to hide his identity. At the age of 80, when he finally revealed his Jewish surname to me, he also said: 'Don't tell anyone.' Later on, in 2005, I made some recordings of my father discussing his Jewish life in pre-war Poland. I tried to convince him that his devotion to Communism represented an escape from his Jewish roots. He thought that perhaps I was right, but he pointed out that he wasn't a psychologist. Then, in 2006, he died suddenly.

I graduated in medicine from Warsaw University in 1980 and became actively involved with Solidarity through work in my first hospital. That short period before martial law was a beautiful time of real freedom and the struggle to change Poland. But, unfortunately, I also learned that it allowed the freedom for more frequent and open expressions of anti-semitism.

In 1989, Rabbi Avi Weiss's confrontation with the Carmelite nuns at their convent in Auschwitz was the straw that broke the camel's back. Cardinal Glemp's anti-semitic comments regarding Jewish opposition to the convent, and his statement that Jews should know how to behave like guests, made me realise where my loyalties lay. My response was that I should be able to live as a full citizen of this country – even as a Jew. And so the process of becoming a Jew continued. By 1997, I had become a member of the Jewish community in Warsaw, officially an Orthodox organisation. My father was opposed to this. 'What connection do you have with that?' he demanded.

'Religion, language? Family – all your Jewish family died.' However, I wanted to prove to myself, and to my father, that it was no longer dangerous to be a Jew in Poland.

My wife is Polish but is not involved with the church – despite her strong Polish identity. I learned that her father was Jewish but, unfortunately, as he died in 1962, she never had the opportunity to discuss this with him.

My sons were baptised and they don't feel Jewish at all. I had been raised as a non-believer and recall having fights at school between believers and non-believers. So I didn't want my sons to be stigmatised at school when they wouldn't understand why they were different from the rest of their class. The decision to baptise them was also influenced by the important role that the church played during martial law and the Solidarity period as a key centre of resistance. Like many other non-religious people, I started to attend church. I met with Jehovah Witnesses every Monday for four years and studied the Bible with them.

Today, I am a member of the Jewish community because the law doesn't require that I must be an Orthodox believer, but rather that I don't practice another religion. I joined essentially because I didn't want to be ashamed of my Jewish origins and have to hide my identity like my father did. But I intend to live out my identity like a free man in a free country. So no one can demand that I should be circumcised. I also wrote to Rabbi Schudrich that I'm against the Jewish ritual of slaughtering animals without stunning.

I'm very happy that Second Generation exists and I participate in all the group's major meetings. In terms of Jewish culture, I'm very involved in the annual Jewish book festival for which I take three days off from work. Over the last 20 years or so, books with Jewish themes have come to comprise 90 per cent of my personal library.

As in other democratic countries, the issue of hidden Jews will become less important in Poland. Under the Communist regime, we grew up with an internationalist ideology which proclaimed that all people were equal, and so it was pointless to discuss who is a Jew. Then, nationality became important for Poles, but their identity was strongly connected to their Catholicism. However, it's not so strong any longer and people now more readily accept the idea that you don't need to be a Catholic in order to be a Pole. So, even if people discover their Jewish roots, it's not such a traumatising experience as it was in the past.

AGNIESZKA MARKOWSKA

In my family there was never any mention of Jewishness. But when I was a 20-year-old student I started thinking about it; I suspected there must be a secret involving this. It was a gut feeling. Before my grandmother died at the age of 99, I asked her on many occasions about our possible Jewish links. I was particularly curious about some of my great-grandparents' names. Yet she maintained that they had absolutely nothing to do with any Jewish origins.

I was born in 1969 in Warsaw but grew up in Berlin. We returned to Warsaw at the beginning of the 1980s, where I attended high school and later studied German philology at the university. My father was a cameraman who worked on documentaries for Polish television. I was baptised although my father protested. My grandmother sent me a white dress for the occasion, but my father dyed it black. In high school I occasionally heard unpleasant remarks that I looked Jewish; I had dark wavy hair. But no one really knew about my origins.

My grandmother was very proud of the fact that we have our roots in a very good, noble family called Rawicz-Niedziałkowski. Our family tree, which hangs in the houses of all our family members, goes back to the sixteenth century. The names on the family tree sparked my curiosity. For example, my grandmother's mother was called Weiss. But she would explain it all away by saying they were German, or else she would say she had forgotten the history. I found this very suspicious as she has an excellent memory, like a computer, and knows everything about everyone.

That may have been the end of it if not for a series of coincidences and events that led to one goal – explaining this issue. It was uncanny. It was like playing solitaire: you uncover subsequent cards that lead you to victory.

Although I'm from Warsaw, I moved to Kraków around eight years ago to work as the director of the Austrian Institute. My mother's sister had refurbished her flat and found a pile of documents. As she was not interested, she gave them to my mother. Knowing that I've always been interested in stuff like this, my mother scanned the documents and sent them to me in Kraków. And that's how my investigation started, in December 2012.

The documents were in Latin. Having studied Latin and also being a German philologist, I managed to understand some of the documents. I found the information very strange because they included baptism certificates issued in Kraków for my great-grandparents when they were in their forties. I was very curious as to why someone of that age would be baptised.

The documents also revealed that they were converting from the evangelical faith to Catholicism and their birthplace was stated as Friedland. They also provided the Polish and German names of the parents and grandparents of my great-grandparents and these included many famous names of the Polish aristocracy such as Sobańscy, Wielopolscy and Czartoryscy. I sent these names to the Jewish Historical Institute, seeking some explanation, but they replied that these were not Jewish names.

I didn't give up, however, because I was sure something was amiss. At this point, when my grandmother learned I had started searching for family roots, she said: 'Hitler didn't search them out, but my granddaughter does.' This proved she knew something and that inspired me to keep looking.

Initially, I contacted all three Friedland locations in Poland, one in the Czech Republic and one in Germany, asking them to search in their parish records. In the Czech Republic I perused birth records online, which was time consuming. Unfortunately, I couldn't find anyone with those names. So I thought: what else? I went to the national archives on Sienna Street in Kraków and looked at the census. That's where I found them, but their birthplace was recorded as something completely different – not Friedland. My great-grandfather was born in Andrychów, near Kraków, and my great-grandmother in Rzeszów. So the whole family comes from Galicia.

I then searched for them on JewishGen with their birthplace, and the whole family history came up. It turned out that my great-grandfather's name was not Hieronim Weiss – the name he used – but Rachmiel Weiss. I also contacted the technical university in Leoben, Austria which confirmed that a Jewish student called Hieronim Weiss had been a student there and that his parents were Samuel and Riesla Weiss from Andrychów.

According to JewishGen, my maternal great-grandmother was not Salomea Weiss, but Zertl Weiss, née Brandt. My grandmother became hysterical with this revelation. I also approached the research centre for Jewish history in Rzeszów and it uncovered my entire Brandt family.

It appeared I began my search with a forged document which helped the family to survive the war. All these discoveries caused lively family discussions, and somehow helped us to unite. Part of the Weiss descendants felt compelled to adopt a Jewish identity, while others decided to remain, as it were, on the Aryan side; and we respect that too. So the family has been moving along two parallel paths.

My paternal great-grandparents with the family name of Borys were born in Tykocin, which was a very Jewish town. I still need to conduct some research on my father's family in the archives of Łomża and Białystok. My father rejects religion in general and, as a family, the church didn't play a role in our life – apart from attending family events. We always found the church's actions incomprehensible and, interestingly, there were never any crosses on our walls. But I don't have much information about his family because I have been focusing on my mother's relatives. So I'm searching for people who are still alive in the Weiss and Brandt families.

My 80-year-old grandmother's cousin lives in Florida and, once the whole story came to light, she called me from the United States and told me what she had known since childhood. When the war broke out, she learned about her Jewish roots. Her parents hid her in a convent and forbade her to ever mention her Jewish origins. They told my grandmother the same thing but as she was eighteen when the war broke out, she was too old to be hidden in a convent. So she was sent to Hungary to stay with relatives.

Something happened that might have caused her to be silent until today. She had a fiancé who was in the upper echelons of the AK (underground Home Army) here in Kraków. He told her they can't remain together because they came from two different worlds; too much separated them. He was the love of her life and she hasn't made peace with this setback. She still curses her mother for being Jewish.

In the 1970s, after my sister Małgorzata was born, my grandmother received an anonymous letter. It said: 'It was supposed to be Itzik!' The letter said that my sister was given a Catholic name, but it should have been a Jewish name. Grandma only related this story to us recently.

My husband is Polish but has a very positive attitude towards my family background and our Jewish activities. My younger son attends a Jewish summer camp run by the American Jewish Joint Distribution Committee. When my older son comes to Kraków, he joins me and my younger son at the Shabbat dinners in the Jewish Community Centre. As he is studying in Rzeszów, he has been searching for documents in the local archive relating to the Weiss family because that is where my great-grandfather lived for a few years after his marriage to Zertl. This archival work has been a very emotional experience for him, and he has become fascinated with his Jewish roots.

My mother strongly encourages me to continue my search. During one of her visits from Warsaw she joined me at a Shabbat dinner at the JCC, the first she ever experienced. Even my grandmother says: 'I was born a noblewoman and I'll die a Jewess.' She says if this goes on, I'll eventually bury her in a Jewish cemetery! She has never gotten over the trauma of her fiancé. What has also become clear to me is that her cooking has always been very Jewish. So it's absurd to believe her claim that she didn't know anything about her Jewish ancestry.

For now, my connection with the Jewish world is primarily cultural and secular, but I have started going to synagogue. Last Friday I went with my children to the Tempel and Kupa synagogues. Nobody ever taught us anything about Judaism, and we'll see what path my children eventually choose to follow.

People are starting to search more openly for their identity. The conditions are increasingly favourable in Poland and people are getting rid of their old fears. I have no problem saying I have Jewish roots, and that's why I go to the synagogue or the JCC.

My search began with a sort of gut feeling. But now, after coming to Kraków and discovering so much, I have an awareness that I am truly in the right place, that perhaps I'm following in the footsteps of my forebears who were once here. I have a need to continue what was shattered by the war, also out of respect for the past.

PIOTR KOWALIK

I am 50 years old and a native of Wrocław.

I have a Jewish mother and a non-Jewish father. They were married in Wrocław in 1966.

My mother and her family came from Drohobycz, which is now in Ukraine. Miraculously, nearly the entire family survived until the Red Army entered that area in 1944.

After the big border changes, when they learned that Drohobycz was going to be part of the Soviet Union, the family refused to take Soviet citizenship. So they were forced to return to Poland. Along with many other Poles and Jews who survived, they were given 24 hours to gather their belongings. They were packed into train wagons and sent to the western territories recently expropriated from the Germans.

During the journey, my grandfather told the family he'd decided they would all disembark at the last train station. And that station was Wrocław. It was almost empty because the Germans had fled. The houses were waiting to be occupied and so they took one of them.

In Wrocław, my Jewish grandfather attempted to live an ordinary life devoid of Jewishness. It was a very unstable situation in Poland at that time. They found that by assimilating, pretending to be ordinary Poles with a very shallow Catholicism, they would help the children to adapt and lead normal lives.

This is how my mother was raised. Yet my grandfather didn't send the children to religion classes which, even in the most Stalinist times, were obligatory. So my mother and her siblings didn't attend church or religion classes. My mother says they suffered as a result because they were attacked by their peers – even with stones. This happened to other children, since they lived in a kind of Jewish neighbourhood and had some Jewish friends who, one by one, left Poland for Israel and America in the 1950s and 1960s – especially given the ugly events in 1968. However, they stayed because they were so assimilated that they didn't suffer personally from the anti-semitic purges.

They ran their own private business, which was difficult under Communism. As they were gardeners and fruit sellers back in Drohobycz before the war, they knew that business well and were very successful in Wrocław. There was a great demand in Communist Poland for vegetables and flowers. Of course, there were times when life was hard due to poor harvests or very high taxes imposed by the Communist authorities, who were always suspicious of private enterprise.

My mother recalls my grandparents quarrelling in Yiddish when they didn't want the family to understand the conversation. From time to time, they also visited the Jewish theatre, which was the best one in the 1950s before it moved to Warsaw under Ida Kamińska. However, in the 40s and 50s, Wrocław and Lower Silesia were the main centres of Yiddish culture in Poland. Sometimes *gefilte* fish and *matzo* were on the table in their home – not in any religious context, but rather as a food. In terms of religion, however, the family didn't practise anything and didn't impose Catholicism on the children. So my mother was never baptised.

My parents were a very sweet, loving couple and I had a wonderful childhood, but unfortunately my father died of illness in 1990. My mother still lives in Wrocław. My father's family was strongly Catholic, especially because they lived in the countryside, where people were not very favourable towards the Jews. So a deal was struck between my parents not to discuss nor reveal anything about the Jewish background. That's why my young brother and I knew nothing about the Jewish origins of the family right up until the end of the 1980s.

I was baptised and grew up as a Polish Catholic. Because of the pressure from my father's side of the family, it was decided that we should go to religion classes. I also remember my paternal grandmother was a deeply religious Catholic. But it was also a positive experience because she taught me good things regarding the relationship with God – for example praying, being a good person. She taught me to pray before bedtime and I still know and understand the meaning of the prayers. I went to church regularly on Sundays. Although my mother didn't attend church, she wanted me and my brother to participate in Catholic services just to pacify the Catholic side of the family.

When I was fifteen or sixteen something happened. It was a difficult time due to my father's illness and also because we were facing economic hardship. It was then that I began to seek the meaning of life. The typical Catholicism, and answers from the outside world, no longer satisfied me. During my searches some sympathetic men gave me, for the first time in my life, a Bible containing the Old and New Testaments. I started to read the Bible and was completely overwhelmed and fascinated.

I felt I had to understand the message, and how it is translated in practice. Captivated by Jesus' ethical teachings, like the Sermon on the Mount, I put more emphasis on the New Testament. I decided I had to treat it seriously. Either you play at being religious or you do it. I just can't stand the pretending.

Later, I had my first encounters with more advanced religious people from Protestant circles in Warsaw, like the Pentecostals and the Baptists. One day a friend from high school told me: 'I have another colleague who attends a very interesting religious group. They are quite strange because they combine the New Testament with the Jewish element.'

I was really shocked. I was met with a warm welcome from the group, and encountered a great atmosphere and spirituality. It was like a heaven on earth, precisely what I had been seeking. I saw a real hunger in the souls of these people. They were really dipping into the Bible, interpreting what Jesus meant, how to live your life to be a really good Christian. When I was among these people, I didn't want to go home or back to high school because it was a difficult reality we faced – especially in the 1980s when the economic situation seemed hopeless. Even as a Jew today, I can really appreciate the spirituality that they imbibed and the striving for the highest ethical conduct. I can't stand it when religious people pretend to be devotional. I say openly: that's bullshit, either you pretend or you truly live that life. As a result, people sometimes don't like me because of my perspective. But this is what I learned and internalised and I can't change it.

My parents were furious when they discovered about this group, which I hid from them. It was a very small group, like a sect. We formed great friendships.

I haven't eaten pork since 1984 because it's forbidden in the Bible. Also, in 1984, I started to eat *matzo* and to live in a tent – a big army tent that we bought – because I didn't yet know about the *Sukkot*. In the Polish translation, it's not written as *Succos* but as the festival of tents or tabernacles. It's written that you should take the willow branches from the tree. So we cut branches from the willow tree and waved them. It was lovely, authentic, a wonderful spiritual experience of discovering new things. Holiday after holiday, we wanted more and more. But the rest of the group felt it was enough. The message was: don't be too Jewish.

We then started a smaller group of young people within the group to pursue real in-depth studies – for example, the history of the early church. And we discovered that Christianity is really an invention of the apostle Paul, who changed all the theology. Jesus was probably an ordinary Jew with perhaps some unconventional ideas – a kind of Jewish hippie or a wandering teacher – but he didn't change Judaism. That was the work of Paul, who completely changed the theology. We decided we preferred the Torah, which is the source. This must guide our lives.

At the outset, we created our separate congregation in which we conducted, in our own way, services and prayers. We gradually introduced more and more Jewish content; we started to use the *Siddur*, for example. But this was still happening outside the synagogue, outside the formal Jewish community in Wrocław. However, over time, we realised we can't continue to be outsiders; we have to join the family and return to the roots. So we started to attend the synagogue in Wrocław. At that time, it was a small *shul*. These poor old guys looked at us and wondered: what are you doing? They were accustomed to thinking that Jewish life was over. Now a group of young people were coming who wanted to be Jewish. Finally, they realised we were not some freaks. Then we had various first encounters with Michael Schudrich, who started to come to Wrocław as a director of the Lauder Foundation.

I discovered my Jewish origins in the course of time. Eventually, when I was observing most commandments and had joined the synagogue, my mother finally gave up and said: 'OK. I will tell you the real story. Our family name is Bernstein.' Then I said: 'Maybe this is the missing puzzle in my story. Perhaps I have travelled full circle.'

My mother's confession didn't shock me because I felt that I was already a Jew. So it was more like God's funny way of doing things; I felt God's smile. For me, it's very important that I found my Judaism. It's not like I just inherited it. It's really important for me that Judaism was a real, very valuable discovery and a process in my life which is not finished. I treat it as a life-long process.

The rest of the group found some Jewish connections, but couldn't prove it with documents. And some just went through a full conversion process – either in Poland or completed it in America.

At this point in time, my brother was not interested in reclaiming our Jewish identity. 'Me, I'm not Jewish! Give me a break! Jew is a dirty word.' In 1991, however, we were installing fencing around a Jewish cemetery in Wrocław. We needed some extra help and my brother joined us. He became curious about the tombstones, what they said. His curiosity grew and within three months, he was studying in a yeshiva in Israel. An observant Jew, he returned to Poland and said he needed a full infrastructure to have a full Jewish life and a Jewish wife. He went for the first time to America to stay with our friends in Borough Park in Brooklyn. There he said he felt most at home. He lives there with his Polish-born wife.

My mother also found her way back to the Jewish world and is now the head of the senior club at the Jewish community in Wrocław. It's funny that my brother and I were first to return to the Jewish world, and our mother followed us.

My wife, Marisa, who was raised as a Catholic, was part of the same Judaism/Christian group and we experienced the same spiritual journey, including baptism. We married in 1990 in a civil ceremony. Shortly afterwards, we moved to Warsaw at the beginning of 1994 when I started to work for the Lauder Foundation to establish the first Jewish day school in Warsaw since 1969. I had already been active in Wrocław as an educator and a *chazan*. However, my discovery of my Jewishness was also a big surprise for Marisa. She agreed to move to Warsaw in 1994 and live a more Jewish life. But I didn't push her in any way. She decided on her own that she will convert and so we had a Jewish wedding in 2007.

Since I became an outwardly religious Jew, I have not suffered from anti-semitism. In fact, I've had the opposite experience; people greet me and say *Shabbat Shalom* when I take my *Shabbos* walk in Warsaw. Unfortunately, my son has suffered because he has worn *Tzitzit* and a *kippah* since he was a small child.

The current situation for Poland's Jews is dynamic. However, I'm very sceptical in terms of any expectations for positive changes. I still maintain hope because I'm optimistic by nature but I've become less naïve in regard to what is actually going on. This concerns the low level of Jewish leadership in Poland. There is no cross-organisational institutional thinking about the absolutely fundamental issue – namely, how to build and support Jewish families in Poland. This is the most crucial aspect in normal functioning Jewish communities around the world. Yet, in Poland, it's very hard to find practical thinking and activities directed towards the future among the Polish Jewish leadership. This is a disaster. No one is thinking about what we want to achieve for our children and grandchildren over the next 10, 20 or 50 years. Instead, everyone is concerned about how to cope with very current issues such as the size of the communal budget. It really makes me despair.

BARBARA CZACHOWSKA

I was born in Bytom, Silesia in 1985 and grew up in Gliwice. My mother had Jewish ancestry on her mother's side, but I'm not sure about my father. His family surname was Hirsch; they came from Linz in Austria, where there was a big Jewish community. Hirsch was a common name there. My paternal grandfather changed his last name after the war to Czachowski, but my father was born in 1949 with the name of Hirsch. When he was two years old, his surname was changed to Czachowski.

My grandmother, Renata Teich, was born in Przemyśl in 1920 and came from an assimilated family; they didn't practice Judaism. Renata met her husband after the war but he was not Jewish. After she died in 2009, when I was clearing up her things, I found some documents. I looked at her photo and thought it was obvious that she was Jewish, something I hadn't previously realised. That convinced me that I was also Jewish.

My great-aunt Alma, Renata's sister, also survived the war. She and Renata discussed their future and came to the conclusion they had two options: either to assimilate into Polish society, or emigrate to Israel. Having decided to remain in Poland, they changed their surname and were baptised.

After the war, my grandmother came to Kraków to study chemistry at Jagiellonian University. She had begun her studies in Lwów but they were interrupted by the war. At university she met my grandfather, Zbigniew, who wasn't Jewish. But, most interestingly, his father was the president of the National Democratic Party in Zakopane, which meant he was an anti-semite. I think Zbigniew was also an anti-semite, but he nonetheless fell in love with my grandmother, whom he knew was a Jew. After they married, my grandmother would tease her father-in-law by saying: 'I am your punishment for your political views.' They eventually moved to Gliwice, and my grandmother asked her husband not to tell anyone she was Jewish. He took this secret to his grave.

I recall my grandmother telling me that she had planned to destroy all the documents proving her roots, but fortunately she didn't do so. I found documents revealing that she had changed her name from Teich to Trzebicka. At that moment, I realised more fully that I was not only Jewish, but halachically Jewish. Once my grandmother also confided in me her experiences during the war and told me about her parents.

After my grandmother's death in December 2009, I cleaned her flat and discovered a large piece of paper hidden under her bed. It contained many genealogical trees, put together by my grandfather, and was very detailed. However, it only involved my grandfather's side of the family. There was nothing about my grandmother's side as it appears that he would not expose her genealogical secrets.

My mother and her brother were raised in Gliwice as Catholic children, although the city had a Jewish cemetery and synagogue. When my uncle started school, the teacher sat him with another Jewish child by coincidence. Ironically, the teacher later apologised to my grandmother for having done that.

In 1968, during the turmoil unleashed by the anti-semitic campaign, not only did many Jews leave Poland, but some Jewish graveyards were destroyed. At that time, the Przemyśl graveyard was also wrecked, including the gravestone of my grandmother's grandmother as well as a memorial gravestone which Alma had created for her parents whose fate is unknown.

My great-aunt, Alma, maintained contact with her cousin Edith Weisz, who lives in Cambridge, England. Her husband is Hungarian but her maiden surname, Teich, was the same as my great-grandfather as well as my grandmother.

After the war, Alma and Edith corresponded through letters but eventually decided to meet. So Edith came to Gliwice around 1992. It was Easter; my uncle and his family were visiting my grandmother's flat, where Edith was staying. They were on their way to church. Edith asked them why they were going to church and they replied because it was Easter. She said: 'But you are Jewish!' That was the moment when the mystery was unveiled and it led to a big argument between Alma and Edith.

I was in secondary school when my uncle told me about this incident. I wasn't surprised to learn about my Jewish background because I already, deep inside, suspected this was the case. Although my uncle expected this would lead to a big emotional drama, I was very happy to learn about my roots and told all my close friends. And now I feel even more Jewish.

I came to Kraków to study law at the Kraków Academy. After finishing my last exam a few years ago, I went to Kazimierz with my friends to celebrate. Everyone eventually left and I stayed alone to walk around the area. By chance I stumbled upon the Jewish Community Centre, and decided to find out what was going on. This was really the beginning of my Jewish journey.

I also attended the Kupa Synagogue, where I met Boaz Pash, and told him my story. Boaz had organised a mini-yeshiva and I was fascinated to see how religious Jews actually looked. I've also visited Israel on a Birthright trip but the visit was far too rushed. It was always 'yallah, yallah'.

My family responded to the uncovering of our Jewish identity in sharply different ways. My brother is very interested, and is particularly keen to find any information that can be added to our genealogical tree.

My mother became an apostate and left the Catholic Church some years ago. She is now practising yoga and meditation; she is in another spiritual world. Sometimes she attends Jewish meetings in Gliwice but these are really secular and cultural occasions. She would like me to follow yoga and marry a yogi boy and meditate together.

My mother's brother is very strange because, although he attends church like a fervent Catholic, he would like to be Jewish and wants me to introduce him to the Jewish community in Katowice, where he lives. He had a good relationship with my grandmother, but doesn't want to tell me the family stories.

It's difficult to envisage raising a Jewish family because it would also depend on my husband. I had a boyfriend for six years and we argued constantly. I objected to baptising any children we might have, and also opposed the idea of a Catholic wedding. The situation was even more complicated because I was baptised, raised as a Catholic girl, and continue to believe in Jesus.

DANUTA CELIŃSKA-CEDRO

I was born in Warsaw in 1949 to a Jewish father and a Polish mother. My father's name was Chaba, a somewhat unusual name for a Jew. He came from Wolbrom, a small city in the south of Poland, near Kraków. He was a pre-war Communist who escaped in 1939 to Lwów, only to be sent by the Russians to a camp in Siberia.

When the Soviet Union and the Polish government created the Anders army, my father tried – but failed – to join up. The only papers he possessed revealed that he had been released from a Polish prison before the war, which prevented him from joining Anders' army. Later he managed to sign up to the Polish army led by Zygmunt Berling and eventually fought his way to Berlin.

On his return to Poland in 1945, he met my mother and they got married. As a military man, he was sent to various locations around Poland until they eventually settled in Warsaw. My father always seemed to be away from home and I don't recall him spending much time with my older brother and me. He held a high military rank and worked constantly to construct the post-war Polish army.

When I was a child I asked my mother about the absence of an extended family. All my friends seemed to have four grandparents, while I had only two. She told me that my father's entire family perished in Auschwitz. She said it was a very painful subject for my father, and that I will only make him sad if I asked about it. At school we were educated to believe that Auschwitz was a death camp for Poles. I didn't make the Jewish connection at all.

When I was 17 a friend told me I was Jewish and that made me start thinking it might be true. Shortly afterwards, in June 1967, the Polish government unleashed a hostile propaganda campaign against Israel following its victory in the Six-Day War. I noticed papers on our table at home indicating that my father had asked to be released from military service. The army sought to transfer him to the north of Poland, but he didn't want to make the move.

I found his birth certificate, which stated that his father was Szymon Chaba, but that didn't make me think he was Jewish. Yet when I saw my grandmother's name, Ita Gelbart, on his birth certificate, everything fell into place like a jigsaw puzzle.

I was very proud and felt very good upon discovering my Jewish roots. I was living in a Communist, but also privileged, Jewish ghetto in a desirable 1930s area of Warsaw. Many children at my Gottwald school were from Communist, mostly Jewish, families. Until the discovery of my Jewish background, I partly felt like an outsider. However, suddenly I was part of the group of the most interesting people in my school.

This was a traumatic time for my father. First of all he lost his career and, secondly, he was betrayed by the Communist regime which he had worked so hard to establish. He essentially lost the life he had known because he was a Jew; consequently, he became very depressed. This caused many problems for our family.

Although I knew I shouldn't inquire too much about his past, we nonetheless had some conversations. He told me about his imprisonment in Belorussia for Communist activities, and recalled his family's deep poverty and his father's fervent religious devotion.

I also discovered that my father was married before the war, and had twin daughters born in late 1939. He used to say: 'Of all my daughters, you are the most beautiful' – or 'you are the cleverest'. For a long time I thought it was just a joke. But later I learned about the twins from a list of victims from Wolbrom.

In retrospect, I recall various details that could have provided clues to his past. He would regularly prepare a Sunday breakfast of matzah and eggs, celebrate the anniversary of the Warsaw Ghetto uprising, and visit the Jewish theatre. He also attended funerals at the Jewish cemetery, and welcomed strange dark visitors to our home. I had interpreted these events simply as matzah being a healthy food; my parents' interest in going to various theatres; and the visitors were merely old friends from Wolbrom.

After my father was released from the army, he began to correspond with a cousin who lived in Israel. She came to visit us in 1990, which prompted me to put together a family genealogical chart. I discovered we had other relatives, including cousins living in Los Angeles. My father travelled to the U.S. to visit his cousins, and to investigate whether there would be opportunities for the family if we emigrated there. I was reluctant, however.

Studying medicine had been my dream since childhood. In September 1967, I entered the medical faculty of Warsaw University and graduated in 1974. I received my Ph.D in 1984 and habilitation (assistant professor) in 2004, specialising in paediatrics and gastroenterology. I am now a consultant at the Child Health Centre in Warsaw and a professor at the Medical Faculty of the University of Rzeszów.

Shortly after starting university I lost most of my old friends in 1968, in the wave of emigration that resulted from the anti-semitic campaign. My brother was also expelled from university. After years of rejection, he was finally allowed to emigrate to Canada with his family in 1980, shortly before the introduction of martial law. However, by the 1970s, I increasingly found myself at home within a circle of people that identified completely with the Solidarity opposition. In that milieu, the Jewish issue was not important.

For many years I was deeply involved with family life and work, and didn't have time for myself. It was only when I became a widow in 2009 that I was able to explore my identity. If the war hadn't occurred, I wouldn't exist as the person I am today. It's very important for me to remember those grandparents to whom I feel I owe so much. I want to know as much about their lives as I can, as those are my roots. I'm eager to know more about Jewish traditions, Israel (which I admire) and Hasidism.

Around six years ago those feelings led me to join Second Generation, where I meet people with whom I can share traditions like a Seder at Pesach. It helps me to connect with my Jewish roots; it's an opportunity to engage with others who share similar backgrounds and experiences. Some come from religious families, but most have secular backgrounds. What they recount about their mother or father is often very similar to my experiences with my parents.

Big surprises can emerge from these Second Generation meetings. On one occasion my friend, Ania, a biologist whom I have worked with for the past 40 years, suddenly appeared at a meeting. Despite years of close contact, we knew nothing about each other's Jewish background. At another meeting I met a friend from my hospital, who was a doctor; we also had no idea of our common ancestry.

Now, as I grow older, I'm meeting people I want to be with. When I talk to friends from Second Generation, we all feel we have found a family we did not possess for many years.

MONIKA RAKUSA

I was born in 1966 in Wrocław. My mother's family was Jewish and my father's was Polish. But my mother only revealed that I was Jewish when I was fifteen years old.

Our surname was Kowalski, which was my grandfather's assumed name during the war after he escaped from the Warsaw ghetto and hid on the Aryan side. Funnily enough there were three families called Kowalski in our Wrocław apartment building. Later I discovered they were all Jewish. Lower Silesia was a popular place for resettling Jews after the war. I know that now but it was not obvious to me then.

My family's history had previously been related in a bizarre way which left me with ambivalent feelings. On the one hand the Kowalski family was described as virtual aristocrats, yet there was an ongoing discussion in our household about which distinguished people in the world were Jewish. At the time I missed the point of that discussion.

My mother was baptised before the war and therefore I've also been baptised. Officially, in all the documents, I'm regarded as a Catholic. There was, in baptism, an element of seeking protection; but there was also a desire to belong. As a child I didn't want to be different, and dreamed of having a grandmother in a typically Polish village. I had the impression that there was something wrong with my family. The food, the way of thinking, the jokes – all were different.

My mother decided to move to Warsaw in 1975. I was attending a high school in Szymanów, near Warsaw, which was run by nuns, and there I made friends with two Jewish girls. The three of us were very rebellious and played naughty games. For example, we pretended that a Jewish ghetto had been created and, as the only non-Jew, I had to shout anti-semitic insults. My mother was subsequently summoned to the school because I was misbehaving. I told her that I would actually love to be Jewish, and she said: 'OK, you are Jewish. We are proud of our heritage, but YOU MUST NOT tell anyone about this.' I was in a corridor of the school where the nuns were returning from prayers and, despite my mother's warning, shouted to my friend: 'Marysia, Marysia, I'm also a Jew'.

When my mother was hiding during the war, she contracted polio. She was a well-educated woman, but very lonely; she had to wear crutches. In Warsaw we lived in a working class area and my mother and I were an odd pair because she behaved like an opera diva although she was disabled. For me, becoming Jewish was a good solution to my identity. Although it was traumatic, it also represented a great history of which I could be proud. I had, after all, been the daughter of a single, disabled woman until then and there exists a hierarchy of minorities in this world. It's like when you are gay, you would prefer to be Jewish.

I recall another important reaction to this discovery. It took place in the storage room in the school, when I stood in front of the mirror and stared at myself, thinking: how is it possible that I still look the same having found out I am Jewish.

My mother told me that our real name was Perec (Peretz) and that her family believed that we were related to I.L. Peretz. As I'm also a writer and have published several books, there is nothing I would like more than to be descended from the father of modern Yiddish literature in Poland. However, my mother wasn't sure whether this was true because there is a tendency in all families to create myths, and my mother loved myths. Yet, when I started to search for family documents, I suddenly found that beside the usual Polish names, there were many Jewish names like Dvora.

A few years ago, in the Warsaw Jewish cemetery on Okopowa Street, I discovered my great-grandfather's grave. On the tombstone was written, 'Henryk Perec' although his original name was Zvi Hirsch Perec. That was typical of the Polonising tendency of some Polish Jews like my grandfather, who was very assimilated. I also changed the tombstone in Wrocław cemetery where my grandparents, Roma and Jan Kowalski, were buried to add: formerly Roma and Gustaw Perec.

Over the years my attitude towards Jews, or maybe more towards the Holocaust, turned into a kind of obsession. My favourite writers were Primo Levi and Hannah Arendt for her book *Eichmann in Jerusalem*. I started university in 1986 in the faculty of Polish Studies and then switched to social psychology. Both my MA dissertation and my Ph.D project dealt with Polish attitudes towards the Holocaust.

I've been married twice but neither of my husbands was Jewish. My previous husband's family, named Suszczewski, are very proud of their aristocratic heritage. I believe they are also hidden anti-semites but, as they belong to the intelligentsia, they don't express it – of course. Both my children have been baptised but my teenage daughter, Clara, is more sentimental about her Jewish background than my older son, Antoni (Antek), who is very anti-clerical and is regarded as a leftist in the family. However, I'm very proud of my son because he says the only family he identifies with is the Perec family. So I joke that the first and only grandson in the anti-semitic Suszczewski family is a Jew.

I feel the tension that Jews in Poland experience regarding whether to be a Polish Jew or a Jewish Pole, and the difficulty of integrating Polish and Jewish identities. This question is very important to me. In reality I identify less with my Jewishness because, as the poet Agnieszka Osiecka once said, my home country is Polish grammar and this is my homeland. So in that sense I feel very Polish.

At the same time I have a big problem with my Polishness. The 11 November Polish national independence holiday, which is so important to Poles and to me, has been taken over by right-wingers and thugs who call themselves patriots. So we have to organise counter marches against their attempt to take our Polishness and history and turn it into a farce. I have a big problem even when I hear the church bells signifying only one religion in Poland. Maybe I have a bigger problem with my Polishness than with my Jewishness.

Although I go to Limmud and I find the activities there very interesting, the group I really identify with is the Second Generation because my Jewish homeland is the Holocaust. Perhaps, if the Holocaust hadn't happened, none of this would be of any significance at all. As an atheist and feminist, I only dislike Judaism a bit less than Catholicism.

Polish Jews, particularly among the Second Generation, carry a strong feeling of guilt for everything. There is a big range of members in Second Generation because some were born right after the war while others were born in the late 1970s. Some come from very Jewish homes whereas others didn't know they were Jewish and therefore didn't have any idea of Jewish life and culture.

I am more or less optimistic about the revival of Jewish life in Poland, partly because there are a number of Jewish organisations that are working towards that goal. Also, the general atmosphere in Poland is changing and, hopefully, the widespread and shoddy kitsch folklore about the Jews will eventually disappear too.

PIOTR STASIAK

I was born in 1947 in Katowice to a Jewish father and a Polish mother. My father became a Communist in the 1930s and was imprisoned twice before the war in the internment camp of Bereza Kartuska. Although his parents and siblings died in Treblinka, he avoided their fate by having been arrested as a Communist and sent to Buchenwald.

He was later transferred to Auschwitz. As the Russians approached the extermination camp in January 1945, he was forced to join a death march. He was in a group of twelve prisoners who managed to fall behind the main column until they escaped into the woods. One member of the group was a Polish Communist from the region who led them to a hut where the family living there was expecting them. One of the people who looked after this group was my mother, Erna Kostka, who was 20 years old at the time. This is how my parents met.

They married after the war, and my father became a senior Communist official in Katowice and later in other Polish cities. By 1956 we had settled in Warsaw. My mother and her two uncles were later given the Righteous Among the Nations award by Yad Vashem for having hidden and looked after Jewish prisoners.

As a youngster I wasn't aware of my Jewish background. The knowledge came in bits and pieces; it was a slow process and is still going on. It wasn't like a bolt of lightning or a sudden discovery. For example, even though there was a menorah in our home, I didn't realise it was a Jewish religious symbol. People frequently came to visit my parents and the one country they always talked about was Israel. Someone was always going to Israel or coming from Israel. So you then start asking yourself: Out of so many interesting countries in the world, why do they always discuss Israel?

Over time I began to connect things. Although my father was not religious, he always observed Yom Kippur on 22 September because the deportation of the Jews from the ghetto of Częstochowa, his home town, took place on Yom Kippur in 1942. Regardless of when Yom Kippur actually fell in any particular year, my father only acknowledged it on 22 September. In a similar vein, I was regularly taken by my parents to the annual ceremonies commemorating the Warsaw Ghetto uprising.

When you are young you are curious, and sometimes search for family secrets in places like drawers. One day, when I was about fifteen, I noticed my mother had neglected to lock a drawer. Inside, there was a small pre-war photograph of my father as a young man. I turned it over and it said: this was to certify that this is a photograph of Lazar Sylman. I was astonished that the man I knew all my life as Leon Stasiak was actually Lazar Sylman. I didn't mention my discovery to him because I couldn't admit I had been sneaking around. Unlike previous hints regarding the possibility that he was Jewish, this was actually evidence.

In 1968, after the onset of the anti-semitic campaign, my father resigned at the age of 53 from his position as head of the propaganda department in the Central Committee. He told Gomułka, the head of the Communist Party, that he was not going to put up any more with the propaganda rubbish that was being promoted by the party.

By the time I went to Warsaw University, where I studied in the physics faculty from 1965 to 1970, I already knew about my Jewish background. Of course, knowing about your background is one thing, but identifying with it is another. In 1968, following the student revolt, our studies were suspended and 300 students in my class were expelled. Then we had to re-apply to be re-admitted.

After graduating, I practised as a physicist for a short while. But in the 1980s, I started to work for Sigmund Rolat, an American philanthropist and businessman who originally came from my ancestral town of Częstochowa. Rolat has been very active in supporting the revival of Jewish communal activity here, and also has economic interests in Poland. Working with Rolat also reinforced my growing sense of a Jewish identity.

About 10 years ago I got involved with Beit Warszawa, the Reform congregation in Warsaw. This was a significant development for me as I grew up in a household which was anti-religious to a certain degree. During the past few years, I have also been active in the Second Generation organisation.

Embracing my Jewish identity has been a long and winding road which goes up and down. At one point you feel quite connected, while at another time you feel less so. I recall a very important moment occurred when Israeli flags were flying on the main streets of Warsaw welcoming the president of Israel in 1992. The two countries had established diplomatic relations and now enjoy strong military, political and economic ties.

EWA WOLAŃCZYK

I was born in Kraków, and educated at the technical academy. I work as an environmental engineer. My father was an engineer and he inspired me to pursue this profession.

My mother's story, so far as the outside world was concerned, did not exist. She told one importunate cousin that she was raised in an orphanage. However, the version for her daughters was that despite not having a mother, she was raised in a family, not an orphanage. She told us that her mom died while giving birth. As for her father, he apparently died during the war. We knew nothing about our family because whenever we asked about her past or her family, she replied it was very painful for her. She insisted we don't ask questions or the whole trauma would return to haunt her.

My sister and I stopped asking questions, and I no longer thought about it. But my sister invented a story that our mother resisted questions because she was born as a result of a rape.

My father was Polish and born in a village near Kraków. His mother, a simple woman and very devout Catholic, did not harbour good feelings towards Jews. Yet, despite my parents' very different backgrounds, they were very close and enjoyed a good marriage. We had loving parents, which contributed to a happy childhood. But we were a religious family that regularly went to church. As part of a normal Catholic family, I was baptised and had communion.

Many years later I learned that our grandmother had been possessive toward her son, as often happens between mothers and daughters-in-law. On one occasion she disapproved of something my mother did, and said: 'You are behaving like a Jewess!' My father, who was very strict about the deal he made with my mother regarding her background, told his mother never to speak like that. Apparently it didn't happen again.

Growing up I had no reason to doubt my mother's story because everything was hidden. There were no cracks in the edifice; nothing was revealed. Whenever I raised questions about the war, even my father cut the conversation short. The issue of war, including his own experience, didn't exist in our household.

However, my mother introduced a custom in our family that on 1 November, All Saints' Day, we would go to the Rakowicki cemetery in Kraków and light a candle at the monument for those killed in concentration camps. Another custom was to light a candle on a tombstone for someone who was forgotten and never received visitors.

Another thing that intrigued and saddened me occurred in 1968. I had a good friend in primary school, Irena Horowitz, who suddenly disappeared without saying good-bye. When I divulged my feelings to my mother, she replied: 'Why are you so sad? She was a Jewish girl who had to move to Israel or somewhere else.' Her reaction was so calm and natural that it didn't allow us to start a conversation about the meaning of this event.

When I was about fifteen years old I read a memoir by David Rubinowicz, a child who was confined to the ghetto. It mostly depicts how he suffered from constant hunger, and was eventually killed. My mother also read the book. She wasn't pleased that I was reading such sad memoirs, and wanted to know why I was so interested in this material.

Never in my youth did I pursue my desire to ask my mother deeper questions about her background. I was always a very polite and well-behaved girl, and understood I might hurt her. I only knew she was an only child. One day, however, I decided to visit my mother's Polish friend from Lwów, where they had both lived before the war, to get more information about my mother's past. My aunt, because that's what I called her, refused to say anything, and contacted mom as soon as I left. When I returned home my mom accused me of interfering, and warned me against repeating this kind of behaviour.

I wasn't too suspicious about the lack of an extended family on my mother's side and I never raised an issue that often brought up questions for other hidden Jews. Looking back, I think my parents consciously chose to make our family very small. We lived in a detached house and limited our contacts with other people. When a child came to play with me, the main gate was locked and we always played in the house or back garden.

As I grew older and went into higher education, nothing changed. My parents continued their policy of protecting me. After I got married, suddenly, out of the blue, I became a total maniac about the summer Jewish Festival in Kraków which started in the 1990s. I would take a 10-day leave from work and spend all that time attending the festival. It wasn't just the music that attracted me, but also the various meetings and lectures. My husband started raising questions about this fascination with Jewish culture, and once said to me: 'I understand your mother doesn't want to tell you anything. But you don't even know your grandparents' names; you don't know anything about this family. Your behaviour is strange.'

At the time I worked in a company headed by my father. He advised me not to talk about my interest in the festival, or the staff would become suspicious or even label me a Jew. That was a key moment when everything began to be revealed. I vividly recall asking him whether there is any reason to suspect something. He froze, and did not speak. When asked once more, he remained speechless. Then he replied: 'Ask your mom.' His answer made everything clear. It was like someone opening a door wide.

I took his advice, and approached my mom. It proved to be a very difficult and painful path, like walking down the Via Dolorosa, as she warned me that I was opening old wounds. It was a serious problem because my mom had been living her life totally concealing the truth. Yet, by opening up, she could finally unload the burden of having deceived her children.

I started asking questions and she told me more and more stories. Because my mother had repressed memories and facts for so long, initially she could hardly remember anything. There was also a great deal of resistance on her part. For example, she complained when I tried to get her to utter her real name. With great difficulty she finally told me it was Sydonia Magenheim. I wanted so badly for her to remember everything. I too was in an emotional state; I wanted to remember every detail and to ensure the information wouldn't slip my mind, I kept saying: 'Wait, wait.' And I would go to the bathroom to write down all the crucial bits of information. There, I felt safe knowing that no one would enter the occupied bathroom.

So this is what I learned, or as much as could be established. My maternal grandparents were quite well off, and ran a restaurant in Lwów. My mother's father used to go to synagogue from time to time, and her mother performed some religious rituals at home. It was a big family; there were 18 children in the immediate and extended family when the war broke out. My mother was the only survivor, apart from her cousin, but they didn't know that. My mother was in the Lwów ghetto, and later hidden by a Ukrainian man. When a female neighbour started to get interested in my mom's Jewish identity, the man took her to the train station so she could flee. She got on the train to Kraków, and found herself among Wehrmacht soldiers returning from the Eastern front. The train was stopped by a German patrol searching for Jews, but the soldiers shouted they were coming back home wounded and wouldn't hide any Jews. So my mother was saved.

In Kraków she got a job as a housemaid at an SS man's house. She lacked decent clothes, so he took her to the ghetto in Płaszów and Jews from there sewed her a dress and a coat. I have a few photographs from 1945 of my mother wearing these clothes.

My mother didn't know exactly when she was born, thinking it was 1926. In fact it turned out to be 1927. We discovered it just this year, when my mom's birth certificate was found in the archives of the Jewish Historical Institute. A few years ago I met my cousin who responded to a notice my husband had posted on the internet that he was looking for people called Magenheim. Ela's grandmother and my grandfather were siblings, which means we and our mothers are cousins.

Thirty years ago my sister moved to Canada with her Polish husband. My mother wanted to reveal her background to my sister. Because I already knew, I couldn't resist telling her myself. When my sister came to Poland on a visit, I showed her my notes. She was terribly upset and still holds a grudge against our mother because she found out the truth from me, rather than hearing it from her. I once asked my sister why she never shows any further interest in our family background and she replied: 'I don't ask because our mother wasn't interested in telling me.'

My mother often cried when talking about her past, and told me how she couldn't sleep at night. She worried my Polish husband would stop loving me because he would regard me as a Jew. She could never utter the word 'Jew'. In fact my husband accepted everything, and goes with me to the Jewish Festival, albeit to a lesser degree. We both read many books about Jewish history and hunt for television programmes about Jews. Although my husband is a religious Catholic, he will happily go to an event, like a concert, at the synagogue. He is very respectful of tradition. On one occasion, when I asked him to accompany me into the Jewish cemetery in Kraków, he hesitated because he didn't have anything with which to cover his head.

I told my daughter about my background when she around 20 years old, despite my mother's protests. My daughter cried while we were talking, probably due to shock. While her boyfriend, whom she later married, didn't have a problem with her Jewish roots, they decided not to tell his family who don't have a friendly attitude towards Jews. I hope she will raise her daughters to respect Jewish culture and honour the Holocaust; I think her home will be less Catholic than the one she was raised in. I expect she won't hide her Jewish family background from her daughters. I wear a bracelet with the Star of David, which I show to the girls.

I'm not particularly worried whether the Jewish link will extend beyond my daughter's generation; the choice will be theirs. I am very pleased that once, when my daughter was in a group and someone told anti-semitic jokes, she reacted sharply. She insisted she wouldn't tolerate people who were disrespectful of Jews.

I remain a disciplined Catholic, and attend some religious celebrations as my religion commands. Deep faith, however, is a great gift which I possess only in some measure. At the same time, I definitely regard myself as a Pole of Jewish origin. Yet it's easier to say not what I feel but how I feel in certain situations. For example, when someone tells me they were with some Żydziak, I get angry and make it very clear that the word is offensive.

I'm not involved in the Kraków Gmina although I attend meetings at the Jewish Community Centre. Perhaps when I retire, I will get more involved in their programmes for senior people. However, it's very difficult to get involved in this milieu as you have to know people.

I joined Second Generation after meeting my cousin. At that time, she was also participating in therapeutic sessions for Second Generation members in Kraków that were run there by Maria Orwid, a psychiatrist from Jagiellonian University. Orwid was very famous for her work with Holocaust children, but sadly, she has died. I had wanted to participate in this kind of therapy but unfortunately I was too late.

JACEK MŁYNARSKI

I learned about my Jewish roots a year ago, and about the tragic stories of my father and grandmother. My father died in 1963, when I was three years old. He drowned, probably due to a heart attack.

I was brought up in a typical Polish Catholic family. My mother was Catholic. Later I had a step-father who was an ardent Communist, but he came from a Polish Catholic family too.

Nobody spoke about Jews in my house, and the subject of my father was also taboo. If I asked my mother about him, she got upset. As a child, I thought something traumatic had happened between my parents. Even now, when I ask, she says she didn't know anything about my father's wartime story. Perhaps she had an inkling, but didn't know for certain that he was Jewish.

The first internal conflict occurred when I was 30 and officially decided to give up Catholicism. But even then nothing was said about religion, just that I am making a mistake in leaving the community. It wasn't a religious issue but more to do with the community.

Looking back, many things now appear obvious. But, at that time, it was done without any knowledge. It wasn't only a negative choice, but also a positive one; I was looking for tolerant, open-minded communities and cultures not necessarily connected to a narrow understanding of Polishness.

So the discovery in August 2011 was an absolutely lovely surprise, a gift, as if I had received a birthday present. It was 9 August, my birthday. I started talking to my mother once again about my father and my paternal grandparents, whom I had never met. She didn't say much that was new, but she mentioned my grandmother's name, which I heard for the first time at the age of 51. It was Gabriella Hertz from Częstochowa. So the first thing I did when I returned home was to google Gabriella Hertz. Two websites appeared. One was the Częstochowa-Radomsko Research Area Group and the other, of course, was JewishGen.

A sort of puzzle opened up, which led me to the story of my family reaching back to the mid-eighteenth century. The genealogy department at the Jewish Historical Institute in Warsaw helped me find Gabriel Lubowski, my only living relative in Israel, in Holon. He is the grandson of the sister of my great grandmother. We have become friends and exchange emails and letters.

I went to Israel in the summer of 2012 and we spent two weekends together. He had no doubt that I was a Jew. His family came from Łódź; their name was Zaks (a common Polish Jewish name). My great grandmother, Estera Zaks, moved from Łódź to Częstochowa because she married Shlomo Hertz. When I found all these names, I had no doubt about who I am and where I'm from.

My mother finally admitted this but said she could only guess, she didn't know. She only mentioned my paternal mother's surname. What followed was an explosion that I think she hadn't expected. I found out many things very quickly: many documents were preserved. That was wonderful news for me and everything that happened later was also wonderful. I don't want to use big words but it is something of a miracle.

I don't think the discovery of my Jewish ancestry generally had a negative impact on my relationships. Perhaps only my mother found it difficult to cope. Once she even asked me whether I wanted to convert to Judaism. I told her that Judaism is a very attractive religion. I'm not excluding this possibility, but will keep it to myself.

The funniest reaction came from my half-brother who does not have Jewish origins and had rather anti-semitic views all his life. Suddenly he saw a Jew in his family and stopped being anti-semitic altogether. Now we can meet and no longer talk about Jewish conspiracies. We used to argue about it all the time, but that has stopped.

My partner accepted everything easily; she was very positive from the beginning. She is half Russian and half Polish and grew up in Moscow.

But she has always been against anti-semitism and every kind of intolerance.

I also have three children from two marriages with Polish women. They are 30, 27 and 20 years old and their reactions to my Jewish journey have been varied. The oldest daughter accepted it with enthusiasm. She says that now she knows why she always found Israel interesting, why she found it easiest to talk to Jews, especially those from Israel. The middle daughter also reacted calmly. She lives in Copenhagen with her husband and child. To her it was completely natural.

The biggest problem was my 20-year old son. He has a very close relationship with his mother, who is a militant activist with the Law & Justice Party. So I decided to send him on Birthright Israel and he was enthusiastic. When I gave him a lift to the airport, I noticed he was sad. I told him he was heading for a lovely holiday, so why is he sad. He said: 'Oh, you know, I'm sure they will indoctrinate me there and I feel Polish after all.' I told him that he would see that one thing doesn't cancel the other. Then, after his return, he said: 'You know, Dad, in the Six-Day War we really defeated the Arabs.' I thought: he may not yet know whether or not he is a Jew, but he already is a Zionist. Unfortunately, I was wrong then.

In the course of my family research, I learned a lot about my father's story. It started with documents in the JHI and on the JewishGen website. I knew that before the war, the family lived in Warsaw. The first document I found was the registration of my grandmother and her son in the Częstochowa ghetto; they were resettled there from Warsaw in December 1940. It is possible they transferred them there because they had lived in a relatively wealthy area of Warsaw and had to be moved and Gabriella was from Częstochowa, so they moved them there.

My grandfather, Gabriella's husband, was evacuated in September 1939 to Romania with employees of the Polish Radio. She ended up alone, and perhaps wanted to join her mother and brother.

I also found documents about my father and grandfather in the archives of Warsaw University. My father studied there, and my grandfather was a professor. He lectured on the history of journalism. Both sides of my family were intelligentsia – both the Hertz and Młynarski families. The latter was a family of teachers.

Zygmunt Młynarski married Gabriella Hertz. Their son Andrzej was my father. So I kept my Jewish father's name (Młynarski). It was suggested I change my name to my step-father's, but I declined.

I'm sure my father was only a Communist for career reasons. But my grandfather, Zygmunt, was definitely an idealistic Communist; I read some articles he wrote. He also spent some time in prisons in inter-war Poland. I have read a lot in order to understand all this. Communism in my biography was definitely more difficult for me than Jewishness. Jewishness was a gift, but I had to struggle to understand the Communism.

Of course there is an internal dilemma between my Polish and Jewish identities. The first thing I'm trying to pass on to my children is that there is no balance between Polishness and Jewishness. There are enough people to remember about our Polish roots. But when it comes to the Jewish ones, there is only us. Only we can bring to life all those people who were murdered between 1940 and 1942.

I found many documents and personal belongings of my father's. Among them is a notebook of poems he was writing when he was eighteen. It was with my grandfather's family. They kept it safe, and gave it to me. That's another miracle. All of this is extraordinary.

My grandfather died of a heart attack in December 1963, shortly after my father drowned. I didn't know I had any family, and it turned out I do and quite a big one. For example, I didn't have any pictures of my father but I now have photos of him from before and during the war.

In the notebook, my father didn't write much about his mother, but what he did write was striking. Of course I'm paraphrasing, but when the police took his mother, she said in farewell: 'Look, remember and describe everything.' I kept that promise on my father's behalf in the sense that I would like to discover what I can and describe everything. That's another reason why, after all these years, Jewishness is closer to me.

On the other hand I was brought up in the Polish culture, in a world of very characteristic Polish ideas. I think in Polish and when I happen to pray, I do so in Polish. When I stood in front of the Kotel (Wailing Wall) in Jerusalem, I wondered if God understands me as I was praying in Polish. So Polishness is close to me. I'm thinking of the Polishness of Tuwim and Słonimski. Or Aleksander Hertz, whose surname is close to me. That's how I would like to perceive my Polishness. A bit of the Haskalah attitude: integration.

Gaining an understanding of my Jewish ties is a process, it's not finished. I'm trying to read as much as I can. I'm not sure whether I'm ready to go to the synagogue to pray. I'm trying to understand, to know what my ancestors believed in. I don't know what the outcome will be.

Almost immediately after learning about my Jewish family, I was browsing the internet for Holocaust survivors and found the Second Generation association. I thought: that's wonderful, there are people who probably have some experiences that were denied to me and that I should have had.

The concept of Second Generation is more about people being together in this unique situation than working on a psychological level. Without the Second Generation contacts, I wouldn't have gone to Limmud or to Israel. Had I been alone, I probably wouldn't have dared.

I don't have to struggle to integrate my Polish and Jewish identities. My Polishness was given, my Jewishness was chosen and they work together quite well. I reject a certain conception of Polishness. I don't see why someone should take away my Polish passport, as was done to many Jews in 1968, and I don't see any reason why I can't be a Jew here. I nurture the hope that there are good prospects for creating a stronger Jewish community over the next couple of generations. Poland without its Jewish traditions is impoverished.

ZYGMUNT STĘPIŃSKI

(Deputy Director, Polin Museum, Warsaw)

The terrible events of 1968 and the subsequent emigration of many Jews from Poland constituted an absolutely critical moment in my life. I was a student in the History faculty of the University of Warsaw and became involved in the student strike of 8 March. Adam Michnik, well known as one of the leaders of the student revolt, was my very close friend. During this period I observed the rising anti-semitic atmosphere in Poland, which had grown a great deal worse since the Israeli-Arab war of 1967.

Along with most of my friends, I could hardly believe what was happening around us. Until then I had been surrounded by Jewish colleagues, a pattern that began in 1954, at the age of seven. I attended the Karol Świerczewski ('Walter') school, which taught both elementary and high school students, and my classmates and I had close relations for eleven years. We lived in a neighbourhood where a large number of high-ranking Communists resided, many of whom were Jewish. As students we spent most of our free time together and, in a sense, you could say I lived in a secular version of a *shtetl*. But in 1968, amidst the widespread anti-semitic persecution of Jews, many of my best friends started to leave for Western countries, mainly Sweden and Denmark. Even my girlfriend emigrated to Sweden.

Prior to 1968 my mother's Jewish background was hidden. As I don't look Slavic, many people were curious about my family's origins. My mother insisted her father was Italian, but years later I learned he was an Italian with Sephardic roots. The family name was Loria, but my great grandfather had changed it to Lore. He didn't regard himself as a Jew since the family was very assimilated.

In 1971 my twin brother met a Jewish girl whom he later married. As a result, I started to visit my brother's father-in-law, and we discussed issues relating to Jewish identity and how he survived the war in the Soviet Union. His family came from Łódź, the same city where my mother and grandmother lived before the war. Consequently, they knew everything about my mother, including the time she spent teaching at a Jewish school in Łódź.

But it wasn't until 1982, shortly after martial law was declared in December 1981, that my mother spoke to me for the first and only time about her Jewish family. It was a very dramatic encounter because it occurred on the day of my father's funeral, combined with the imposition of a repressive martial law regime. We returned to my parents' home to have dinner and I decided to stay there for a couple of nights. I went to my father's room and filled a glass with his Johnny Walker whiskey – a kind of ritual to remember him. My mother entered the room and said: 'You are drinking your father's whiskey!' I was shocked at her comment and replied: 'Father is dead. Today we had a funeral. But you are acting, as the Poles would say, like a typical Jewish wife.' She was very surprised and said: 'How do you know?' So I told her that my brother's in-laws knew about her family in pre-war Łódź. Then I asked her: 'Why did you hide our identity from us? We should have been aware of our background much earlier, especially in 1968.'

She explained that she did what she could to protect us. As a high school and university student, she witnessed so much anti-semitic behaviour in the 1930s that she wanted to ensure her children would never go through the same experience.

I later learned that my mother spent the entire war in Warsaw, and managed to hide her background due to her 'good looks' (non-Jewish appearance). She spoke German fluently and worked as a secretary for one of the highest ranking German officers in Warsaw. Her first husband was Polish and died from his wounds during the siege of Warsaw. My father, her second husband, was also Polish; this didn't present any difficulties for them since her documents revealed only Aryan names.

I asked her about her father, a Polish war hero and one of the highest ranking Jews in the Polish army. As commander of both the Warsaw military airport and the flying school of the Polish army, he was very close to Marshal Piłsudski. Nevertheless, he hid his Jewish identity despite having the name Lore, a typical Jewish name in Poland. Moreover, he would be very aggressive towards anyone who suggested he might be Jewish.

When, after a couple of hours, we finished our memorable conversation, my mother asked whether my brother was aware of our Jewish connections. I pointed out that he had married into a Jewish family in Łódź, who were very proud and comfortable with their Jewish identity. My mother then urged me not to tell my older sister, who was abroad at the time of the funeral, that we are Jewish. She added: 'Leave her in peace.' My mother believed the knowledge would not benefit her in any way.

When my sister returned from France, I decided to tell her about my conversation with our mother. Since then we have often talked about her identity, but she has decided that it remains completely Polish. Interestingly, as an agricultural scientist, she once attended a scientific congress in Israel and decided to stay on for an extra two weeks to see the country. Although she returned from that trip in a very happy frame of mind, she insisted that it didn't change her Polish identity.

After the revelatory encounter with my mother, I wanted to talk about it with my brother. But he was in Zakopane and, since martial law had been declared, it was impossible to reach him on the phone. When he eventually returned to Warsaw, he told me he had known for a long time what I had just discovered. We felt like a big load had been lifted from our shoulders, and that the air had cleared.

During the period of martial law, having been fired from my job, I worked for CDN, one of the largest underground publishing houses. I was also among a group of nine other people to launch *Murator*, the first private magazine to function in an Eastern European country since 1945. Focusing on construction and interior design, *Murator* grew into one of the biggest publishing houses in Poland.

In 2012, shortly before taking up my post as deputy director of the Polin Museum, a friend recommended that I purchase a book devoted to Polish sportsmen who had received high decorations in the military. I found that my grandfather had been an officer in the Virtuti Militari, the most prestigious Polish order. His parents' names also appeared in this book, and I discovered his mother's name was Felicia Fred. I persevered and found her family tree dating back to the eighteenth century.

Two years ago my secretary informed me that a woman called Sophie, who claimed to be a distant cousin, was waiting for me downstairs. I met a young lady in her 30s, who asked if I had a document concerning my father's family because she was preparing a story about the Stępiński family. I said that I was actually more interested in my mother's family. She replied: 'OK. But you will be astonished.'

She revealed that my great-great-grandfather was called Shlomo Steinman, one of the richest Jewish merchants in Suwałki. In the first half of the nineteenth century, his family converted to Catholicism. When one of his daughters married a Jewish boy from another converted Jewish family, the children remained Jewish from a halachic point of view. The situation was repeated in the second half of the nineteenth century when my great grandmother married into the Stępiński family. I am named Zygmunt after my father and grandfather.

All this background information was shocking because I strongly believed my father was mildly anti-semitic. For example, as one of the best architects in Poland, he was commissioned to design a chapel memorialising Maximilian Kolbe, the priest who died as a martyr in Auschwitz. However, Kolbe was also a founder of modern Polish anti-semitism. My mother therefore asked him: 'Why are you doing this? Don't you remember his activities before the war?'

Today I would regard my identity as mixed. It's either Polish-Jewish or Jewish-Polish – it depends on the situation. When I'm confronted with Polish anti-semitism, I'm 100 per cent Jewish. But, in normal everyday life, it's 50-50.

When I visited Israel to represent the museum at Yad Vashem, I went to the Wailing Wall. I expected it would be a kind of revelation, something special would happen to me. Maybe I would commemorate my mother's memory there. But nothing significant happened.

I don't know how many Jews live in Poland. Probably, it's higher than the official figure of 7,000, but considering there are many family stories like mine, it might be 100,000 or even more. However, it's now 70 years since the war ended and it's probably too late for many hidden Jews to really come out. Many people might pursue genealogical studies or go to the Jewish Historical Institute or the Museum to search for family roots. Yet I wonder how many will take it very far. So I'm not very optimistic.

ROBERT CHMIELEWSKI

The core of my Jewish story is a few sentences; the rest is intuition. My mother was left as an infant at a church in the small village of Trzebinia, close to Kraków, during the Second World War. A woman came to the nuns and asked them to watch the child for a few hours. She never returned. The nuns gave the child to a priest, who in turn handed it to another priest who lived with his sister.

The sister's name was Helena Kantor, the widow of a Polish officer murdered by the Nazis. Two weeks later a package with children's clothes was delivered to the convent where the nuns lived: it was addressed to Wanda Zakrzewska. Here ends the early part of the story; my mother never found any members of her Jewish family. But we know that she was somehow connected to somebody named Wanda Zakrzewska.

During the German occupation, my mother was raised in an unusual vicarage. She was the first of many Polish and Jewish children the priest saved; later he was responsible for rescuing a few hundred children during the Warsaw Uprising of 1944.

After the war, when my mother was a few years old, representatives of Jewish organisations came to her Polish home seeking to reclaim her. She became hysterical, and it was agreed she remain with her adoptive mother. As she grew older she acquired a higher education, and became a teacher in Lublin where she still lives.

My mother raised me in the Catholic tradition. I also studied at the Catholic University of Lublin in the 1980s because it embodied my world view as well as my political outlook. I was a young anti-Communist engaged in opposition activities with the Solidarity movement. During this period, the Catholic University of Lublin functioned like an island of independent thought, where students and lecturers of different religious beliefs could study and teach. With the fall of the Communist regime I was even very involved, for a short period, in creating a Polish right-wing party, where I often encountered anti-semites.

My mother retired at the start of the 1990s, and began her quest to discover her Jewish roots. She had time, her children were adults, and she was free to investigate. She managed to find one of the nuns in the convent who remembered her as an infant. She asked the nun: 'Do you know who I am, who my family was?' The nun replied: 'We don't know your real name, nor who your parents were. But we never had any doubt that you were an abandoned Jewish child.' They could not offer any documentation, only circumstantial evidence. Nonetheless it was sufficient proof to convince my mother she was eligible to join the Association of Children of the Holocaust.

In the mid-1990s, my mother told me about our Jewish origins. This news was not unexpected, strange or incomprehensible, despite the fact that suddenly my identity took on a different context. I didn't experience negative emotions, but neither did I feel euphoria or happiness. I was calm, perhaps a little moved by this discovery. After all, a few thousand years of history came knocking on my door. I was aware of that then, and still am.

In terms of my daily life very little changed. My Jewish background seemed distant from everyday concerns. However, when I was working as a journalist for Polish Radio, I met Romuald Jakub Weksler-Waszkinel, the renowned Jewish priest, who had also joined the Association of Children of the Holocaust where he had met my mother. It was an important interview for me because it allowed me to openly discuss my Jewish origins for the first time.

Yet I remained a mildly conservative Catholic until I met Karolina Szykier-Koszucka, who was very active in the Wrocław Jewish community. She belongs to the Third Generation and was the second person with whom I could discuss my Jewish background. We met in my role as a journalist covering the commemoration event of Kristallnacht, which Karolina had organised.

The journey toward becoming actively involved with the Jewish community was a long process.

The situation changed when I got divorced – perhaps because I was lonely and looking for some sense of security with people who were similar to myself. My son and I started to attend meetings for Jewish families organised by the American Jewish Joint Distribution Committee. Sometimes this involved summer camps, while other events would be Shabbatons which are held every couple of months. Although I'm sympathetic to the Second Generation, I haven't joined the organisation yet. But I am an active member of Cukunft, the Wrocław social and cultural organisation.

I think visiting Israel is a spiritual experience, but not everyone has the capacity to take it in. I went for the first time last spring. If I had a rich spiritual life, either Catholic or Jewish, I would have felt it was a pilgrimage. In Jerusalem, I felt better at the Western Wall than in the Vatican. The prayers have soaked up the walls.

Today my Catholicism is almost non-existent. However, I haven't reached the level of knowledge where I can embrace Judaism. Until I cross that threshold, I can only participate on a purely cultural or social level. In fact, I go to the synagogue for social contacts. On one occasion, one of the members invited me to participate in the prayer for my grandfather's *yahrzeit*. I explained that I don't know how to pray, but he replied that it wasn't important; it was simply necessary to be there as part of a *minyan*. So I felt obliged to go to the prayer service. If my mere presence can help someone, I will be there – like in Cukunft. These places bring people together who have Jewish origins but don't have to be registered members of the Jewish community.

My son is now thirteen years old, the Bar Mitzvah age. He participates in Hasmonea, a small Jewish football team led by Cukunft. I realise I can also access my Jewishness through him, and learn Jewish traditions and culture. That's why I send him to one of the private Jewish schools in Wrocław. They offer a course on Jewish culture and, on Friday morning, the students celebrate Shabbat and receive some Hebrew instruction.

It's very important that my Jewish origins and the Polish culture I grew up in don't contradict, but rather complement one another. I don't feel any kind of internal split since I am not depressed about being a Jew, yet regard myself as a Polish patriot. I consider the discovery of my Jewish origins to be a great gift from fate; that I am part of something important and beautiful.

Since the fall of Communism, you don't necessarily have to be brave to regain your Jewish roots because an open society tolerates many expressions of identity. But it's not only an issue of inner courage; it's also a question of inner need. Not everyone has that need. I only got involved in Jewish life when I started to feel an emptiness in my life after my divorce. I had lost my point of reference, which was my family, and found a point of reference in Jewishness. Perhaps people who are fulfilled on all fronts don't need this Jewish point of reference.

People sometimes tell me that Poland is a hard country to live in. But I reply that Eskimos live in more difficult conditions, and still love what they were born to do.

ANIA BOROS

When I was fourteen, in 1968, the daughter of a neighbour said to me: 'You Jew.' That's how I found out I was Jewish. I felt insulted, and went home crying. I told my father, and he admitted he was Jewish and that, therefore, I was half-Jewish. He said it as though he had a guilty conscience. My mother, however, was Polish and even came from an anti-semitic family. I never had a good relationship with my mother, and felt a closer emotional tie to my father.

This Jewish background was always a taboo subject, both before and after 1968. I realised my father didn't want to talk about it, so I never asked questions.

My father was a Communist and a political officer who taught at the military political academy. In 1967, he was thrown out of his job. He gave a lecture about the Six-Day War, and he must have drawn some information from Radio Free Europe and said something the Communists didn't like. So they used that as a pretext to expel him.

My father was born in Lwów in 1924. When the war started he was fifteen years old and somehow got to Kraków, where he spent the whole war in hiding. After the war, he regarded himself as a Communist and felt he now had an opportunity to improve his life. So he went to college and then joined the army at the age of 21. He eventually became a lieutenant colonel and was about to be promoted to a full colonel. But then he got kicked out in 1967 when he was only 43 years old.

Regarding anti-semitism in this matter, I'm not sure from whom I heard this story; perhaps my mother. There were quite a lot of Jews in this academy and my father's direct supervisor, who was also Jewish, was afraid all of them might be kicked out. So they took the opportunity to blame my father and made up some absurd excuses. At that time, despite being a genuine Communist, they accused him of betraying Communism.

Following the loss of his job, my father had a complete breakdown because that represented everything he believed in. Sadly, he couldn't find a new job for a long time.

In 1968, my parents considered emigrating. They didn't, however, because my father was a historian and they worried whether he would find a job abroad. Also, my mother had a good job at the headquarters for foreign trade, and she didn't encounter many problems as a result of what happened to her husband.

As for my father not telling me about my Jewishness, perhaps he wanted to protect me. But, firstly, he just wanted to forget his background; he didn't like Jews a lot. Even when he told me he was Jewish, he said it with a kind of guilty conscience. I remembered it that way for a long time.

We never had an extended Jewish family. When I was a small child, a cousin stayed with us, but later she went abroad. Over time we lost touch. My mother wondered why my father didn't try to look for other relatives through the Red Cross, but clearly he didn't want to. When he was hiding in Kraków during the war, he was with a cousin who was nine years older and he did stay in touch with him.

My discovery of my Jewish background at the age of fourteen came as a shock. I couldn't get over it for a long time. There was a lot of anti-semitism when I started high school. I shared a desk with another girl whose name was Szycman, which sounded Jewish; she even looked Jewish. I never dared to ask her about her origins. There was also an anti-semitic Russian teacher who must have known I was Jewish because he always made unpleasant remarks. He really didn't like me.

We were faced with a very difficult economic situation when my father lost his job and it continued to get worse. For example, I used to play the piano at a private school but couldn't attend any more.

My brother, who was five years older, was always very proud of his Jewish background. He was never into books or studying, and, after graduating from high school, he started to get involved in business. He feels he has the ability to make money in his business ventures, which he thinks might be related to his Jewish background.

I married a Hungarian and lived in Hungary for over 30 years. Today, I'm a baby-sitter because I couldn't find another job when I returned from Hungary two years ago. But I had a technical education, and also worked as an editor of a technical monthly magazine. I also studied journalism after martial law was imposed before that school was closed. When I lived in Hungary, I was a correspondent for four years for a major Polish newspaper.

I studied at the Warsaw Polytechnic. My father chose that practical course of study for me as he thought it would be better for my future. Yet, at heart, I was more into the liberal arts and never worked as an engineer.

In 1968, I pushed aside the discovery of my Jewishness as I had other problems to deal with. Also, my father had mental health problems which he was being treated for. He went to everyone and told them he was Jewish. Some people replied that they already knew; others chose not to meet him any more.

As a child I felt very lost and lonely. My father was writing his Ph.D. and was always locked up in a room and urging everyone to be quiet because he was working. Later I found out that my mother had been raped by a Russian solder. We never talked openly at home because my mother always said we shouldn't discuss it.

I didn't have any Jewish family to share my feelings with. At same time, I felt fear and underwent psychological treatment. I started to confront my Jewishness only some years ago, when as a first step, I went to Auschwitz.

I only found out about the Second Generation group half a year ago when I read the book *I Accuse Auschwitz* by Mikołaj Grynberg. I feel I have a lot to learn – maybe I will try to track down some of my father's relatives.

I still feel more Polish than Jewish. I really appreciated it when I returned from Hungary because I could use the Polish language. Poland is where I grew up. But there is still a black hole when it comes to Jewishness. Perhaps when I have time to acquire more information it might be possible to feel closer to my Jewish background. I love Jewish music and when I hear *klezmer*, I want to dance. In Hungary, I was involved in a Jewish dance circle.

My Hungarian husband was my second husband. However, my first husband was a Solidarity activist and photographer. After I left Poland, he got in touch with me and arranged the correspondent role in Hungary from 1992 to 1996 with the Polish newspaper.

As for my experiences with the Jewish community in Hungary, when I lived in Poland I always felt fear when it came to any relationship involving Jewishness. In Hungary, I took a Hungarian language class. One woman openly said she was attending the Anne Frank school; she was just so relaxed about it. It was so different.

After a few years, I started to open up about my Jewishness. Then I found out that many of my friends also had a Jewish background but never spoke about it among themselves. Jews in Hungary are more assimilated than in Poland in the sense that they have experienced much less discrimination.

When I initially found out about the Second Generation I was so happy. I had been searching for something and finally found it. So it was very exciting. For five years, I had been a Buddhist. So when I returned from Hungary, my first connection was with the Buddhists. In Hungary, a lot of the members of the Buddhist group were Jewish. The way they practice Buddhism has very little to do with religion; it's more of a philosophy.

I meet with the Second Generation around once a month. These encounters are totally different from my Buddhist practice, but equally interesting.

I was counting on the group to provide psychological help, perhaps also treatment, because many of us are struggling with the same problems. We have all had very difficult experiences due to the silence in our families. But, perhaps I haven't been in the group long enough.

I'm very interested in Jewish culture and I'm very excited that there are all those initiatives, including the establishment of the new Jewish museum. In fact, I went to the opening of the museum. I also think there is a lot of fear, which is being discussed at Second Generation meetings, regarding the growth of anti-semitism in Europe.

After I divorced my Hungarian husband, I had a boyfriend from Israel because I wanted to get closer to Judaism. However, the experience was very negative as he was very chauvinistic. He thought Jews were better than *goyim*. Nevertheless, I recently returned with my children from our first visit to Israel and I was really impressed with the Promised Land.

I would like to have a positive sense of pride in my Jewish heritage, but I think I will have to know more about it. Something more than just my roots. From my father, I only inherited shame. But now I feel my outlook is changing in the right direction.

LESZEK (LESŁAW) PISZEWSKI

(Chairman of the Board of the Union of Jewish Communities in Poland)

I was born in 1958 in Łobez, a small town near the German border, and lived there until I was fourteen years old. I went to a Catholic school; there were no Jews in the town. No doubt I even went to the school's religion classes.

When I turned fourteen, I decided to go to a high school that was about 200 km away where I lived in the dormitory. I wanted to be a forester, and it was the forestry high school.

Later I went to Warsaw University, also to study forestry. In Warsaw I began asking myself questions about my family. In our small town kids used to call me 'Jew', but I didn't look like a Jew. I knew this was an insult, and I was very pleased when the teacher summoned me to the front of the class, and said: 'Don't call him such a bad name.' I was happy she tried to protect me. Only later did I realise that what she said was even worse than the remarks of the kids.

My mother is Polish, from a small town near Lublin. My father was Jewish, and came from Warsaw. He looked very Jewish; perhaps it was thought he was different in some way. For example, he never went to church. As a child, however, he was in the Warsaw ghetto. Before the ghetto was closed, his parents sent him to a little village called Dąbrówka, near Mińsk, where they had spent summer holidays. There he hid in a barn. When I was a boy and he told me this story, I would imagine it was an adventure; perhaps all the children there did the same. He hid in the barn, under the hay where he slept, and only went out at night. He was starving. But as a child I didn't relate this story to a larger picture.

My father didn't want to talk about it once I started asking questions. He refused to discuss this topic. Did he not want people to know he was Jewish? Yes, precisely so.

I asked him how he got from Warsaw to the small town where I was born. He said that when he returned to Warsaw after the war, he couldn't find his family. He was fifteen or sixteen years old, and decided to leave because everything was destroyed. There was nothing to keep him in Warsaw, so he decided to register in Berlin for the American army because he heard they were helping kids go to Israel, America, Sweden – to different places. So he and others travelled by train; it took them a month to get to Łobez. The train made stops and they foraged for food. When the train stopped at Łobez, which was very close to the border, this formerly German town was filled with refugees from eastern Poland, Warsaw and Ukraine. There he met my mother. She was a young woman who had been sent there to work. They started dating, and after a year they married and decided to settle in Łobez.

When my mother took my father to meet her family, they said: 'Please don't marry him; he is a Jew. He will have problems. You never know what will happen to the Jews. You will have a very unhappy life.' But my mother had fallen in love. Later she told me: 'I knew he was a Jew. But I loved him, and decided to stay with him.' My sister was born, and later my brother. We lived a very quiet life in this town.

My father was a mechanic for office machinery. He didn't have a good education because during the war he couldn't go to school.

Although I was born thirteen years after the war, I still thought about it as something very dangerous which I had experienced personally. The war was still in our house. There was the fear of hunger; you had to eat because you never knew when you would have food. But I didn't realise why we had these concerns.

Regarding the 1968 anti-semitic purges, I only remember the situation in our home. We were travelling by car one day in early spring, and my parents were listening to the radio. They spoke to one another in angry, panicky tones. Also, the atmosphere in our home at the time was very tense.

One day in Warsaw I reflected about my college friends, who talked about visiting their extended families on both parents' sides. But we only visited the family on my mother's side. Where was my father's family? I began questioning my father, and he replied: 'You know they all died. We don't have a family and don't ask.'

And so I began to wonder. He'd lived in Warsaw; perhaps there were neighbours who still remember the family. Or perhaps my father could show me some graves. He said there were no graves because they all died in the war. And he didn't want to talk about it any more.

But I didn't give up so easily. I asked him to come to Warsaw to show me places he remembered from his childhood. But he said he didn't remember much – only small details. He didn't feel comfortable talking about this and, when I persisted in my questioning, he became angry and rude and tried to change the subject.

Yet he loved Warsaw because he remembered his happy childhood; he liked to come here to visit. Once he took me on a tour and showed me where he had lived, where there was a market.

He told me about a holiday when they built a tent in the courtyard. It was very enjoyable, with the men sitting outside during the night. The women came to bring food while the children played games. Later my father began to sob uncontrollably. He fell apart and I saw it was very painful for him.

I went to the Jewish cultural society, TKSŻ, because it was the only Jewish organisation I knew of. I told them the story and asked the old people there whether they knew anyone who had lived at my father's old address at 20 Chłodna Street, which had been in the middle of the ghetto. However, they didn't know because they were not from Warsaw. Most came from Russia, where they survived the war. There are very few Jews in Warsaw from the pre-war era.

They asked me to become a member of TKSŻ and I joined in the late 1970s. I met some young people and they told me about a young American rabbi who was teaching basic Judaism in someone's home on Sundays. They offered to introduce me.

At first, when I began delving more deeply into Jewish life, my father was very angry. But later he said he was very proud of me, that I was brave enough to be a Jew. He even came to the Nożyk synagogue on holidays and felt very happy. He felt like a fish restored to water when he heard the old people singing, also when the songs were in Yiddish. I remember from early childhood that he sang a lovely lullaby to me; it's my first childhood memory. It was Szrulik, a variation of Israel, by Adam Aston. It was his favourite song.

Did I have a positive response to my realisation that my father was Jewish, and that therefore I was Jewish as well? First I wanted to know the family story. Everyone has a story.

My mother used to take me and my siblings to church, and I was baptised. When I turned fourteen, I stopped going to church. When I was young my mother forced us to attend, while my father helped us avoid going. He always found reasons to excuse us from church. For myself, going to church was a very negative experience. Then, when I went to high school, I realised I didn't have to attend church at all.

It wasn't a shock to discover I had a family background previously unknown to me. I didn't have bad experiences regarding Jews. In our small town there were no Jews, and no references to Jews. Jews were something unreal – something from the past. Perhaps, in another place where Jews were living, I might have acquired a bad impression.

My father never stopped hiding his identity. The only time he demonstrated his Jewish identity was during his visits to Warsaw, when he went to synagogue for the holidays. But he never revealed his identity in the town where he lived.

I started going to Rabbi Schudrich's lessons. That's when he started to organise the Lauder Foundation activities in Poland. The classes became very important to me. After a couple of years, around 1991, I started working as his assistant. He was the administrative director of the Lauder Foundation. We started building the community. At that time, there was no organisation like the *kehilla* in Warsaw, only the umbrella organisation the Union of Polish

Jewish Communities. There was a *kehilla* in Kraków, Wrocław, Szczecin, and so on.

In 1995, some friends and I began thinking that we need a *kehilla* in Warsaw which would fulfil all the needs of local Jews. So, in 1996, we established the Jewish community of Warsaw. I was elected as the first president of the Warsaw Jewish community for one year. The next term I was a vice-president and Helena Datner became the second president between 1997 and 1999.

At the same time, we started organising the Jewish summer and winter camps in southern Poland that were run by the Lauder Foundation. After a couple of years I became the manager of these camps, and helped people go through the Orthodox conversion process. It usually took place in the summer in the old manor of Rychwałd near Żywiec. We rented the whole manor and it became a place where people could enjoy openly being Jewish, and experiencing Jewish life.

After a couple of years, I decided to go through the conversion process myself. It had not been important because I already felt I was a Jew. But, at that point, it was time to complete – something was missing in my life. So I went through the conversion in the 1990s, in other words, very late.

I was not a professional for the Jewish community at that point, only a volunteer working on behalf of the elderly.

When Michael Schudrich returned to America and a new director was sent here, I left the Lauder Foundation. I started doing volunteer work for elderly people, visiting their homes and spending time with them. They were very lonely, old Jewish people with no families. They were either in old age homes or in their private houses. Perhaps some nurses came from the social services. As time went by, they became my family. I was with them until they died. They often died in my arms. I became a son and they shared all their secrets with me. They were Holocaust survivors. It was a very important time in my life. I loved them. They even knew my mother and siblings.

How did my siblings feel about my becoming Jewish? My sister and brother were very supportive. My brother is an agnostic. I am a religious person who believes very strongly in God. I have a very good connection with Him. I can't imagine my life without God. However, my brother is the complete opposite. He doesn't believe in God and is against all religion. But he was very happy with my decision. He hugged me and said: 'I envy you.'

My mother had grown up in a very Jewish neighbourhood in a town called Wawolica, near Lublin, where Jews once comprised 80 per cent of the population. She saw how the Germans took 2,000 Jews to mass graves outside the town, where they were murdered. She actually witnessed this as a child. Therefore, she believed that being a Jew would cause me trouble and suffering. For example, when we took a photo in the synagogue showing my father and myself celebrating the holidays while wearing *kippahs*, my mother used a marker pen to blot out the *kippahs*.

At first she was very unhappy, and told me: 'I raised you a good Catholic. Why have you done this?' But she is a very tolerant person, and has come to accept my choice.

As for my sister, I think she believes in God but isn't a Catholic. I think she has something in her *neshumah* but hasn't externalised it. She is a good person but doesn't need religious practice. Sometimes she comes for the Jewish holidays, like Purim or Chanukah. All in all, my family has supported me.

My father died three years ago. He is buried in the municipal cemetery in our town. My mother tried to bury him as a Catholic and put the cross on his grave. But we really fought back against this idea.

After a couple of years of voluntary work, I became involved in Jewish education for adults. I started running the private foundation called AtaRA run by an American family, especially by Joy Balsam. She was Orthodox and very righteous, and lived in Israel. She came to the Lauder summer camp as a teacher of Jewish subjects. She was a brilliant person and we became close friends. She appointed me the educational liaison for the foundation; I ran the project for informal Jewish education for adults in Poland.

Once a month, on a Shabbat, she brought very good scholars from around the world and I organised trips for them to cities around Poland. They would give a lecture on a specific Jewish topic – not merely for Jews. For example, once we organised a lecture for doctors at a university. This went on for five or six years, but unfortunately Joy died of cancer and her family didn't want to continue the programme.

At that point, I became involved in private business outside the so-called Jewish world. I was engaged in communal activities but didn't feel connected. Yet I did feel connected to the young people, particularly the very young who I knew from the very beginning, and during their growing up years.

Once, when I was at the Polin Museum in 2014, young people asked me whether I would be interested in the election for the community. After a period of reflection, I decided to participate. There was an election in March that year; I was elected to the board of the Jewish community of Warsaw, and became the vice-president. The board started to change and fix everything that was not good in the community; we have made a lot of positive changes.

Following this, there was an election to the Union of Jewish Communities in Poland. This organisation represents the Jewish people to the Polish government. I decided that as the changes in the community went well, perhaps I'll try to change a bit more. Maybe the attitude of the outside world to the Jewish community in Poland was not particularly good. I won the election, and am now the president of the Union of Jewish Communities.

Regarding anti-semitism, I didn't have bad experiences because I was very openly a Jew from the beginning. I had a lot of non-Jewish friends, and never had any negative reactions from them. I had an anti-semitic experience once when I went to Auschwitz and there was the problem with the crosses and the Carmelite nuns. There was a man sitting in this place, fighting to keep the nuns and the crosses there. He was completely hostile towards Jews. When I tried to negotiate with him, he took a pole to strike me, and called me a 'dirty Jew'. It was very shocking and primitive and I never had such a bad encounter before.

What I will admit is that I feel the anti-semitism in Poland, although not directed toward me personally, is aimed at the entire Jewish nation. People and organisations treat Jews in a bad way; we are still the 'others'. Some people like to call themselves Polish Jews, but the Poles don't like this term. Even educated people make anti-semitic statements in the media, particularly during an election. They use the word 'Jew' or 'Jewish roots' as something negative.

Do I belong to the Second Generation group? No, but we are close friends. Many people like to go to such groups because it's part of their therapy.

As for Rabbi Schudrich's belief that there are tens of thousands of Jews yet to come out, I am not so optimistic. However, there are many more Jews than are actually members of the community. I know there are many who feel they are Jews but are not affiliated to any organisation. I also have friends who feel very strongly Jewish but they never go to any Jewish activities. Yes, they attend cultural festivals, but as a cultural, rather than a Jewish, event. I have worked very hard to bring them closer because I think they will bring fresh blood to the community and help renew it. And they will inject more intellectual content.

Intermarriage is a very big problem. Many years ago, we set up a Jewish kindergarten so that Jewish kids could grow up together. Then we organised the primary school, followed by the gymnasium. Now we are hoping to build a high school. I know if they can grow up together, some of them will marry. It started slowly, but I know a couple, for example, who have married, had kids and live a good life. At the same time, I understand it's a problem here to find a Jewish partner.

It's become very fashionable to know a Jew, to come to a Jewish activity or centre. Yes, there is nostalgia about the past when Poland was much more multi-national before the war. Today, many Poles understand that something is missing in Polish society and cultural life and they realise the Jews were an important factor.

Do I feel positive about the prospects for a growing and stronger community? Of course, absolutely. Otherwise I wouldn't be here.

JOANNA TARASIEWICZ

I was born in Zakopane in 1951, and am an editor by profession. However, I am now retired.

Although my mother was Jewish and born in Kraków, we were never told anything about her background while we were growing up. She worked hard to conceal her past and told people – who survived the war and knew she was Jewish – to never divulge anything to her children.

I recall an incident during my school days, when we returned from the cemetery on 1 November, All Saints Day. My Polish father stood up and began to say: 'There is somewhere …'. But my mother cut him short and, in a fury, told him to never embark on that discussion again. Of course, my brothers and I had no idea what they were talking about. But it left us with a sense there was a mystery connected to something Jewish. If my mother was Spanish or Italian there wouldn't be a cause for suspicion; she would have spoken openly. However, if you say you are Jewish, there is always a strong reaction. I also thought my mother's maiden name, Rudzka, didn't seem to be genuine. Anyhow that's how I, perhaps subconsciously, interpreted these signs.

My mother's uncle, Juliusz Turski and his wife Eugenia, used to come to our home to play bridge. Eugenia had, on her arm, a tattoo number of a concentration camp. We never dared ask why she had this tattoo. My mother told us not to stare nor question it.

The silence was finally broken in the early 1990s when my mother was still alive. She asked me to help my great-aunt with her household chores, because she was elderly and ill. One day I arrived at her home and found a woman visitor who asked me to help my great-aunt fill in some documents to claim compensation from Germany. Apparently, she had been imprisoned during the war. I was greatly surprised and asked: 'What prison?' The woman responded by saying: 'Don't you know your great-aunt is Jewish?'

I started blushing, and felt I was inside an explosion. I was also upset at my response, fearing the woman might think I was ashamed to learn this news. But what was really shameful was the fact that I didn't know until that moment. The woman then repeated: 'Your great-aunt is 100 per cent Jewish.' My great-aunt sat silently – she was mute. She didn't know what to do with herself. After the woman left, I tried to ask my great-aunt to explain everything. She remained silent.

I returned home and called my mother to recount what had happened. My mother also stayed silent. Finally, I said: 'Mum, what is going on?' She replied that I and my brothers should come to her, which we did. She started off by saying: 'First of all, you must vow never to reveal this story. I will only tell you if you agree.' Later I started to read various books, and learned about the trauma Jewish people suffered after the war. They wanted to be cut off from everything that had happened. I think my mother carried this trauma.

My mother was born in 1925 in Kraków, where the extended family lived. Although she called herself Maria, I discovered during my research in the Jewish Historical Institute that her real name was Maryla Mund. The fake documents her family made in 1941 to escape Nazi oppression and flee to Lwów reveal a name change to Maria Rudzka.

In Lwów my grandfather found a job as the main accountant at the famous George Hotel. He was later betrayed and shot in Lwów. But my grandmother managed to send my mother to the Ukraine, where she was hidden by a Polish family. At the same time, my grandmother survived the war in Lwów after her release from prison in order to clean German homes. However, my mother was not forthcoming about those relatives who had perished.

My mother had a cousin, Salome, whose family survived the war in Siberia. Salome and her daughter, Elżbieta, left Poland after the war for Australia and later moved to Vancouver, Canada. Seven years ago I travelled to Vancouver to talk with Elżbieta. She told me a great deal about our family, especially the relatives who died in the Holocaust, and why my mother didn't want to have any contact with the aunt who lived near Warsaw.

When the war ended my grandmother returned to Kraków. But a Jewish man who lived in Montreal, whom they called Uncle Julek, had been in love with her before the war. He discovered she was still living in Poland and contacted her. They married and went to live in Montreal. With the departure also of Salome and Elżbieta, my mother felt very much alone in Poland.

My father was born in Warsaw in 1923 into a normal Polish Catholic family. During the war, he served in the Home Army resistance as a scout. After being captured, he was regarded as a political prisoner and sent to Auschwitz and Mauthausen-Gusen. Despite enduring terrible conditions, he carried on writing poetry in the camps. These were later published in Poland.

When the war ended, he was sent for treatment to a tuberculosis sanatorium in Zakopane, where he met my mother, who was also recovering from tuberculosis. Before their wedding in 1949, my Mum told Dad about her ancestry and asked whether it troubled him. His reply: 'Darling, it doesn't matter a bit.' They got married in a civil ceremony.

According to my brother, there was a pact between our parents that the children would not be raised in any religion. Out of respect for my father's parents we always celebrated Christmas and Easter. But we didn't treat them as religious holidays.

My aunt once explained that my mother refrained from revealing the family's history so that we wouldn't encounter problems in Poland. As one so often hears in similar situations, she was trying to protect my two brothers and me. So I asked my aunt: 'What have you left me?' And she answered: 'Trauma'. Over time I have come to the conclusion that trauma has a greater impact on children than protection.

Nine years elapsed from the time I knew I was a Jew until my mother's death in 1999. A further nine years passed after her death before I began writing my book, *Breaking the Fear*. For eighteen years I wrestled with these issues.

I still can't talk about my experiences; it's very emotional for me. As time goes by I realise I relive it whenever I speak about it.

Each one of us, the siblings in my family, approached this reality differently. I was the most involved in the question of identity. My older brother, Jacek, helped me when I needed his support. The younger one, Janusz, is married to a very Catholic girl. Furthermore he was very opposed to my book; we quarrelled over whether our mother wanted us to talk about it publicly. Janusz believes she wouldn't have been happy if we did. But I assume her ban only applied while she was alive.

I think Janusz feels his Jewish background may be a big handicap within his Catholic family, as well as the Catholic movement to which he belongs. I told him that I have the right to pursue my path while he is free to live his own life. I knew I had to do something with my knowledge. If I was a film-maker, I would make a film or, if I was a musician, I would compose music. For me writing was the means to express my feelings and thoughts.

I think my life may have been totally different if I had known about my origins from the outset. Maybe I would have lived abroad. Yet I have been told I should not blame my mother for hiding our Jewish identity, or for not revealing the whole story.

I used to be married to a Polish Catholic. My son, Marcin, is now forty years old, but he has known about my Jewish background since he was seventeen. He has made it clear that it he is comfortable with it, but he doesn't participate in Jewish activities. On the other hand I have taken his son, who was baptised, to Jewish festivals. While initially I got involved in liberal versions of Judaism, I now go to Chabad.

When I ask my son whether he regards himself as a practising Catholic, he replies in a philosophical way. Although he doesn't formally belong to any particular religion, he claims to take different values from various religions.

In the last Polish census, there was the option to write that you had a Jewish background. But I'm also Polish and would never reject that part of my identity. So I say that I'm a Pole from a Jewish background. Not only do I see the wisdom in Jewish culture, I also perceive my participation as a way for my mother to be involved in all these Jewish holidays. In her own life, she was unable to engage in Jewish events.

So I'm like two people – my mother and me – and it's not schizophrenia. I feel that she somehow lived on a volcano with so much internal tension because she was always afraid to reveal anything. For her, everything was hidden. I feel very happy that the Jewish community has accepted me and I have found my home among them.

ARTUR DAVIDSON

My Jewish roots stem from my father's side. My great-grandfather, who came from Lwów, was the first member of the family to live in Kraków. My mother is not Jewish and her family came from a small country town called Strzyżów in Galicia.

My grandfather was quite emancipated and married a Polish woman before the war. My father's family survived the war here in Kraków because my grandfather managed to obtain Aryan documents for them all. He opened a bistro in the Salwator district of Kraków but, because of his unusual name – Davidson – the Nazis became suspicious. If they suspected a man was hiding his Jewish identity, they checked to see if he was circumcised. My grandfather found a way to put Scotch tape around the foreskin of his penis to disguise his circumcision. The Nazis carried out several inspections of his premises because they also suspected his bistro was a meeting place for members of the resistance.

During the war my grandfather sent his three sons, including my father, to a monastery during the day which ran a kind of underground school. There they learned to behave like good Catholic boys. The family was fortunate to survive the war, but when the Communists came to power in 1948 the state nationalised my grandfather's business and evicted the family from their home.

Growing up as a young boy I was never told about the family's Jewish background. When I was about fifteen, however, my grandfather told me the truth. This news came as quite a shock. Nonetheless I was very happy for different reasons. Even before my grandfather's admission, because of my family name, I used to be called 'the little Jew' or 'Żydek' which is the Polish equivalent of 'kike' and is a very negative term.

I was also relieved because my grandmother's family were very conservative Catholics. Consequently, I was sent to a primary school that taught religious classes at the end of the school day. But I always felt different in that environment. When I was in high school, I decided to sever my ties with Catholicism; therefore, I was the only member of my class who didn't take part in the religious classes. Consequently, most regarded me with some wariness, not sure who I might be. As I grew older I often encountered anti-semitism, primarily because of my name, which was not typically Polish.

After I completed my university studies in tourism, I found it very difficult to get work. In the tourism industry one needed family contacts in the police, or army or the Communist Party to get a decent job. Being Jewish, of course, was always a handicap as well.

Since 1988, I have been in touch primarily with many Jewish tourists, mostly from Israel and the United States. I take them to places of Jewish interest like Kazimierz, including visits to Auschwitz. Since 1992, I have been collaborating with Gesher Tours, one of the leading tour operators in Israel, who have been organising the March of the Living in Auschwitz since 1988. I've always felt more comfortable with Jews, which is why I am happier to work with Jewish visitors. I'm currently the chairman of the association of tour guides. That makes me a small chairman of a small board of a small association.

I was previously married to a Polish woman. At the beginning of our relationship, I didn't tell her about my Jewish background in case it created tension. Our divorce, however, was not related to the Jewish issue.

I started connecting with the organised Jewish community about seven or eight years ago because of my long-standing friendship with Jakub Rympel, who was active in the Ronald Lauder youth club that was established in Kraków at the start of the 1990s. Although I initially kept my distance, I later accepted his invitation to join him at the club's Shabbat dinners. With the subsequent appearance of young people's organisations like Schmooze and Czulent, the Lauder Foundation felt the club was no longer needed and it closed around 2000.

For people in the second and third generations, it's difficult to find a Jewish spouse. For example, there are only around 200 people who are active members of the Jewish community. Even at the Jewish Community Centre, which has about 400 members, many are not formally connected to the community. In Kraków, there are many people who have Jewish names but don't want to be identified as Jews. It's estimated that their numbers could range from 5,000 to 10,000 people. While it has become more popular to come out as a Jew, many people are still wary about revealing their Jewish origins – even in a cosmopolitan town like Kraków.

That said, the environment towards Jews has changed a lot in Poland and there is generally a more positive attitude among younger Poles than in the past. But this improved atmosphere is more noticeable in the cities, rather than in small towns in areas like eastern Poland, where unemployment is high and a very conservative kind of Catholicism holds sway.

BARBARA ROGOWSKA

I'm an only child born in Warsaw in 1979. Having studied marketing in Poland and the Netherlands, I currently run a marketing firm.

My maternal grandparents were Jewish and came from Russia and the Ukraine. However, they were not open about their Jewish background. When I was six or seven years old, my mother told me I had Jewish roots, and that I should be proud. At that time – Poland in the 1980s – it was not a good idea to admit you were Jewish. So I kept this knowledge to myself although I wasn't ashamed. When I was about seventeen or eighteen I grew more aware of Jewish history. I started to feel proud of my connection to an ancient nation; it made me part of something much bigger. I didn't feel a strong connection to the religion but rather the legacy.

My mother met my Polish father in Moscow, where she was studying, and they eventually returned to Warsaw. My family didn't have a religious identity at all. Although my father was raised in a very Catholic household, he isn't a practising Catholic. As a result, I was not baptised – unlike most children in Poland. My mother's family was also not very religious, so my parents decided that I would choose my religious beliefs when I grew older. We celebrated Christmas and Easter but not for religious reasons – more like a national holiday. For us, a Christmas tree was considered to be very nice and it also represented Slavic roots.

Today my mother encourages me along the Jewish heritage path and discusses it a great deal with me. But my parents never pushed any religious dogma during my upbringing.

On one occasion a close friend joked about Jews, so I asked him if he knew any. When he replied that he didn't, I told him about my Jewish roots. He was shocked because I appeared 'quite normal'. From then on I never hid my

Jewishness, and that my grandparents lived in Israel. I don't like to say that I 'came out'. I'm simply open about it, just as people say they have Greek or Italian roots. So I have Jewish roots.

In the current environment it is much easier to talk about these issues, particularly among my generation. I have rarely heard any nasty comments. When I do, I always point out that I'm Jewish and ask whether they think I'm like the people they have just described.

I have a dear friend whom I have known since infancy, and we have become quite close. At one point, I told him about my Jewish roots and he said: 'Finally, I have met someone who is Jewish.' He was so excited and so happy that he had made this discovery.

I don't need a formal organisation to feel that I belong, nor any labels. But it also depends on what the organisation represents. My mother told me about the Jewish Community Centre whose main purpose is to enable people to meet and eat together and enjoy developing a culture. I take photography classes there, and if I had more time, I would go more often because it's an attractive place that offers interesting activities. If there is something interesting as well for my seven-year-old son at the JCC, I will take him there. I would like him to feel exactly as I do: that he is aware of his roots and that he also knows about various cultures. Like my parents, I want to give him the option to choose.

The key thing about religion is your connection to God. I believe religion is in your heart. Maybe I feel that way since I know many people who follow Jewish or Christian rituals, but they are still not genuinely religious. Meanwhile, as a secular Jew, I feel very comfortable in Poland.

My partner, who is not Jewish, no longer practises Catholicism and is also very supportive of my Jewish connection. His attitude has been influenced by the strong reaction of his staunchly Catholic mother, who proclaimed I was the devil because I was very anti-Catholic.

My partner is also very open to the idea that my mother takes my son on Shabbat to the Chabad centre. My son likes to go because he thinks it's fun and feels more like he is going to a playground. Of course, we explain the religious aspects to him. For one year, I also participated in those Friday night events. So now, when he hears that some of his friends are going to church, he knows that he can say he is going to Chabad with his grandmother. They also attend the Jewish summer camps. I have also been to Israel a few times to visit family members. But, if I ever decided to live there, it would not be due to the fact that it's a Jewish state, but because it was a nice place to live.

I don't share the need that many people have to put themselves in a category. I'm celebrating my Jewish as well as my Polish roots. I'm trying not to define myself as Jewish in terms of the Holocaust, but with the more positive and joyful side. I know I should visit Auschwitz and Treblinka because this is a huge part of our history. However, I'm a very empathetic person and I know that if I went there, it would probably overwhelm me.

I would like the next generation to not have to feel 'tolerant' towards Jews. After all, people don't tolerate Greeks or Italians. It would be much better if Jews were regarded as normal without creating a specialised category for them. And I'm also hoping that Jews will celebrate together not because they are Jews, but because they actually want to be together.

JACEK JURKOWSKI

I was born in Warsaw, in the toughest part of Praga, in 1952. My Polish father comes from a peasant family while my Jewish mother, who is a doctor, was born into a family of the intelligentsia in Czortków, near Lwów. My father nevertheless benefited from Communist rule, which enabled him to attend university and gain a degree in Polish philology. He worked in the Ministry of Culture and later as a professor at the actors' academy. He is now a professor emeritus.

As for my mother, before the war her family had a Jewish surname, Koerner. During the war they moved from place to place, trying to escape not only the Germans but also the Poles. Every now and then someone would discover they were Jews and they were forced to flee once more. In the process, they changed their ID papers and my mother took a Polish name.

Until I was 20 we never discussed my mother's origins. She belongs to the Holocaust generation and didn't want to speak about that period. While I learned about the family history later on, what actually happened during the Nazi occupation is still vague.

Although my parents were not practising Catholics, I was sent to religion classes and received the greater part of a Catholic upbringing. Like many children with some Jewish background, I was also baptised. This phenomenon has given rise to a Polish joke: A guy who was not Jewish asks his Jewish friend: 'How is it possible that you produce so many good musicians and bankers?' And the Jewish guy replies: 'It's very easy. When the child is born, we observe his hands. If he is gesturing in one direction, we pay for the best classes and eventually we get a very good musician. But if the child is gesturing differently, he goes to the London School of Economics and becomes a good banker.' So the non-Jewish guy asks: 'And if he doesn't follow either path?' The Jewish guy explains: 'Oh, then we baptise him.' Since I couldn't be a good musician nor a banker, I was baptised.

At the age of 20 my mother told me, very casually, that my maternal grandmother was Jewish. At the time, I didn't react. I was more preoccupied with my studies for chemical engineering at Warsaw Technical University. But after giving it some thought, I realised that having a Jewish mother meant that other Jews would regard me as Jewish. Therefore I could belong to a group of interesting people.

Meanwhile I set aside the Jewish theme. It surfaced a few years ago, when we went to the cemetery on 1 November, the traditional day for visiting cemeteries in Poland. We visited the graves of my mother's parents in the Catholic cemetery of Bródno. Why did she bury them in a Catholic cemetery? My mother knows she is Jewish, but she has a problem. Because of the Shoah, God doesn't exist. If he did exist, there wouldn't have been a Shoah. I don't know why she chose Bródno; the most important thing for her was to have a place to come and visit her parents' graves.

The trigger that propelled me to increasingly identify myself as someone with a Jewish background happened a couple of years ago. My brother had some friends from work, and also from Solidarity, who had encouraged him to attend Limmud. He then got me interested as well, and so Limmud was a way of getting to know Jews as well as Judaism. I attended a lecture given by a rabbi at Limmud, who explained how Jews conduct morning prayers. I told the rabbi that I had a Catholic background and he explained everything in a very sympathetic way. This kind of Jewish environment offered a lot of intellectual stimulation which I found seductive.

My second wife, who is not Jewish, came with me to Limmud. Because she doesn't believe in God, she was somewhat cautious at first. However, despite her reservations, the atmosphere strongly drew her in. After Limmud we attended lectures at the Jewish Community Centre, and took our children and grandchildren to Boker Tov on Sunday morning.

Nevertheless, my children and my wife's children were baptised. Yet I don't think they will baptise their offspring. They say they want to give their children an option. The Jewish option hasn't been discussed; it's unlikely they will choose it.

By birth and upbringing I'm part of a Polish community. But I also regard myself as a member of a Jewish community that accepted me. I was happy to learn from my mother that we have family relations in Israel. In May 2015 we made our first trip to Israel, where we spent 10 days. It was a fantastic trip and our relatives welcomed us warmly. I found Israel both beautiful and complicated.

I believe in God but I'm fighting the Catholic church wherever and whenever I can. For example, religion classes don't belong in public schools, which are essentially secular institutions. Yet the problem doesn't stem from the schools, but rather from our society and politics. Poland is unfortunately becoming a religious state. Currently, I have been helping a campaign to put together a petition with 100,000 signatures; if we succeed it will go to parliament. State schools which receive public money should be free of religion.

I believe the outlook for a Polish Jewish revival is positive. However, the Jewish community is more or less in the same situation as the LGBT movement and, perhaps, the left-wing elements in our society. They all have to confront the pressures generated by stereotypes in Polish society of different minorities.

PIOTR KADLČIK

(Council Member of the Union of Jewish Communities in Poland)

My mother is a native of Warsaw. She met my Czech father when she worked as a guide for foreign students. They were married and went to live in Czechoslovakia.

My mother returned to Poland in 1962 so I would be born here. She wanted me to have Polish citizenship, which proved helpful when I was involved in opposition activities in Poland. If I had had Czech citizenship, the Polish authorities would have shanghaied me back to Czechoslovakia. In 1968, shortly after the Prague Spring, my parents decided to return to Poland.

My maternal grandfather was a lawyer who fled to eastern Poland after the German invasion. He was then caught up in the Soviet invasion but managed to survive the war. My maternal grandmother and my mother were forced into the Warsaw ghetto. Eventually my mother escaped to the Aryan side but my grandmother perished – either in the ghetto or in Treblinka.

When I was thirteen or fourteen years old I asked my mother if we were Jewish. I began to perceive holes in my family's biographical story. She straightforwardly told me the truth, because she realised that sooner or later I would find out and it would be much better to learn it from her. She also explained that my 'grandmother' was not actually my biological grandmother, who had been killed in the Holocaust. The woman I had known as my grandmother is a Gentile who rescued my mother from the ghetto. She received the Righteous Gentile award from Yad Vashem.

I later realised I was raised in a society that is not sympathetic towards Jews because my first reaction was: I can't be Jewish. I have blond curly hair and blue eyes and don't look like a Jew. I inherited these features from my mother, whose Aryan 'good looks' helped her to survive the war. But, at that stage of my upbringing, being Jewish just didn't seem to be a part of my life.

During the anti-semitic campaign of 1968, my mother worked in a hospital. However, she was not directly affected by the purge of Jewish professionals because she had kept the false identity papers she had acquired during the Nazi occupation and had never returned to her original name. Also, she was not involved in any Jewish organisations or activities that might have identified her as Jewish. While my family did not practice Christianity, I was nonetheless baptised in 1968. It was probably due to the hostile anti-semitic atmosphere of that time.

The process of reaching the point where we are now – sitting in the offices of the Union of Jewish Communities in Poland on Twarda Street – has been a long road. It started in the late 1970s when I had become involved in various anti-Communist activities. Among the many things happening at this time was the Jewish Flying University. I participated in those lectures to become better informed about what it meant to be Jewish. In the 1980s, the main struggle was the fight against the Communist regime. I was involved in practical activities, such as printing leaflets. Because I was half Czech and fluent in the language, I could transfer messages between the opposition movements in Poland and Czechoslovakia.

In 1987, there were two Jewish organisations functioning in Poland, including the Religious Union of Mosaic Faith. I was involved with the official organisation, the Social and Cultural Association of Jews in Poland, which was led by officials who were approved by the government. People are now saying that we are experiencing a Jewish revival, but I insist that a Jewish revival took place 25 years ago with people coming out of nowhere. Today, we have a generation of people who are now in their 30s and grew up in Jewish summer camps and Jewish institutions. So we are really talking about continuity when we speak of the current Jewish scene in Poland.

The revival kicked off because people perceived that the changing political climate made it actually possible to meet and organise activities. I was one of the founders of the Jewish youth club in Warsaw. We renovated the cellar in the neighbouring building and it was charmingly code-named 'morgue' because it smelled like one. In 1988, I was the first person from Poland to be sent to Israel on the Buncher family leadership programme. It was my first time in Israel and I immediately fell in love with the country.

At the same time, other initiatives were under way. A friend and I established one of the first private travel agencies in Poland, which was also the first Jewish travel agency. It was called 'Our Roots: Jewish Information and Tourist Bureau'. We published the first guidebooks to Jewish Poland in the mid-1990s, which included Łódź, Lublin, Kraków and Warsaw.

Initially my mother was not very happy about my growing commitment to Jewish activities. However, she soon changed her mind and became involved with the Association of Children of the Holocaust, as well as the Jewish welfare system.

I can't say that I have experienced much anti-semitism. Although I'm very much part of Jewish society, I pursue quite a few extracurricular activities, involving combat and dynamic shooting and survival, and I also participate in various discussion groups. In all these areas, everyone knows I am Jewish. For example, there is a pub very close to my apartment where I like to drink a couple of glasses of beer after work. The regular crowd know that I have held various Jewish public positions and sometimes they have seen me speaking on television. On one occasion someone made anti-Jewish comments. But when I returned to the pub a couple of weeks later, I was told the man who made the comments had not returned. The regulars had informed him he was no longer welcome.

Frankly, I believe that Jews are currently safer in Poland than in the UK, Western Europe or Scandinavia. In December 2009, I received one of the highest Polish state awards, the Commander's Cross of the Order of Polonia Restituta, for my contribution to the democratic transformation of Poland. However, there is still cause for concern over the recent demonstrations organised by right-wing or neo-Nazi thugs.

Many people are worried that the lack of potential Jewish partners makes it more difficult to build stable, Jewish family life in Poland. Yet my wife is not

Jewish, nor did she convert, but she makes great *challah* and *gefilte* fish and blesses candles on Friday night. My children have never had any problem regarding themselves as Jewish, so we don't struggle with identity problems within the family. Moreover, our Reform congregation, Etz Chaim, acknowledges my children's Jewish identity because of the Jewish lineage of their father.

VIKTORIA KORB

I was born in Guriev, Kazakhstan in June 1945. My father had escaped from Poland to Boreslaw in the Soviet Union, where he worked at the only oil refinery in Europe. When the Nazis invaded the Soviet Union, all the refinery staff were transferred to Kazakhstan. There he met my Russian mother, who was not Jewish.

After the war, when I was six months old, we moved back to Poland and settled in Wrocław where my father became an entrepreneur. After the Communist takeover of Poland, he surrendered his enterprise to the state. When he was subsequently appointed a senior director for electricity generation, almost akin to a minister's role, we moved to Warsaw in 1952.

My father was a leftist all his life and identified with the liberal wing of the Communist Party. He also took part in the demonstrations of 1956. Then someone wrote a letter accusing him of having travelled to Egypt in order to smuggle gold to Poland. He had never been to Egypt and the charges were absurd; yet he was arrested and imprisoned for a few months.

When I was growing up my father never spoke about his Jewish background, but he liked to tell Jewish jokes. Once, during an argument, my mother went around the house saying 'Stupid Jew, stupid Jew'. You know how married people sometimes quarrel. I didn't take it very seriously.

Our social world was very international, with friends from different countries, like Russia and Hungary. One of my mother's best friends, for example, was a Spanish woman, as a number Spaniards moved to Poland when the fascists came to power in Spain. In this kind of environment, I didn't care about people's nationalities.

I attended the exclusive Gottwald school in the centre of Warsaw which included many children, often Jewish, from the *nomenklatura*. But even those who may have been aware of their Jewish backgrounds didn't speak about it. Living in this somewhat sheltered environment, I never experienced anti-semitism.

In 1956 we visited Vienna, my father's home town, where he searched for his relatives for the first time. None were found; they were probably killed in the war. Being so young and unconcerned about nationality, it never occurred to me then that these relatives might have been Jewish.

In 1963, I finished gymnasium and entered the prestigious Main School of Planning and Statistics (SGPIS), now known as the Warsaw School of Economics. In retrospect it's clear that the School employed many Jewish professors. It contained a number of faculties, including foreign trade, which nurtured most of the future ministers and ambassadors who were taught Western theories of economics and various languages. In March 1968, during the big student demonstrations, we held a meeting in our school. Due to the efforts of our Rector, the police did not enter the institute but, later on, disciplinary trials against the so-called 'Zionists' began.

In the spring of 1968, just before I was due to finish my studies, I was subjected to a disciplinary trial along with other, primarily Jewish students, such as Marek Borowski, who is currently a left-wing member of the Polish Senate. I was not penalised: the professor who questioned me admitted that my jokes about the Communist Party, and Polish politics, greatly amused him. But I was unable to finish my studies because various anti-semitic professors refused to examine me.

The whole affair proved to be very dramatic for me. It was only at the disciplinary trial that I guessed I was half-Jewish. That prompted me to research my family's true identity. When my father was away, I looked through his private documents and found his birth certificate, issued by the Jewish community in Lemberg (Lwów). This was a key moment because I learned he was Jewish. My reaction was two-fold. I was very proud of my family history, but also frightened because I understood the authorities would not leave me in peace.

At this time my father was the head of Huta Warszawa, the steel mill which was a key industrial facility for Warsaw. Yet he also started to encounter political problems. For example, they demanded that he condemn Israel for the June 1967 war, but he refused. The only reason they couldn't throw him out was due to a doctor's certificate that he was ill. Furthermore my sister's attempt to study German philology, although she already knew the German language very well, was blocked by Warsaw University because she was falsely told that she had failed her entry exam.

At this point I had enough of all the insults, and felt very depressed and frightened in the face of such an insecure future. So I called a family meeting and it led to the decision to emigrate. My mother was confused by the turn of events; we decided to initially emigrate without her. Being of Russian origin, she was not prosecuted by the Polish Communist authorities. They even allowed her to keep her scientific job in the Pharmaceutical Research Institute. But she joined us a year later.

We left for Vienna; there my sister decided to leave for Israel. My father's friends in Vienna arranged visas for us to remain there for half a year. I also received a grant from the International Rescue Committee in order to finish my studies in Vienna. Later my father moved to Cologne to take up a business position and managed to get my mother to Vienna and then to Cologne.

I joined them in Cologne, but hated the town and escaped to London. An American friend in London suggested that I move to Berlin. I received a grant to finish a Ph.D. at the Free University of Berlin. After four years in Israel, my sister joined me in Berlin. She eventually married a grandson of Heinrich Mann, who was Jewish, and had left Czechoslovakia for Germany during the Prague Spring of 1968.

Living now in Berlin, my sister and I socialise mostly with Poles. We are not religious Jews; moreover, German Jews are rather arrogant towards Polish Jews. My sister's elder daughter emigrated to Israel because of her anger towards Germany, while the younger one followed and stayed a few years. She married an Israeli but they currently live in Berlin.

Although I prefer to live in Berlin because it is so cosmopolitan, I also have a second home in Warsaw. Due to my extensive writings on Poland through fiction and autobiography, I get invited to Jewish events in Poland and have given lectures about my books in Jewish cultural centres. I'm also a member of the Second Generation organisation.

ZBYSZEK SOKULSKI

I was born in Wrocław in 1953. My father was Polish and grew up in the countryside. My mother, who was Jewish, was born in 1930 in Lublin. Her father was shot by the Germans in 1943. She spent the war in hiding, along with her sister and grandmother.

Following the liberation, my mother decided to hide her origins because of the trauma she endured during the war. Her reluctance to talk about her Jewish background also arose from a fear of the anti-semitic attitudes that many Poles harboured.

Unlike many Catholic children I was not baptised, nor did I take communion. But I was jealous of other kids who received communion gifts. When I asked my parents why everyone else was going to communion, they simply kept silent. To some extent my father's approach to religion was due to the fact that he was a Communist, and an active member in the party. He worked for the militia until 1971, when he left with the rank of captain. I shared his Communist views until I went to Wrocław University to study Russian philology. My ideas underwent a change as I developed close ties to some Solidarity supporters at the university.

For years my mother claimed her brother and sister lived in Australia. However, her sister actually lived in Israel; she came to visit us in 1979. Her arrival in Wrocław was unusual at that time as Poland had broken off all bilateral relations with Israel in 1967. Although her visit came as a great surprise, it wasn't shocking and didn't cause an upheaval for my brother and myself. We were no longer impressionable youngsters, and reacted calmly to the news about this previously hidden Jewish family history. Yet it was the moment when, at the age of 26, I discovered I was Jewish. The ice also broke for my mother, who became more open about her ancestry. It was a great relief for her as she no longer had to bear the burden of hiding her identity.

After that visit my mother made three trips to Israel; on the first occasion she lingered for two months. Since then I also met some Israeli cousins who visited Poland.

My mother's older sister, who lived in Łódź, was less secretive about her background and would occasionally make hints about her Jewish roots. That is why my brother and I often suspected there were Jewish origins in our family. This aunt also wrote a testimony in 1955 about her wartime experiences for the Jewish Historical Institute in Warsaw but, unfortunately, I didn't get to see this document until 1984. That proved to be an unsettling experience; I finally realised the magnitude of the suffering my mother and her family had undergone. It also made me aware that, due to the horrific times they lived through, I was never given a chance to know many family members who perished in the war.

After 1979, I became increasingly interested in all things Jewish. It was a gradual process. But I would only reveal my Jewish ancestry to my closest friends. My mother tried to convince me to join the Wrocław Jewish community but I only became a member in 2012, one year after she passed away. By that time I realised something was missing in my life, and felt the need to know the community and contribute to it.

I joined the Second Generation in 2014 when, unusually, they held a meeting here in Wrocław. I also attended the annual gathering at their retreat outside Warsaw. My involvement with Second Generation gives me an opportunity to meet people whose parents also survived the Holocaust.

My current participation in Catholic rituals is of a passive, symbolic character. I only take part because my brother and his family, who are Catholics, want me to spend time with them on Christmas Eve and Easter.

Other Polish people who discovered their Jewish origins, but remain hidden, need to be made aware there is a support network available if they come out of the closet. But you can't pull them out. They have to sincerely wish to make the move.

The outlook for Jewish life in Poland depends on the next generation. It's a question of how people of Jewish origin, or people with no Jewish roots at all, see their future role in this country. I'm sure there will be some people who will be interested in converting to Judaism and they can add something worthwhile to Jewish life. Yet there are so many countervailing forces, with people moving abroad and the attractions that globalisation offers. Like the rest of the world, Poland is a much more open society now.

I believe I have found my place in the Jewish community. I have told my family that I want to be buried in the Jewish cemetery, and was assured my decision will be respected. No one from my father's side of the family questioned my religious choices, nor have I encountered any criticism. On the contrary, I feel they have been supportive every step of the way.

PART 3

Third Generation

JAN KIRSCHENBAUM

My grandfather was raised in a Jewish, unobservant home in the Chełm area of eastern Poland. When the war broke out he fled to the Soviet Union, and was sent to the Gulag. At the end of the war, in Odessa, he met my Polish grandmother who was not Jewish. They married and, in 1946, were repatriated to Poland and settled in Wrocław. My father was born nine years later.

My grandparents changed their surname in 1954 from Kirschenbaum to a more Polish-sounding name. I didn't know my grandfather was Jewish until the age of eleven or twelve, when I was told about the name change and his Jewish origins. I was also told to keep it a secret. It was a huge shock for me. I simply didn't know what to do with this information; I couldn't relate to the word 'Jew'. It was a profane word: if I encountered it in a newspaper or book I would cross it out.

My parents didn't want to baptise me or Mati, my twin brother. We came from a family that is secular on all sides, although my paternal grandmother sometimes went to church. She was the only one who occasionally performed religious practice. Compared to most Polish families, we were unusual for being completely secular. My maternal grandmother, who will be 90 in a few months, never went to church – nor did the rest of the family – except for funerals.

However, when my brother and I were two years old we were baptised, but only because my mother was asked to be a godmother for her nephew. In order to allow this to proceed, she had to baptise us. For the same reason my parents got married in a church. Yet nothing followed our baptism. At Christmas we had a tree and, in the beginning of the 1990s, my parents sent us to religion class so we wouldn't stand out as the only kids who didn't attend. But they didn't pressure us to do so.

Only my brother and I knew about our Jewish roots. It remained a secret until my last year in high school. I met a girl who was a member of the Wrocław Jewish community and we dated briefly. It turned out she was in the same position as myself in terms of having a hidden identity; it made me realise I'm not the only person with Jewish ancestry. We soon split up and she went her own way. My grandfather was still alive and, at that time, was actually a member of the community, a fact I was unaware of. Everyone knew him, which made my integration into the community much easier.

I decided to formally join the community. I also took a major decision to convert to Judaism and underwent a three-year process in Łódź. It culminated with my circumcision at 23 by a *mohel* in Warsaw. Having gone down that route, I thought it was an irreversible change. There was no going back.

My brother also converted to Judaism but in the Liberal way. He was quite observant for a while and is now studying at the Abraham Geiger institute for Liberal Judaism in Berlin. He occasionally travels to Warsaw to assist in the services of Beit Warszawa.

I believe part of my drive to take on the challenge of conversion was my age; at nineteen or twenty you are still seeking your identity. However, two crucial experiences also played an influential role. One occurred when I went on a school trip to Auschwitz when I was around 17. I felt the visit was more relevant to me than the others; this history belonged to me more because so many members of my grandfather's family were killed during the Holocaust.

The second event took place during the summer vacation before starting university. By then I had become interested in the Jewish community, and had visited it a few times. But that summer I went on a road trip with my brother and a couple of friends around the Czech Republic. We planned to visit the beer factory in Pilsen, but it was closed. Instead we went to the Pilsen synagogue, which is one of the largest in the world. It was neglected, but not destroyed. I felt this was part of my heritage, and I should know more about it. So I began to explore. These were the early stages of acquiring my Jewish identity.

At nineteen I went on a Taglit trip to Israel, which made a great impression on me: I fell in love with the country. After completing my undergraduate degree at Wrocław University, I returned to Israel to gain a Master's degree in Holocaust Studies at Haifa University.

I feel that I am continuing the Jewish tradition on behalf of the 70 people on my grandfather's side who died in the Holocaust. In the last conversation with my grandfather before he died, when I was 21, he was very happy to hear I was embracing a Jewish identity. It meant he was not the last Jew in the family. I sat with him and he wept as he drew the family tree. Even my father never knew the family names because my grandfather never shared this knowledge with him. At least I now know there is a record of these people in someone's memory confirming they had existed.

My parents have been incredibly supportive of my return to Jewish roots. My father says that my brother and I are the first people in our family in 70 years who found joy in being Jewish. He has followed our example by joining the community and participating in meetings of Second Generation and Limmud.

I'm no longer very active in terms of religious observance, which I needed previously to build a strong Jewish identity. It provided me with the structure to learn traditions and culture. But having acquired this, I no longer had the incentive to remain religious. However I'm involved in Cukunft, an organisation I founded for younger people who want to identify as Jews in a cultural sense. Initially, we met with strong opposition from the established community. It was really a power issue because these people were not members of the community and so the leadership could not control us.

I'm still debating whether I will ever make *aliyah* as I don't see a Jewish future for myself here in Wrocław. The community is tiny and I don't really like the direction in which it is moving. I've tried to draw the attention of the community leaders to the demographic issue, whereby there are not enough young people to sustain the community. If you want to build a viable community, you should speak to the older members who have children and grandchildren and at least try to get their offspring involved. There could then be potential Jewish wives and husbands who would create growth and stability for the future. It might fail, but it's worth trying. Yet there hasn't really been any organised outreach effort.

In order to build a Jewish identity, you need to make the community more welcoming. For a person coming from a secular or Catholic family, it's probably not the best idea to have them sit through a Kabbalat Shabbat conducted entirely in Hebrew. They will never come back. You should start by inviting them to a Shabbat dinner without any prayers and, in general, be more accommodating.

I know people who have come forward because of their Jewish roots, but it's from the father's side. Then, all of a sudden, they miraculously find out they also had a Jewish grandmother. So the narrative evolves, but there is little evidence of any documentation to prove it. The next thing you know is that they have quietly converted to Judaism abroad. I have never tried to be anyone other than who I am. I had a Jewish grandfather and I don't happen to have a Jewish mother and grandmother. My 90-year-old Polish grandmother is alive and kicking and I don't see why I need to Jewify her.

Is the political climate in Poland becoming more anti-semitic since the rightward change in government? I feel nervous as a liberal, human rights/gay activist who also happens to be Jewish. But what I find to be more oppressive is that because there are so few Jews in Poland, you are a kind of an exhibit in a glass cage. Older Polish people know, or think that they know, who a Jew is. After a while, it can become tiring. I sometimes wish Poland was a more multicultural country. That's one of the reasons why I wouldn't mind moving elsewhere.

What I also find annoying at times is that while I'm concerned about anti-semitism, I'm also afraid of philo-semitism. I'm not sure if these enthusiasts of a Jewish culture, that is now long gone, would be happy if there was a significant population of 'others' currently living in Poland. There is no real threat of the Jews returning to Poland. It's a safe minority to like because it's not very threatening. The 10,000 Jews in Poland are statistically irrelevant. Yet the whole industry of Jewish renewal depends on keeping alive this image of a massive revival.

I think the Jewish revival has missed the boat in terms of large numbers of hidden Jews coming out. Throughout the 1990s, there were many more but they could only turn to old-fashioned structures, like TSKŻ, or Orthodox institutions. It was therefore difficult to hold on to people with their secular or Catholic backgrounds. Yet this is the last moment to get people, like the grandchildren, involved in Jewish life. The last survivors are passing away and there will soon be no immediate connection to the Jewish past.

JAKUB WASILEWICZ

I was born in 1988 in Częstochowa to a Jewish mother and a Polish father. My parents separated when I was very young; I was mostly raised by my mother.

She wasn't a hidden Jew; she always knew her parents were Holocaust survivors. Although her father was not religious, her mother ensured she had a Jewish upbringing by maintaining some religious observance. After the war, Częstochowa attracted a number of religious Jews.

My grandmother wanted to move to Canada, but she met my grandfather right after the war. They had survived a labour camp in Częstochowa. My grandfather was a native of the area, but my grandmother came from a city near Łódź. She was on the last transport from the Łódź ghetto headed for Auschwitz. For some reason, it wound up in Częstochowa.

When the Germans took Jews away on the train as the Red Army approached, my grandmother realised she had to escape and went to the end of the line. She and others walked to the city to find refuge. She was directed to an apartment building but it was packed, with no room for her to sleep. Weeping, she went downstairs. Just then my grandfather appeared. He recognised her from the labour camp, and offered her somewhere to stay. That was the beginning of their relationship.

When I was six years old, I came home from school one day and told my mother we would be going to church the following day, and the priest will pour ashes over our heads to commemorate Ash Wednesday. My mother took me aside and said: 'Kuba, I have something to tell you. You can't attend church or religion classes. Although you sometimes go to church with your father, you must not go with the class.' When I asked her the reason, she said both she and I were Jewish. But as all my friends were Christians, I was puzzled over what it meant to be a Jew.

One day I told a girlfriend that I'm Jewish but urged her not tell anyone. Yet she informed all my friends, who started bullying me. That experience made me conclude it would be better not to tell anyone again. I knew I was a Jew but also understood it was not a good thing.

After I left pre-school and went on to the next level, some kids remembered me from pre-school but kept quiet about my Jewish background. When I didn't attend religion classes, I explained my absence by claiming I didn't believe in God. But there were incidents of bullying. In the 8th grade there was a boy who knew me from my neighbourhood, and bullied me quite often. One day a girl in my class, who was passing by, told him to let me go. And he said: 'Why are you defending him? He is a Jew!' And she replied: 'So what? Let him go!' That really surprised me. It was the only incident I recall when someone tried to help. Otherwise there were a lot of incidents at school involving bullying on account of my Jewishness.

The main activities of the local Jewish community centred around the TSKŻ club, a cultural and social association, with branches all over Poland. My mother was the head of TSKŻ in Częstochowa for many years, and occasionally took me there for Jewish holidays or performances by the Yiddish Theatre from Warsaw. I was the only Jewish child going to TSKŻ. All the older members were happy to see me but I felt isolated.

When I was twelve my mother decided to contact Rabbi Michael Schudrich in Warsaw to prepare me for my Bar Mitzvah. He explained I would first need to undergo a circumcision. Was it not a big commitment? I realised it was something a Jewish boy must have. Rabbi Schudrich joked that when he had his *bris,* he couldn't walk for a year.

We went to Warsaw where the operation was performed by Rabbi Fisher from the United States in a meeting room of the main Nożyk Synagogue. At the time, many Hasidim were returning from Leżajsk in Galicia where they had been observing the *yahrzeit* of Rabbi Elimelech and decided to come to the synagogue when they heard about my *bris.* One of the Hasidim held me in place of my absent father. Since I didn't have a Hebrew name, the Hasid gave me the name of Yaakov. Unwittingly, he named me after my grandfather, who was called Yankel.

The following November, on my birthday, I went to Moldova to have my Bar Mitzvah. There was a yeshiva in Kishinev that was run by Rabbi Herschel Lieber from Borough Park in Brooklyn, whom I had met earlier at a Lauder summer camp in Poland. Another rabbi at the yeshiva taught me enough to enable me to recite the blessings before the reading of the Torah. It was fun when my mother and all the girls threw candies at me after I had finished my Torah reading.

When I was fourteen and already in gymnasium, we decided to move to Warsaw. I had told Rabbi Schudrich I needed to leave Częstochowa, which lacked a synagogue or a Jewish school, because I wanted to learn what it meant to be Jewish. He found us a place to live near the synagogue so I could attend the Lauder Jewish school in Warsaw.

I expected to be going to an Orthodox school where the boys wore yarmulkes and the girls dressed in long skirts. As it turned out, I was the only boy wearing a *yarmulke*. In fact, 70 per cent of the students were not actually Jewish. Nevertheless, it was a very good school with a high level of education. In addition to the regular classes, it also offered courses on Jewish history and culture.

I was very happy with our move to Warsaw as I made a lot of friends and was able to observe Shabbat and celebrate the main holidays. But when it was time to apply for high school, I didn't know where to go because I was keeping Shabbat and kashrut and there was no Jewish high school available. As a religious Jew, I didn't want to attend a public high school since I was hoping to continue my Jewish studies and remain observant.

In 2004, the Hasid rabbi from my *bris*, Rabbi Yaakov Yosef Neushloss, invited me to his home in New York for *Pesach*. Since I couldn't afford to pay for the journey, a free ticket was arranged. I took the opportunity to visit Rabbi Lieber and explained the difficulties I faced in order to continue my Jewish education. After my return to Warsaw, I was told to travel to New York once more to take a place in a Hasidic yeshiva run by the Bobov sect in Borough Park. Following two months of studies, the rabbi there said I wasn't suited to become a Hasid and sent me to a Baltimore yeshiva which I didn't like.

I then transferred to a regular Orthodox yeshiva in Baltimore where I completed my high school studies. My mother came for my graduation, at which I spoke in Polish and English, and thanked her for allowing me to go to the U.S.

After graduation, I transferred to a baal teshuva yeshiva in Lawrence, New York, and after nine years, I'm still there. Having not been raised religious, I feel more comfortable in this environment, but I expect this will be my final year there. During this time I also graduated from college with a degree in Psychology and Education.

I have thought of giving something back for what I have received by returning to Poland to teach. However, I have some doubts about going back as it's not easy to live as a religious Jew in Poland. Also, many people in Poland have advised me not to return, pointing out there are few people to work with. They insist that many people have tried and failed and, ultimately, I will regret it.

Despite having lived in the U.S. over the past twelve years, I still describe myself as a Polish Jew – not an American Jew. My family has lived in Poland for hundreds of years; I continue to feel part of Polish history. I miss my mother and Polish Jewish friends and I also miss speaking and reading in Polish. Although I had to leave Poland to study the Torah and become observant, I would never have left Poland if I could pursue a religious life there.

KAROLINA WAŃTUCH-GAZDA

My grandmother, who wasn't Jewish, often told us about her war memories. She helped Jews and carried parcels to the ghetto, often risking her life. Only a few years before her death at 90, she started saying repeatedly: 'It's very important that you remember your grandfather was a Jew.'

My grandfather survived the Płaszów, Auschwitz and Mauthausen camps because he had a strong constitution, despite the fact that he was used for medical experiments. Of his entire family he was the only survivor. He went to Kraków just before the war, to go to university, and met my grandmother. After the war he changed his name, and they got married. It was a secular wedding. He never changed his religion.

My father comes from a Polish family in Kraków. My mother learned she was Jewish when she was about thirteen, during the anti-semitic campaign in 1968. She confessed this only a few years ago; she had been very frightened of anti-semitism. My grandmother would talk about my grandfather, while my mother said: 'Grandma is old and gets confused. Take it with a grain of salt.'

My mother and her siblings lived in a sort of double world: they knew their father was Jewish, went to strange meetings on Saturdays, and ate different food. Yet nobody spoke about it. Like myself, my mother's siblings, who are older, were both baptised. She was born in 1954, during a political thaw; my grandparents hoped they might raise at least one child as a Jew. Two years later the political situation became unsettled again. Just to be safe they baptised her quickly, somewhere in a dark church at 6 o'clock in the morning.

I was born and raised in Kazimierz, in a Polish family. Yet Jewish culture was present and very important at home, although in an intangible way. I never knew why my family always attended the Jewish Cultural Festival. My grandmother told me about Jewish holidays.

We didn't practice Judaism. It was obvious that we're Polish and embedded in Polish culture, but the Jewish one was actually equal to it. It was important and we needed to respect it. Not because we're Jewish, but it was important.

It was only after my grandmother died that I started discussing these matters openly with my mother: for example, my grandmother's repeated insistence that my grandfather was Jewish. In 2009, my mother admitted it was the truth.

I found some items in the house, like *Kiddush* cups, the *megillah* of Esther, *kippas*, *siddurs*, and documents about my grandfather, including his circumcision certificate, the name change papers and school reports. I wondered who they belonged to and was told it was my grandmother's friends. Other items were shown to me after 2009 by my aunt, who had kept them at her home.

When my Jewish background came to light, I had problems with bullying at school. My mother, a psychologist, works in a psychiatric hospital. In the 1990s, there were many staff members who were Jewish. Someone from my school was a patient in that clinic, so information leaked out that my mother had Jewish origins. Children from my school learned about it and I was bullied.

Once a girl locked me in a basement room that had bars on the door. I was the smallest in the class and said I have to sit there and get used to it, because this is the Jewish fate.

Another incident occurred during a school Christmas play. One of the children said Karolina should play Holy Mary because she was Jewish. The teacher said she should apologise to me because she had used such an offensive word: Jewish! I just couldn't understand why it was so offensive.

When I found out in 2009 about my Jewish background, I was very sad and upset. I've always wanted to be Jewish but felt I am not entitled to it. In the beginning, I decided to distance myself from it all. Then, while going through documents with my aunt, I felt that these people lost their names, their past, their right to memory. It was a kind of Holocaust of memory. I decided to do something for them, for now only for my family, for my grandpa whom I'd never met.

The first thing I decided to do was to learn Hebrew and that's why I came to the Jewish Community Centre. At the same time, by coincidence, I met Rabbi Boaz Pash, who used to be the chief rabbi here. (He left for Warsaw.) He said that I had the right to be Jewish; he showed me that it's not only my right, but my duty to take on a part of this heritage. I had the right to own this. He introduced me to everything, asked me to tell him all about my feelings and family, and said he will teach me everything I want to know about Judaism.

During that period, I also met my boyfriend at Jagiellonian University. He suggested that we go to synagogue together. It was still alien to me then, and I was scared. My boyfriend, whom I subsequently married in 2014, is Lemko Rusyn and Polish and belongs to the Polish Eastern Orthodox Church. Yet the idea had come from him. I had been in a synagogue before, but only as an onlooker. He offered to accompany me, to make me feel more at ease. When we went, in December 2010, it was Chanukah. We have been together since then and Chanukah is our own special holiday.

He does not want to change his religion. We haven't thought how we'll raise our children. We'd like to – maybe it's a bit utopian – raise them to respect many religions and cultures. Respect most of all – combining all religions would be impossible, but respecting all of them is key. We had debated whether to marry in an Orthodox or Catholic church, but finally we decided on the Orthodox option, particularly as we had some difficulties with the Catholic priests. Our wedding party was beautiful and combined Slavic and Jewish aspects.

As for my family and the Jewish issue, in the beginning it was I who was involved and interested; then they picked up on it. My mother gradually stopped being so secretive and scared of anti-semitism. She realised there are many Jews in Kraków, that various people visit the synagogue and she won't be stigmatised if she goes there.

My friends responded very well to my growing interest in Judaism. Fortunately friends are friends; you can trust them. They didn't let me down.

I asked my female friends for advice as to whether I should get involved and they were helpful.

It's different for my cousin; he has a different approach. His mother is Jewish – she is my aunt. So we have the same roots. But he keeps a distance from his Jewishness. He knows about it and respects it. He likes to look at the old documents, but, for example, he wouldn't go to the Jewish Community Centre.

I'm working on a Ph.D in regional studies – a continuation of Ukrainian studies which I studied before. That's why I went to Zbaraż (Zbarazh) a few times, searching for my family's roots and found three family *matzevas*. It was a *shtetl* that is now in the Ukraine.

This process of becoming more Jewish has been very positive; other family members became involved. Even my paternal grandmother – who knew previously – started talking to me openly about it. Sometimes she comes to lectures, particularly if I am the presenter. But my father's sister-in-law, the widow of his brother, came to hate our family because of this development.

It's still hard to say how I perceive my identity as a Pole and a Jew. I wouldn't say I feel Jewish because I'm afraid I would be accused of making an outlandish discovery, or even fabricating all this. Yet I do have a feeling of being connected to a larger Jewish world. I was helped in this by the community and the rabbi. And I'm very grateful for that.

I've been to Israel twice. The first time with Birthright in 2010 and then with Shavei Israel. Shavei is interested in the hidden Jews. It tries to deal more with religious education; they took us to Israel so that we could spend a real, proper Shabbat in Jerusalem, with families. There were about 30 of us from Poland. But only two or three were religious. We spent time learning, travelling, and in the city. A bit of everything.

I've heard of some cases where Shavei succeeded in encouraging people to become more religious after going on the Israel trip but, in my experience, people usually stayed away from the religious occasions. There was more of an avoidance tendency.

My grandfather never wanted to go either to Zbaraż or Israel. Zbaraż reminded him of his family, who were killed. Israel wasn't good either because he believed you shouldn't uproot an old tree. He knew Hebrew, but only the religious kind, as well as Yiddish and Ukrainian. But, as an old man, he wouldn't have adapted. He was 18 years older than grandmother, who wasn't Jewish.

I wasn't raised particularly Catholic. My grandfather was probably sympathetic to Communism whereas we found documents proving that my grandmother was actually in the Communist Party; she was repelled by religion. It was only at the end of her life that she started praying. So I'm not from a very religious family. Of course we have Christmas and Easter, for grandmother and other family members. But I think that the issue of faith is too complicated and multi-faceted to make any drastic decisions. When the whole family comes around for Christmas, we go to midnight mass. We don't want to cut ourselves off.

The JCC has played a very important role in my personal development. It's hard to find another organisation in Kraków that would be sympathetic to people who are not fully defined, who don't know whether they feel more Jewish or Polish. Here, nobody needs to define their faith in one word; I wouldn't be able to do that. To me faith is so complex, composed of so many influences, that I couldn't define myself fully as any one thing.

MAGDA GUDZIŃSKA

I was born in Warsaw in 1980, and work as a doctor in epidemiology. My mother came from a mixed family: my grandfather was Jewish, and my grandmother was Catholic. My mother, who was a doctor, had an arranged marriage: her father asked one of his friends to find a husband for her. My father was a historian who came from a small *shtetl,* Joski, close to Białystok. However, the marriage didn't work out and my parents divorced when I was three years old.

My father was not religious at all but my grandmother wanted my parents to have a Catholic wedding. Yet my father didn't have a baptism certificate. My mother told me his family were not Catholics; she thought they were Eastern Orthodox. I only discovered following my father's death that he wasn't Eastern Orthodox at all. He may have been Jewish; in his birthplace most of the families were Jewish. I had no contact with him as he was deeply disappointed that I wasn't a boy, and consequently showed no interest in me. Since he wasn't a father to me, I didn't wish to claim a heritage from him.

My grandfather took on the role of a real father, and played a very important part in my life. Not only did he not come from a religious background, but his family were socialists. Before the war my great-grandfather even spent time in prison for his political activities. In contrast, my grandmother came from an upper class family that had its own coat of arms. Unsurprisingly, her parents weren't happy at all that she married a Jew. When she was angry with my grandfather, she would call him an old Jew.

My grandmother was quite devout and sent me to religious classes at church, which I didn't enjoy. When I was twelve I refused to attend any more classes. My grandmother also insisted on having me baptised. My father, who was a devoted Communist, was opposed to it while my mother was indifferent. In the end my grandfather paid a student priest, a neighbour's son, to arrange a baptismal ceremony.

While growing up I thought everyone was either Catholic or an atheist; I didn't know one could be Jewish. So I saw myself as someone who didn't quite fit in. For example, I had an ongoing problem with food. Although I knew nothing about my origins, I hated the smell of pork and refused to eat it. It's interesting that my grandfather always insisted that my grandmother prepared meat in the kosher manner, by soaking it in salt. Sometimes he slaughtered chickens and drained the blood. Furthermore he never ate meat with dairy products, and refused to celebrate his name day, only his birthday.

My grandfather raised me in quite a traditional way. He didn't allow me to wear mini-skirts, for example, or have my hair loose when going outdoors. I put on make-up for the first time when I was 20, but even that, in his view, was inappropriate.

One day at school a boy pushed me down the stairs, shouting: 'Dirty Jew'. I returned home and asked my grandfather if we were Jewish, and what it meant. He replied that it's not something I should ever admit to anyone because it's dangerous to be Jewish. Even though some people may say I'm Jewish, he was sure it wasn't true. He wept on that occasion, because he always tried to hide his own Jewishness.

When I was sixteen, I was sent to Kraków to spend my holidays with an elderly couple who were my grandfather's friends. They showed me around the Kazimierz quarter, including the synagogues and the cemetery, and explained it was part of my heritage. When I returned to Warsaw, I started to read increasingly about Jewish subjects and literature. I even began to try to keep kosher.

My mother was a professor in nuclear medicine at the Marie Curie Institute, where many Jewish doctors continued to work after 1968. They regarded my mother and myself as Jews. This was based on cultural aspects: what you ate, whether you went to church, how much you enjoyed Jewish humour.

When I was a medical student at Warsaw University I had a Polish Catholic boyfriend who was studying history. Whenever he got angry with me, he said mixed race people like myself should be exterminated. There was clearly something very toxic between us; I had no sense of my personal worth and felt very insecure. I was feeling Jewish by then but practising Jews wouldn't accept me; and yet I didn't feel Catholic. The relationship somehow lasted four years until we split up in 2007.

A couple of years later I got involved in another bad relationship. My boyfriend was a rock musician and said he wanted to have a family and lead a quiet life. So we got married in 2011 in a civil ceremony. But his anti-semitic mother said she would not recognise me as her daughter-in-law nor regard our children as her grandchildren.

When I was six months pregnant my husband attacked me, which led to contractions and heavy bleeding. Because he refused to help me, my mother rushed me to hospital. As I struggled through the worst night of my life, I prayed to Hashem, saying that if he had to take one of us, he should take me. I promised I would live a proper Jewish life by keeping kosher and going to the synagogue. The bleeding and contractions stopped; my daughter survived. Of course, my husband and I are divorced.

By the time I graduated from university in 2014 I felt Jewish, yet believed practising Jews would never accept me. Basically I was a person who didn't belong anywhere, and that's a bad feeling.

I decided I was ready to undertake a formal conversion with a Masorti congregation. On the internet I found a website, the 614 Commandments Society. They suggested I approach the Reform congregation, Beit Warszawa, where the rabbi, Gil Nativ, was actually Masorti. He proved to be a great rabbi and a very compassionate person; I became friends with him and his wife. I never presented my ancestors' documents, but decided to go through the whole conversion process. My grandfather had gone 'down' from being openly Jewish to the degree that he hid his identity from his friends, fearing his wife would reveal his secret. I felt I had to 'climb up' from hiding: to embrace my identity and make it public.

I joined Gil Nativ's conversion class in 2014. I'm still embarrassed when I talk about my Jewish roots because the fear of revealing myself remains so deep. As there is no Masorti congregation in Poland, I had my Beth Din in London in April 2015, along with my little daughter, at the New North London synagogue. It was a very emotional experience, particularly when the rabbis mentioned it was a *mitzvah* to bring people back to *Am Israel*, as part of the process of mending the damage inflicted by the Nazis.

My mother was very pleased with my conversion as she considers herself to be Jewish. As a lifelong atheist, however, she chose not to go through the conversion process since she believed that would be hypocritical. Yet she occasionally takes my daughter to the synagogue to meet other people and show my daughter where we belong.

Because I was raised by my grandfather, I think I should be described not as the second or third generation, but as the two-and-a-half generation. He used to say that if he ever left Poland, he would have fulfilled the Nazis' goal of eliminating the Jewish presence in Poland. Unlike my grandfather, who was a Polish patriot, I don't love Poland as a country because there is still a lot of anti-semitism. Yet there are tolerant Poles who understand that you must allow other people to live their lives. After everything I have been through, I now call myself a 'recovered Jew'.

MARTA ANSILEWSKA

My background is very complicated. I'm an only child born in Szczecin in 1982 to parents who were physicians. My biological father was Jewish, although I never met him nor his family. When my mother was pregnant with me, she had an affair with my step-father. He was also a physician, and they all lived in the same accommodations for doctors in Szczecin. Because her affair and break-up with my Jewish father were mildly scandalous – as they had all worked and lived together – my mother and her new husband, my step-father, moved to a small town south of Szczecin, shortly after my birth. There I spent the first seventeen years of my life.

My mother divorced my father but her marriage to my step-father was not a happy one. Their time together was marked by constant fighting. The main reason was that they didn't want me to learn the truth; they hoped I would believe my step-father was my father. It was an upsetting home atmosphere.

My parents were secular and had a largely tolerant outlook. They only attended church at my baptism, then my first communion, followed by my confirmation. As a child I was very religious and suffered a great deal because, unlike me, all the other children were regularly going to church with their parents.

My mother's family were not actually Polish but Tatar, and lived in Vilna before the war. When they moved to Szczecin after the war, they became very religious Catholics. In fact, my grandmother would never tell anyone about her background because the Communist regime was not very sympathetic towards minorities. It was not only the Jews who felt compelled to hide their identity.

My parents were very open to other cultures and their initial encounter with Jewish culture occurred when I was fifteen, during a trip to Kazimierz in

Kraków. This was also the first time I visited Auschwitz. My mother had been there previously, but found it so upsetting she couldn't bear to return. So I went to Auschwitz by myself. Since then I have been to many other concentration camps because my work as an historian requires me to do so. Yet, throughout this period of my life, I had no knowledge of my Jewish heritage.

When I was seventeen my parents were again quarrelling with one another. My maternal grandmother told me I shouldn't be too upset about their squabbling because my mother's husband wasn't my real father. I was in a state of shock, and told my parents what I had just learned. However, they strongly denied everything.

A few weeks later I was on a student exchange programme in England. There I received a text message from my step-father, in which he admitted he was not my real father. I couldn't believe it, and re-read the message several times. I thought he must be drunk; I had been certain he was my father. Toward me he was a very good parent. He really loved me, and I know he loves me still.

Shortly after, when I was nineteen, my parents divorced.

After primary school in my small town, I won a competition to attend secondary school in another town called Gorzów. I studied there for three years before moving to Frankfurt-on-Oder. I now know that in Gorzów I had some Jewish friends, because of their surnames. But no one would tell you at the time. One of my best friends in high school there admitted to me that his grandfather was Jewish. For me it was OK, nothing special – neither good nor bad. He was very interested in Jewish culture, and so we went together to see the Jewish cemetery in Gorzów. But he didn't know anything about Jewishness. When I went to Frankfurt-on-Oder, after winning a German-language prize to study for my high school diploma, one of my best friends was also Jewish. She had come there with the Russian Jewish emigration to Germany. She told me that she was Jewish because her father – who had been a professor at the university in Minsk – was Jewish, although her mother was not. So I had some contact with Jews.

I studied in Munich and Vienna but decided to pursue a degree in Berlin in order to be closer to my Polish home town, and spent six years in the Jewish studies department at the University of Potsdam. Following my graduation, I received a fellowship from the German government to work on a Ph.D at Humboldt University in Berlin. My thesis dealt with the national and religious identity of hidden Jewish children in Poland after the Second World War.

For many years, my mother didn't want to tell my anything about my Jewish father and his family. Instead she played wicked games, saying: 'You have such Jewish eyes' – or she called me 'my little Jewish girl'. It was never negative, but annoying as. I felt I had something of a Jewish soul. She would play a game, saying something and then dismissing it. Nonetheless I kept asking questions about my biological father and his family.

It was always a very hard job extracting any information from my mother. When I was involved in my Jewish studies, she once said that she thought my paternal grandparents were Jewish. But she added: 'Please, I beg you. Never ever tell this to anyone.'

On another occasion, she did reveal that my father's family came from a *shtetl* in the Kielce region which had been 80 per cent Jewish before the war. After the Kielce pogrom in 1946, the family became terrified by the surge in anti-semitism and moved to Szczecin where they became very zealous Catholics. They were truly hidden Jews who would never admit their origins to anyone.

A few years ago I felt the desire to convert to Judaism. My mother reacted by saying that if I converted, she would never speak to me again. In retrospect I completely understand her attitude. In Poland people have to be very courageous to admit their Jewish roots – even in big cities like Warsaw or Kraków – because to be Jewish is to be different.

In a normal situation being Jewish is not special – neither negative nor positive – but we don't have such a situation in Poland. If you are Jewish, you are different. There is still so much prejudice. Jews never know how non-Jews will react; people can be very impolite, or ask stupid questions and make stupid jokes. Even in Germany it was very hard for me to be open about my identity because it's always an atmosphere where it's not normal.

Is it easier in Germany? Many young Germans still don't know how to deal with Jews. They would never be anti-semitic because it is not permitted. In Poland anti-semitism is permitted; it's still okay. If you have a very strong personality, you can deal with it. As for Germany, I heard so many anti-semitic jokes from my colleagues at the University of Potsdam and sometimes I was really embarrassed.

I'm not sure now whether I really want or need to go through a formal conversion. While I grow closer to Judaism every day, it's a rather intellectual approach. If I were to undergo a conversion for religious reasons, I would do it in an Orthodox way because I'm the sort of person who has to embrace something 100 per cent.

Even without a conversion, I like to light candles on Friday night and say the blessings. Sometimes I go to the synagogue if I feel inclined to do so. It's like being a liberal Jew without actually being a Jew. I feel somehow Jewish because of my paternal grandparents. If I were to convert, it wouldn't change anything. Although I would be more halachically Jewish, this has nothing to do with my feelings. My sense of Jewishness is already so strong because of my interests, my friends and my profession. And the more I'm into Jewishness and the more Jewish friends I have, the less I feel the need to convert.

I tend to be very suspicious when people of my age who were brought up in a Christian tradition, like myself, decide to convert in the Orthodox way. They take on an exaggerated identity by becoming more Jewish than the Jews. However, I don't have to prove anything to anyone to be Jewish. If an Orthodox person asks me, I will say that I'm not halachically Jewish although I have a Jewish background. If someone else asks me whether I have Jewish roots, I would always reply in the affirmative because I would otherwise feel like I'm hiding something important.

Conversion is a huge responsibility and that's why I'm critical of the Third Generation. They think it's fashionable but, after one or two years, they don't want to be Jews any longer. There are also people in the Second Generation who often decide to become Jewish. Currently, we have two trends in Poland; on the one hand, people choose to be Jewish in a religious way, while on the other hand, many people opt to remain secular and only become a member of a community.

Of course, I'm very happy about the positive growth of the Jewish community in places like Warsaw, especially compared to ten years ago. A great deal of the activity revolves around the young people in the Third Generation because they have never been oppressed like their parents and grandparents who often had such traumatic experiences; so it's easier to for them to take on a Jewish identity. Also, places like Beit Warszawa are very attractive to young people because they stem from America and are perceived as cool or fashionable. People in my generation would rarely go to an Orthodox synagogue which they usually regard as boring and grey.

If I decided to convert, my husband, who is a religious German Protestant, would not object. He is prepared to raise our children in both religions. What I know for sure is that I believe in God and can't live without religion. In a sense, that's my personal tragedy.

EMIL JEŻOWSKI

I was born in Warsaw in 1989. I'm currently completing a degree in social policy, which is connected to the Department of Political Science and Journalism at Warsaw University.

In terms of the challenge of seeking out family roots, it's often the third generation that pursues the story. In my case, it was my father who started asking questions. The process began after he left Poland in 1970 with his parents, following the 1968 purge, when he was 14 years old. The family emigrated to the United States; my father studied violin at the Manhattan School of Music. When he was 20 he returned to Poland with his ill sister, who needed the treatment available to her in Poland. My father was supposed to attend the music academy in Warsaw but it didn't work out. He met my mother, a non-Jewish pianist who was originally from Kazakhstan. Her mother was Russian and her father was Polish.

My paternal grandparents also decided to return from the U.S. in 2000 to be closer to their grandchildren.

I believe my father began to have suspicions about his Jewish background when he spent time with my great-grandmother, Emilia, after whom I am named. She was very assimilated and lived in the south of Poland, which is the ancestral area of the Jewish members of our family. Her husband had a German name and came from a mixed Polish-German background, which is probably how they survived the war. My father's discussions with Emilia sparked a deeper interest into the family's origins.

By the time my father left for the U.S., he understood there was something unusual about our family. Despite being Protestants they didn't eat pork, and regarded Friday night and Saturday as something special. My grandmother, Bronia, says that these practices were passed on by her mother, Emilia, and are very important to her. Although Bronia considers herself to be Christian, and would never admit to possessing a Jewish heritage, she respected the fact that her son eventually decided to become Jewish and raise his children as Jews. Furthermore, she believed if this was his final decision, he ought to become fully Jewish.

When I was growing up we still celebrated some Christian holidays, like Christmas, but also Shabbat. We were very confused. As Protestants we were more connected to the church, because it offers a stronger sense of community compared to praying on one's own in a Catholic church. Over the years I recall going to church, but also celebrating Shabbat. It was a big mess in my head. I even thought we might be Messianic Jews.

The turning point came when I was thirteen and had my first experience of attending a Jewish summer camp. I was the first member of my family to do so. This gave me the opportunity to meet other kids of my age who came from Jewish families, most of whom had mixed identities, and helped me gain a different perspective. I realised that I didn't need anything from Christianity and felt more connected to the Jewish community. My older sisters later became involved in the Polish Union of Jewish Students (PUSŻ), the precursor to ZOOM.

By Polish standards we are, with six children, a rather large family. When I was sixteen we decided as a family to convert: my parents and four of us children, including myself. It was a Conservative conversion, performed by Harry Levin, a rabbi from New York who was connected with Beit Warszawa. At the age of seventeen I had my Bar Mitzvah in the synagogue.

One brother, who didn't go through the conversion process, lives in London with his Christian wife and has remained a Protestant. Another sibling, Paul, is not involved in any religion. By contrast my older sister, Josefina, is married to a Polish-Jewish man; they have four children. Their marriage was the first non-Orthodox marriage in Poland since the war. So we have each taken a conscious decision on whether to be Jewish or Christian.

Around fifteen years ago my family was involved in the establishment of Beit Warszawa, the first post-war Reform congregation in Poland. At the time the only religious community for Jews was the Orthodox Nożyk synagogue. Beit Warszawa represented a movement that was separating from the Gmina because the latter only comprised either Orthodox or secular members. Beit Warszawa also tried to register with the government as an official Gmina of progressive Jews in Poland. This proved to be a big issue and, despite the fact that the process has been going on for a number of years, it still hasn't been resolved.

Over time, Beit Warszawa experienced its own crisis as various members found it difficult to work with Seweryn Ashkenazy, the founder of the congregation. That led to a split which resulted in the creation of Eitz Chaim, a progressive community which is more traditional than the Reform movement in the U.S. but is very open to the members' non-Jewish partners. It's also part of the Gmina and has become more powerful in the organisation than the Orthodox community. I am now associated with Etz Chaim and my sister works for the congregation.

I'm currently pursuing three areas of part-time work, which includes working two days a week in the office of Michael Schudrich, the Chief Rabbi of Poland. I also attend a leadership programme, *Minyamin*, run by the Jewish Agency, which is designed to get young people involved in the Jewish community, often after they leave youth organisations like ZOOM. *Minyamin* led to my deep involvement with Makabi, which promotes sports and Jewish values. Nonetheless we are open to non-Jews who want to play with us; we don't see ourselves as gatekeepers for the community. It's remarkable that non-Jews want to represent a Jewish football club and it indicates that many young people in Warsaw are highly tolerant.

In December 2014 I launched a branch of Hashomer Hatzair, the Zionist and democratic socialist youth movement affiliated with the Meretz party in Israel. This represents the organisation's rebirth since its presence in Poland ended shortly after the war. Its recent reappearance is symbolically important. We are very committed to its Zionist and Tikkun Olam values. A great deal of the movement's history emanates from Poland, where it also played a key leadership role in the Warsaw Ghetto uprising. However, in Poland's post-Communist environment, it's somewhat more complicated launching an organisation that is rooted in socialism.

I generally feel positive about the future for Polish Jewry – otherwise I wouldn't work so hard in various areas of the community. Hidden Jews will continue to emerge, but not in such spectacular numbers as after the fall of Communism. By now, most Holocaust survivors have also revealed their ancestry.

At some stage I think I will want to travel or work abroad. One constantly hears people in the Third Generation expressing this feeling. Yet there are a number of factors keeping me here. If I start something like Hashomer Hatzair and leave at this point, I know it's only going to succeed if I can find someone to replace me. I also want to be here for my grandmother. The longer I stay in Poland, the more deeply rooted I become. There is so much to do and many things that need to be changed.

KRZYSZTOF GUTKOWSKI

My mother is halachically Jewish, but she was raised by her mother who was determined to completely assimilate into Polish society. Although her mother survived the Warsaw ghetto, where she studied in an underground medical university, she chose to have her daughter baptised, undertake communion, and regularly attend church after the war. In later years my grandmother was a well-known activist in Solidarity, and would often take my mother along to mass Catholic prayers held in support of the underground opposition movement.

My mother grew up in a household where it was taboo to ask any questions about the war. This was somewhat strange as it was a family where virtually all subjects were open for discussion. Growing up in a secular Jewish milieu in Łódź, however, my mother slowly became more conscious that she was not getting a complete picture about the family's history. For example in 1968, feeling tension in their home as many friends began leaving Poland, she asked my grandmother whether the anti-semitic campaign would affect them as well. On another occasion, when she was still a teenager, she returned home one day to find her grandfather murmuring prayers in Hebrew. She figured out it must have been Hebrew. Also when he died, they found his Jewish prayer books in the house. Then my grandmother cleared the books away; they never reappeared again.

By the time my grandmother died, she had rarely been open about her Jewish origins. But there were small signals which gave some indication. My mother knew, however, she couldn't ask questions. When she did, it was always something like: 'I will tell you later.' Or else: 'Don't ask me.' Just before my mother's wedding, my grandmother wondered whether she should tell my mother's fiancé, Piotr, that she was actually Jewish. Yet nothing was mentioned; my mother went ahead with her church wedding.

As my mother grew more aware of the family background, she was left with angry feelings about the manner in which my grandmother handled the whole issue. It subsequently took her a significant length of time, after her mother's death, to acquire the knowledge that was denied for so long.

I was sent to one of the first private schools to open near our house. As the school was run by nuns, religion played an important role in the curriculum. However, the religious element turned me off but, paradoxically, also helped me to understand the attraction of atheism. That type of school was an ideal factory for manufacturing atheism. Almost everyone I knew who went there failed to become religious. Fortunately my parents came to the conclusion that the educational standards were declining, and moved my brother, Marek, and myself to a non-religious public school. By that time Marek and I had begun to revolt against going to church every Sunday.

At Warsaw University I studied anthropology, which led me to write a thesis about Hasidic Jews who make a pilgrimage to Poland on the *yahrzeit* of Rabbi Elimelech, in order to visit his grave in Leżajsk, Galicia. My thesis was built around the concept of collective memory. Apart from going to Leżajsk every year, I also started to interview people in New York to trace how they imagined Hasidic life in Poland may have been in the past.

The key moment the door opened on our family background was in 2005 when I was 23. I was reading an article in *Polityka* about young people in Poland who had suddenly discovered their Jewish background in a variety of different circumstances. One person, for example, recounted how his neighbour told him: 'Your family should be nicer to us.' He was baffled, and approached his parents for an explanation. It turned out the neighbours had helped that man's parents during the war because they were Jews, something that had been hidden from him until then.

I told my mother that these were amazing stories and it was a pity that we had nothing to discover in a similar way. She replied: 'Well, actually we do because your grandmother was Jewish and survived the Warsaw ghetto.' It was the first time my mother had shared this information with anyone. I was utterly amazed, and also very happy to learn I had Jewish origins and was a part of Polish-Jewish history. It also made more sense of my interest in Rabbi Elimelech and his Hasidic followers.

I had to rush back to university, but suddenly stopped and returned home; we just talked for the rest of the day. I constantly kept asking: 'Why didn't you tell me before? Why didn't you talk to her about it?' The answers were always the same: 'Because I couldn't.'

Eventually I left for university. On the way I started texting all my friends with the news that I just found out I'm Jewish. In Anna Bikont's important book on Jedwabne, she recounts how, in her 20s, she called her friends when she suddenly discovered her Jewish background. But her friends replied that they already knew, and were not surprised. I had a similar experience with my friends, including my ex-girlfriend, saying they already knew or suspected this to be the case.

Even before receiving this knowledge, I always felt like an outsider in Polish society. I didn't like many aspects of Polish culture, especially its conservative manifestations, nor the way people treated one another. So discovering my Jewish identity fitted very well into my outlook.

Because the Jewish members of our family were dead, I had to turn to the Jewish Historical Institute for some background. They located documentation about my family, including the family history forms my great-grandfather filled out after the war for the Polish Jewish Committee. The information was fascinating and enabled me to find my grandparents' graves in the Okopowa Jewish cemetery. Further genealogical research led to broken family graves which we began to restore.

Given my Jewish origins I decided to remove myself as a member of the Catholic community. I went to the church where I was baptised, to tell the priest I was an atheist and very opposed to the Catholic church as a public institution. Although it proved to be a difficult task, it confirmed my divorce from Catholicism.

Increasingly, I became more interested in Jewish culture and history, which steered me to a greater involvement in Jewish life. Apart from a Taglit trip to

Israel, I was active in the youth organisation, ZOOM, which no longer exists. But I also was involved in closing down ZOOM as it disappointingly evolved into a drinking club for people who just happened to know some Jewish people. At present I regard the Jewish Community Centre in Warsaw as the best place to connect with the Jewish community, largely because it's essentially a secular organisation with more intellectual content.

One of the most important moments in my journey to forge a Jewish identity occurred when an Israeli genealogist phoned us in November 2011. The call turned our lives upside down. He was searching for my mother to inform her that her grandfather's sister, Pnina, who died in Israel, left her some property and money in her will. However, the genealogist also pointed out that there was a Russian branch of our family which was also entitled to the inheritance. We knew that we had family in Moscow but contact had been cut off decades before.

Because I knew Russian, I immersed myself in research to locate the long-lost relatives. One month later, I found the number for their Moscow apartment and contacted them. After overcoming their initial suspicions, they understood that we were genuine family relations. Two weeks later I flew to Moscow for a very emotional reunion. We are now in regular contact with our Russian relatives.

We also travelled as a family to Israel to meet the other relatives with whom we had been out of touch for so many years. These discoveries inspired me to create a family tree dating back to the beginning of the nineteenth century. It has allowed me to develop a broader picture of our family ties, which include relations in various parts of the world.

Despite the difficulties Jews are experiencing in reclaiming family assets in Poland, I launched a drive to regain the apartment house on Złota Street which had been owned, before the war, by my mother's grandparents and the grandmother's two sisters. They all died in the ghetto. After two years of hard legal work, we succeeded in reclaiming ownership in 2014. Unlike other similar property disputes, our case was somewhat easier as there were few people involved. We were effectively the main owners who had claims to the building. However, one of the sisters had sold her share during the war. As it was illegal for a Jewish person to do so under Nazi rule, a false document was created showing the transaction to have taken place in 1938. That meant we had to locate the person who was the current inheritor of this sale and he remains a minority owner. For my mother, the Złota building represents an important symbol for redeeming her family's pre-war life.

The opening up to our Jewish past has had a profound impact on our family. My mother decided to write her memoir, which she describes as putting together a jigsaw puzzle of the big family picture. I also encouraged her to join the Second Generation group because I saw her wrestling with a great deal of anger. She needed to share it with people who had a similar history and it has worked out very well.

I celebrate some Jewish holidays, but only with my mother, and I always take the initiative. It's unusual that our roles have been reversed because it's typically the parents who push the kids to attend religious festivals. There are so many layers of meaning here; we understand one another and are quite supportive. We enjoy sharing these occasions together, and often go to the Nożyk Synagogue at Purim for the reading of the *Megillah* or perhaps to a Chanukah celebration.

My brother Marek is also aware of his Jewish background and describes himself as both Polish and Jewish. When I found the destroyed grave of our great great-grandfather, whose wife bought the house on Złota Street, it was in a terrible state. Marek readily contributed his share to the great expense of restoring it.

Shortly after the discovery of my mother's family background, my parents turned their attention to my paternal grandmother. Apparently, before the war, she had changed her name from Wind to Winiarz in order to marry Seweryn Gutkowski, my grandfather. When my mother once asked her the reason for doing so, she stopped the discussion very abruptly by saying: 'Who would want to have a German surname in those times?'

Yet my mother remained suspicious about this reply. I therefore began to research the name, Wind, at the Jewish Historical Institute and on the internet. It was easy to find and I eventually learned that she had converted from Judaism to Catholicism in order to marry her husband in Lwów. They managed to survive the war on the Aryan side of Warsaw and she spent the rest of her life as a very devout Catholic. Unsurprisingly, she also raised my father to be a practising Catholic. Although he never questioned his mother about her origins, he harboured his own suspicions. This was partly because her brother, who disappeared during the war, is mentioned in a book on pre-war Lwów as having to conceal his Jewish roots.

At present I'm not very active in the Jewish community. In general I'm very depressed at the political atmosphere in Poland, and don't think it will change for the better. I'm still active in the campaign to create proper urban space for cyclists and pedestrians. But I'm also fed up with fighting for leftist and LGBTQ causes because I don't want to spend my life in a constant struggle. Given this environment, I don't believe that Poland is a country with a promising future for Jewish people.

GOSIA SZYMAŃSKA-WEISS

I was born and raised in Łódź. I am 35 years old.

My father was Jewish and, although my mother was raised as a Catholic, she is not in any way religious. The last time she attended church was probably when she went for Holy Communion at eight years old.

My father had a Master's degree in economics, and worked in middle management at one of the big factories in Łódź. As a young teenager he organised Jewish summer and winter camps under the auspices of the Peretz school. While he didn't have any religious affiliation and could be described as extremely secular, he had a strong sense of Jewish cultural identity. In 1968, having managed to retain his job and apartment, and wanting to stay close to his mother, he decided not to emigrate. However, many of his Jewish friends chose to – or were forced to – leave Poland at that time.

I was twelve or thirteen years old when I discovered my father was Jewish. I had noticed he was disturbed at the news coverage of the *intifada* that was raging in Israel and Palestine, and asked him why he was so concerned about people living so far away who were killing one another. He replied that he cared because it was happening in the Jewish state of Israel, and he was a Jew. My jaw dropped; I was in a state of shock. I recall staring at my dad and wondering if this conversation had really just happened; and whether my father was still the person I had always known. I was confused, and found it difficult to absorb this information. I knew the word 'Jew' was not a nice one and that if you wanted to call someone a 'moron', you would call him 'Mosiek'. But I was not aware this was a Jewish first name. That's how clueless I was.

My father explained that he and my mother had decided against telling me sooner because there were many people who didn't think well of Jews. My parents simply wanted to protect me. They urged me to keep this knowledge to myself, and not to discuss it with my friends. Of course, as a young girl, I didn't listen to their advice. I had a close friend at school and wanted to share my secret with her. When I told her, she announced: 'We don't like Jews.'

In retrospect I always knew there was something different about our family. For example, I was one of only two kids in my class in elementary school who didn't go to church or religious classes. Unlike most Catholic parents, my mother was perfectly happy that I was not baptised and that was not typical of Polish families. People usually had grandparents and extended family, and many often travelled to the countryside to visit relatives. But, on my father's side, we only had my grandmother, who was an assimilated Communist and anti-religious, and my father's half-brother who lived in Berlin. There was also a cousin in Canada, who emigrated in the early 1980s. Six out of eight siblings of my grandmother's were killed but we do not know how or where. Out of the two that survived, one died when I was a baby (her son is the cousin who lives in Canada) and another died in the early 1990s. She had no children. We know very little about my dad's biological father other than that he was killed before my dad was born. So although I thought we were different, it never occurred to me I might be Jewish. It just wasn't on my radar screen.

As my new identity began to emerge, I kept it hidden from my friends. I didn't want people to know, and didn't understand where it was going. I was toying with religion; eventually a relationship with the Jewish community became increasingly important to me. Gradually, I started to share with my non-Jewish friends that I had begun to be involved in the Jewish community. To my great surprise many were happy for me, while some were just indifferent; I had braced myself for a negative reaction. It was probably largely due to my attendance at a prestigious school in Łódź, High School No. 1, which was the oldest one in the city and renowned for good academic results. The students usually came from the educated homes of the intelligentsia, which probably accounts for the absence of negative reactions. They weren't anti-semites, or if they were, they were smart enough not to show it.

In 1996 I visited my Canadian cousin's family in Montreal, and that proved to be a watershed experience. He and his Jewish wife held Friday night dinners at home. They lit Sabbath candles, socialised with Jewish friends, and went to synagogue. I saw how other Jews lived and it proved to be my first real introduction to Jewish life. I loved the concept of a community: how people were tied together by personal and Jewish experiences. I never encountered anything like that because I had never seen Catholics form a community in quite the same way. That experience propelled me to find something similar in Poland.

When I returned to Łódź I joined the Lauder Foundation club, which had recently been launched in Poland. I began learning Hebrew, and took an introductory Judaism course. The leaders of the club were actually converts to Judaism; the teacher of the Judaism class was Simcha Keller, now the leader of the religious community in Łódź. In the Lauder classes and Jewish holiday events, I met young people who had only recently discovered they had Jewish roots. Through these friends, I became acquainted with other Jewish people across Poland.

Later I went to Warsaw for my university studies. I became more involved with the Jewish community, and joined the board of the Polish Union of Jewish Students (PUSŻ). The American Jewish Joint Distribution Committee, which had become active in rebuilding Jewish life in Poland, invited me to attend leadership seminars in Israel. I also went to Israel for conferences of the World Union of Jewish Students. Although I was very moved and loved Israel, it was clear from the outset that I didn't want to make *aliyah*.

In the late 1990s I became more curious about religion, and felt a spiritual longing. At that time I was disappointed in the Nożyk synagogue, which I found not to be the welcoming place I had hoped for. The opening of Beit Warszawa in 2000 was a promising alternative. The atmosphere was not intimidating; it was acceptable if you didn't understand the service or weren't ready to confront the question of whether you are Jewish – or how. Nobody was going to judge you if you were in the early stages of your journey. It offered the possibility of a place that would really open its doors and make people feel comfortable.

I spent the next few years working on a full-time basis for Beit Warszawa. My last year with the congregation was 2007-2008, when I returned for one year after studying in Los Angeles. Since then I suspect those initial expectations have not been fulfilled.

At the outset, I didn't really understand the premise of Reform Judaism and tended to think of it as Judaism lite. My work there was less about religious experience, and more about the community and creating access for people to learn about Judaism. Over time I realised that, from an intellectual and spiritual point of view, Reform Judaism wasn't for me.

I initially came to Los Angeles for a visit as a guest of Seweryn Ashkenazy – the founder and main backer of Beit Warszawa – to speak to Jewish audiences about the revival of Jewish life in Poland. Through Mr Ashkenazy, I met people who connected me with the School of Jewish Communal Service (now the Zelikow School for Jewish Nonprofit Management) at the Hebrew Union College -Jewish Institute of Religion (HUC-JIR), which offered me a scholarship to study for a Master's degree. After graduating, I was expected to take my knowledge and experience back to Poland and put it to good use for the benefit of the Jewish community in Poland. That's why I returned to work there in 2007.

I originally met my American husband while a graduate student at HUC and returned to Los Angeles in 2008. I left Poland feeling tired and disillusioned, and was quite happy to get away and start a new life. I underwent a Conservative conversion before our wedding in 2010 because I felt it was the right moment to do it. It also symbolised a closing of the circle, a sort of pinnacle of my Jewish journey.

I could easily imagine living a Jewish life in Poland again because I love being there and, especially, spending time in Warsaw. Although I'm primarily living in the U.S., I speak to my daughter exclusively in Polish. When I'm in Poland, I spend a good deal of time in Łódź where my mother lives (my father passed away in 2011). However, since my American husband doesn't speak Polish, it would be quite challenging for him to move there.

It's extremely exciting to see all the fantastic changes that have taken place in Poland's Jewish community in recent years. In particular, I'm impressed by the cutting edge work being done by the Jewish Community Centres in

Warsaw and Kraków. There is a tremendous energy driving these centres which has enabled them to get a lot of people involved in communal activities.

I'm hopeful that the process of revitalising Polish Jewry will continue. New people are constantly 'coming out of the woodwork'. But the future of Jews in Poland boils down to demographics and whether Jewish girls will meet Jewish boys and whether they will have Jewish children. So far I haven't seen much evidence that this is happening to a degree that will ensure a stable and strong future for the Jewish community of Poland.

PAWEŁ BRAMSON

A shochet – ritual slaughterer – Paweł was born in 1976 into a Catholic family. Today he is an Orthodox Jew. He is the subject of a documentary film, 'The Moon Is Jewish'.

How did I discover my Jewishness? It was my wife. She went to the Jewish Historical Institute to check her documents and decided to also check mine. As for the reason, we have to go further back. My wife knew she came from a Jewish background because her mother told her. But I didn't know about this. I found out on our wedding day; my future mother-in-law told me. She said: 'You know your wife is Jewish.' I thought she was joking.

My family was assimilated. I was baptised, and went to church. I stopped going to church when I was fifteen or sixteen. As a teenager, there are more interesting things to do like going to football games. It still is a passion. As for Legia Warsaw supporters chanting anti-semitic slogans, today they don't. But there used to be quite a lot of it. I was also a skinhead chanting those racist slogans. I was a fan but I was also stupid like a young man can be.

As for my wife's discovery at the Jewish Historical Institute, I took the documents to my parents and confronted them. I wasn't kind to my parents; I didn't approach them in a pleasant or courteous way. I used harsh words. I was in a big state of shock.

And they confirmed the truth of the documents. My wife's family knew; my mother-in-law admitted it. But my wife's grandmother never admitted it – even though a lot of her family were killed in Auschwitz. She said her brother had brought food to the Warsaw ghetto and was shot trying to escape.

My father's family were also Jewish. In 1968, my grandfather had to take early retirement because he was an army officer. The only reason they allowed him to stay in Poland was because he had some military merit that he achieved during the war. But he had to leave his work.

I have no control over any of these developments: such as the fact that I married a Jewish woman, and that I became a Jew, and how we just connected with other Jews. The Almighty is somehow connecting all of us.

As for my wife and the discovery of our Jewishness, she had already been going to the Nożyk synagogue and also attending a winter camp run by the Lauder Foundation. It was wonderful when she would go to synagogue and I could stay at home. The football matches took place on Friday and Saturday. It was beautiful: my wife was away, a full fridge, a lot of beer and a football match on TV.

Now I learn the score after Shabbat; I can't watch the match. Sometimes I just walk by a kosher restaurant where the TV broadcasts the game and just peek. Now I go to the synagogue – that's my stadium.

I didn't plan the process of becoming an Orthodox Jew. I don't know how it happened. I lost control over it. It's an ongoing process that has been taking place for sixteen years. I became a truly Orthodox Jew eleven or twelve years ago. When I started going to the Nożyk synagogue, I asked Rabbi Schudrich: 'Who is a Jew? How should I start to live now?' He gave me books to read. I finished one book and came back for the next book and then step-by-step… Also Przemysław (Israel) Szpilman (who runs the main Jewish cemetery) helped me a lot, as well as other friends who know more about Jewishness. So I looked up to them as role models.

If I was working outside the Jewish community, it would be difficult to observe Shabbat and the Jewish festivals. However, in my work, they are always observing these festivals and so it's easier for me.

As for working as a *shochet*, I'm waiting for my certificate. I hope to pass the exam and get the certification. However, for the past two years, there was a ban on kosher slaughtering in Poland, and so it was problematic for me to practice. The Polish government overturned this ban and now kosher slaughtering will be allowed.

I also organise the place where kosher food is prepared, and also catering for outside groups. I'm renting a place from the Gmina where I serve dinners, mostly for seniors, but also for other members of the community.

In terms of maintaining an Orthodox life in Poland, I've gotten so used to it that's it's difficult to tell whether it's easier or difficult. It's just the way I live. I'm sure for those who are *teshuvah*, going back to Judaism, it's easier because there are now at least three kosher restaurants. Actually four if we count my catering business. Also, many Orthodox Jews visit from abroad. They have been bringing their own kosher food because they don't know there are kosher restaurants here. Then they say: 'Really, in Warsaw? No way!'

No, there isn't a growing number of people interested in the Orthodox approach. It would be nice; but you have to be quite crazy to choose to live this way in Poland. Many people look at me – even in the synagogue. They say maybe you are exaggerating, maybe they read different books than I do. For them Judaism is still like 'Fiddler on the Roof'.

That's why many decide to become Conservative or Reform Jews. I don't want to offend anybody but for me it's like playing at being a Jew. OK, it's Shabbat, so I'll dress up like a Jew. But when Monday comes, they take off the *kippah* and dress normally and pretend they are not a Jew any more. For me the law is one – we have one Torah for everyone.

In the past, I had *peyot* and a long beard. Every week I went from Warsaw to Poznań – sometimes in a car and sometimes on the train. Monday morning I went and Friday I returned. Not as a *shochet* but a *mashgiach* (supervisor). And I never encountered any problems. Sometimes people would smile. I used to fly often to Gdańsk and every time they would come up to me and, in English, offer to help. 'Hello sir. Can I help you?' Ah, come on, speak Polish – I would reply. They were very surprised to find out I speak Polish. Sometimes also at petrol stations the same exchange would take place. They are very surprised to learn I'm Polish. 'How very well you speak Polish.' And I would say: 'Thank you so much. I was born here.'

So I cut off the *peyot*. I got very tired of everybody looking at me with curiosity. It started to irritate me.

My 20-year-old son returned from the U.S. last year where he studied for two years in the Talmudic academy in Baltimore and then two more years in the Manhattan Talmudic academy. Now he will finish his college education in Poland because he also needs a secular education. My daughter, who is seventeen, goes to a normal state school since you need lots of money to send your child to the Lauder school, which is very expensive.

I met the film-maker of 'The Moon is Jewish' in Częstochowa. I was there with Michael Traison who is very involved with Jewish projects in Poland; we were preparing the Sukkot festival. Michał Tkaczyński, the film-maker, was attending a film school there. So Michael asked him to come and film the preparations. He called me and tried to talk me into doing a movie but I was reluctant.

At the time, I was overseeing the building of the Jewish museum during the excavations. I was gathering the bones buried in the ground from the Warsaw Ghetto uprising. We filled four cartons with bones. Everything is now in the Okopowa cemetery. When they were excavating here, someone had to supervise it. After the war, they didn't take the debris away; instead they just spread it around. So this area is actually higher than other parts of Warsaw. When they were excavating here, they had to start by removing the first layer and then they found bones in the basements.

Michał called me when I was in the middle of supervising this work. He said he wanted to make a documentary. At first, because I was so reluctant, they said they would just cover my image and I wouldn't actually be shown in the movie. That's how he talked me into it, by assuring me he wouldn't show my face. But then it evolved into a normal film. It even got an award at some film festival.

Here it was shown on TV. But it has gone all over the world. I was interviewed by the *New York Times* and also CNN but I rejected requests for interviews from the Polish media.

When people ask me whether I'm optimistic about the future of Polish Jewry, I tell them that I have to be. Otherwise I wouldn't be doing this.

Katka Reszke

It all started with a hunch I had probably around the age of fifteen. I woke up one day convinced I was Jewish.

I had a childhood memory of my maternal grandmother calling me 'meshugeneh'. When I divulged the hunch to my parents, my mother spoke of her own childhood memory involving my great-grandmother. She would open the door of the closet where my great-grandfather was hiding with a big cloth over his head and a box on his forehead and he would say: 'Shalom Aleichem, Shalom Aleichem.' He did this repeatedly as a joke. He was teasing her because he knew it made her crazy. She would literally chase him around the kitchen with a rolling pin, saying:'What a fool! What if someone sees you!' My mother remembers it being funny. This was her memory when she was a child in the 1950s.

Following my hunch I went on to ask everybody on my mother's side, because there my suspicion lay, whether we had Jewish roots. Sadly, my great-grandmother died just a few months later and I never got a chance to confront her about this in a direct way. But I did ask my grandmother and I did ask my mother.

When I started confronting members of the family, including people on my father's side, all I ever heard was how great everybody thought Jews were. 'Jews are great, but we? No.' It took me a few years to realise that people saying Jews are great was not the standard response to inquiries about Jewish ancestry.

Because I couldn't find any confirmation about members of my family, I began seeking other 'real Jews'. So, in the mid-1990s, I ended up finding the Jewish community in Wrocław where I lived. Here I was, a young blonde girl who nobody knew and visiting the Jewish community back then was not for the faint of heart. The synagogue was a ruin, the services were held in a tiny Beit Midrash. The members of the community were very suspicious of new visitors, so the fact that I persisted and went again and again is something which still bewilders me when I think about it. There was something very familial about it; I felt very drawn to that place. At the same time, I decided that it was probably not a good idea to tell people that I had a hunch that I had Jewish roots, because I didn't want them to think I was crazy. I knew people were suspicious of me yet I didn't want to say I was Jewish because I didn't know that I was – even though I felt it. But it was a crazy kind of feeling.

So I decided that in order to be accepted, it would be best to make myself useful by becoming a volunteer. I became the community photographer and I would take pictures for free. I think I was around 20 at the time when I became this non-member member, sort of by osmosis. I also realised at that time that the other young folks, who were all around my age and were members of the community and who became my friends, were not very different from me. Essentially, the difference between myself and them was that they <u>knew</u> they had a Jewish grandparent and it was often their father's father, but they were still considered legitimate members of the community while I didn't know but I was <u>convinced</u> that I too had a Jewish background.

Interestingly, the majority of the younger members of the community were not halachically Jewish or were unable to prove that they are. That is why when an American rabbi, Ivan Caine from Philadelphia, showed up and started talking about conversion, we all started discussing this and mostly agreed that while we may not necessarily need it in Poland, if we wanted to go some place else, it might not be such a bad idea to have some sort of a 'certificate'. Even though none of us were really religious nor seriously thinking about becoming religious, we thought it would be a good idea to do this. There were a bunch of people of all ages in that group who ended up going through the conversion process. It was a Conservative conversion.

Just around that time, I got a fellowship to do my Ph.D in Israel. Previously, I had received my Master's in Cultural Studies from Wrocław University. Throughout my studies, I wrote all my seminar papers about Jews. Naturally. And my Master's dissertation was actually on the Jewish community of Wrocław.

So in 2002, I entered the Hebrew University in the Department of Jewish Education at the Melton Centre for Jewish Education. It was great. As soon as I moved to Israel, I got a call from my parents who said they had just visited my Dad's mother and she was very excited that I was in Israel and she just happened to mention that her father was Jewish. My dad was quite surprised. I honestly doubt my grandma would ever have mentioned this if I had not gone to Israel.

In Israel, I decided to become an observant Jew. I was not interested in being religious; I don't feel equipped to be a religious person, but I was fascinated by Jewish practice and wanted to learn it. I didn't want to learn it from books though, so I decided to throw myself into the deep water and just do it. It lasted for about eight years. I like to call it my little private yeshiva and, after eight years, I will have decided that I have graduated.

Because I insisted in keeping 100 per cent kosher and I visited Poland frequently, of course, it wasn't easy to maintain kashrut. But my mother would keep separate dishes for me and she essentially learned how to cook kosher for me. During one of my visits, she said to me: 'Listen, there is nothing you can eat anymore, why don't I bake a loaf of bread.' So I began explaining to my mother that baking bread in the kosher way is actually quite complicated, because there is this ritual call *hafrashat challah* – for example, you have to separate the dough. I began to explain how it goes and then I could see my mom's face turning white and she said: 'That's exactly what my grandmother did.' The same grandmother who was so upset about Shalom Aleichem, the same one who used to call me 'meshugeneh'. For me, this was a breakthrough. I thought: 'This is it! I have my proof.' But my mother tried to convince me that it really doesn't prove anything. My great-grandmother had died and so I couldn't confront her about this, but my grandmother was still alive.

So eventually I decided that I should put my grandmother in front of a camera. At that point, I was already living in New York and working on documentary films. I had learned that sometimes people can open up more easily in front of a camera. I talked to my grandmother for two hours. I asked her about her mother and what she did and why. She said that when asked about her curious rituals, great-grandma would reply that it was just a custom. My grandma never confessed to anything. The stories I heard were stories I already knew. One of the more traumatic stories was from Nazi-occupied Czernowitz, where she lived during the war, which was then in Romania and is now in the Ukraine. My grandma recalled how the Gestapo would stop her on a daily basis and ask her where her Star of David was – they obviously thought she looked like she should be wearing one. So every time, she would pull out her perfectly good 'Aryan' Polish papers. I remembered that as being the only story she would tell. I never heard any other stories from the wartime.

And then, I was finishing my book (on the Third Generation), where I mention my grandmother. I thought that when the book comes out, that will be the last shot at this, that perhaps seeing the book will break her if there is something to be broken.

As I was making the final edits to my book, I got a call from my parents. This time it was my dad's father who was on his deathbed and who had just announced to my father: 'I'm not going to take the secret with me to my grave that I'm Jewish.' I just laughed. I had been digging on my mother's side, because that is where my hunch continued to haunt me, and then I was discovering more and more Jewish roots on my dad's side.

Unfortunately, just before the book came out and only a few months of one another, both my paternal grandfather and my beloved maternal grandmother died. When my grandmother died, I assumed she had taken the secrets to the grave with her.

I came to Poland in 2013 to launch the Polish translation of the book. When I arrived in Wrocław, my mother sat me down at the kitchen table and said: 'I've got something to tell you and don't kill me.' It turned out that when my great-grandmother was on her deathbed almost 20 years earlier, she called my mother in and started crying and said to her: 'You have to vow you won't tell anybody, especially your mother, what I'm about to tell you. Keep it a secret at least as long as your mother is still alive.' My mother promised she would keep the secret. And then my grandmother pronounced: 'We are Jewish.'

My mother drove back home from the hospital that night and started thinking to herself: 'This is absolutely ridiculous. It's the 1990s. There is no way I am going to keep this secret. I'm going back there the next morning and I'm going to talk my grandmother out of this because not only will nobody be upset about this. There will be some people who will actually be very pleased.' She was thinking of me because I had just started my investigation into our Jewish roots. When my mother arrived at the clinic the next morning, she was ten minutes too late.

My mother kept this a secret for almost two decades while I was going through everything I was going through – the hunch that we were Jewish, joining the Jewish community, conversion, moving to Israel, writing a book about Jewish identity. She had taken a vow. I cannot even tell you how crazy I think it was of her to have kept it from me for so long. But it sure does make for a good story.

When I told this story at Limmud UK, a guy in the audience – a psychologist – commented, saying: 'To be honest, until it becomes clear that you were right about your hunch, your story sounds like the onset of psychosis.'

How do you wake up one day with the feeling that you are not what you thought you were, or really that you are someone different from what everyone has ever told you that you were. I have since actually met several people, mostly women, who have had a very, almost disturbingly, similar experience. And now I'm writing a book about it and it's called 'The Meshugeneh Effect'. A small tribute to my grandmother.

Both my parents were always very supportive. My mother was clearly hiding something. But today, she is pretty Jewish herself, in the cultural sense. In fact, nowadays both my father and mother are very keen on telling people they are Jewish. Because in Poland it's a bit of a mission: you have to come out as a Jew every day. That's how they fulfil their Jewish identity in a way. My mother always jokes that it's the best way to put a filter on your circle of friends.

I think the Wrocław community is in direct competition with Kraków and probably Kraków is winning today, partly because of the Jewish Community Centre. Wrocław was for many years, and may still be today, the official second largest Jewish community in Poland after Warsaw. There was a great

Rabbi, Tyson Herberger, who unfortunately left a few months ago. Although he is actually Orthodox, he is also the most liberal Orthodox rabbi I have ever met.

I've really had difficulty defining where home is in recent years. But I do find myself between the U.S. and Poland – those are the two places where I spend most of my time. If you're lucky enough not to have to spend 100 per cent of your time there, Poland is an awesome place. I don't get to miss it because I keep coming back. Yet there are things about Poland that are insufferable. However, you do get to see some of the best things when you are away. There is a Polish sense of humour which I miss very much. There is this Polish cynical, depressing kind of intelligentsia which I'm very fond of.

What I like about Poland most are the Jews; I really like Polish-Jewish life. I don't feel at home in American-Jewish life. So I miss that. I've told people that I've lived in Jerusalem and New York, possibly the two most Jewish places on the planet, but I never feel more Jewish than I do in Poland.

There are only two Jewish communities in Europe that are actually growing – Poland and Germany.

Being Jewish in Poland is a queer identity. It's different from being Jewish anywhere else. People like to impose foreign models on the Polish-Jewish community. But what is happening in Poland doesn't fit any American model and it is by no means a bad thing.

The major problem in Poland is the fact that we need to constantly prove to people that we are 'real'. We have to constantly defend our authenticity because people come here, look at us and they think we are not real Jews. Whatever their reason may be, it is quite patronising. And I think a lot of the discussion we are having here has been partly in response to this type of questioning that we are faced with constantly. Yet I also think that it is precisely the discussion – between ourselves and the outside – that accounts for the vitality of the contemporary Polish-Jewish community.

JAKUB GRUSZCZYŃSKI

I run my own company which deals with the statistics of websites of the online business. I work mainly for one company which involves collecting data and integrating them and creating reports based on e-commerce data for big companies.

I grew up in Płock, where my father and grandfather lived. My father's side was Jewish but my father didn't feel any Jewishness until a few years ago.

My grandfather died before I was born in 1984 and everything I know about his Jewish heritage I personally found in many Polish archives. I discovered a lot of documents. In my father's house, my grandfather's Jewishness was a silent topic. He and his siblings told me it was never discussed.

My grandfather's father and his siblings were killed at the very start of the war. He and his mother lived for a while in the Płock ghetto until they were transported to the ghetto of Częstochowa to work in the factory. I have no further knowledge about my grandfather's story. I assume his mother died in Częstochowa but I don't know for sure.

Then my grandfather was transferred to a concentration camp in Lwów. He hid in a transport of human bodies and managed to escape from the place where the bodies were dumped. Somehow he managed to return to the Kielce region, and find or prepare some Aryan papers. He hid in a village until the end of the war, then he returned to Płock and married a Polish woman. I believe the marriage occurred shortly after my grandmother became pregnant.

My grandfather, as far as I know, started to work in the Polish militia. I read in his CV, which he wrote to join the militia, that he believed the militia and the new Communist government in Poland should be supported because of their opposition to Nazi Germany. From some reports I've read, there were two or three attempts to murder him by the anti-Communist resistance. There is a lot of discussion about this in Poland today, but I have very mixed feelings. The people who are now part of society and are called heroes were, in some cases, simply killers.

There was only a small Jewish community in Płock after the war. I found some documents with my grandfather's name from that time and they indicated there were about 30 Jews in Płock. But they left in 1968. My father's family also considered leaving for Israel. My grandmother wanted the whole family to leave, but my grandfather was opposed to the idea. He didn't wish to leave Poland and I think he still had a strong belief in Communism. I believe he wasn't very much into his own Jewishness. As far as he was concerned, that ended during the war.

My first contact with Jewishness occurred when I was about twelve or thirteen. I was talking to my grandmother and I think I told her some kind of Jewish joke. My grandmother was very sad; she told me I shouldn't joke like that because my grandfather was Jewish and the joke was horrible. It might have hurt him even if he hadn't concerned himself with his Jewishness.

My grandfather was no longer alive. The revelation was shocking, but I didn't connect it with myself. It was connected to my grandfather.

Something changed when I moved to Warsaw to attend university in 2003 at the age of nineteen. The first apartment I rented with friends was located close to the Nożyk synagogue. I think it was a factor that got me thinking. During my studies, I started to feel it's part of my heritage and something I would like to have more knowledge of. It was a feeling; I talked to my friends about it. I had to consider my Jewishness and it took time.

When I started work in 2008, I began to research various Polish archives and to talk to my father's older sister about our grandfather and his times. My aunt had memories about the Jewish part of the family; I learned from her that my grandfather's aunt survived the war, as well as some distant relatives from a village near Płock. My aunt recounted spending Jewish holidays with that part of the family. She showed me some old photographs. For example, she showed me photos of my great-grandparents and I learned my great-grandfather had the typical look of a Polish Jew with a long beard. In late nineteenth century Poland, I think the majority of Jews were religious. So my aunt was the first source from which I received first-hand knowledge, as well as the information I obtained from the archives. The bits of knowledge were exciting. It was like putting together Lego bricks.

I don't have siblings. I decided to become a member of the Warsaw Gmina. To begin with, I'm not a religious person. I decided to become a member to preserve the heritage because according to the laws of the Gmina, and the Law of Return in Israel, if I didn't do that my children can't do it at all. So I felt it was my responsibility to my family and my ancestors to preserve that. I will have a daughter in two months. I wish to nurture that option for my children and for myself because you never know. It can only be good to have that option. The crisis with Russia has made people here nervous.

At the very beginning, I had a meeting with Rabbi Tyson Herberger who was based here. He is a great personality and I spent a lot of time with him. He examined my documents and said he honestly didn't have a clue but he would help me. He arranged a few meetings with Gmina members, because you require signatures from two members and one rabbi to be eligible for membership. At that time I didn't know any Jews in Warsaw. Later he invited me to meet with him and a few girls who were preparing for conversion. He invited me because I was hungry for Jewish knowledge. I felt that you can't be a Jew without some knowledge of the religion. We met on a weekly basis and went through a few books about how to be a Jew. It was my first exposure to Jewishness. Later I started to study on the internet yeshiva, Yeshiva Pardes, with Rabbi Sasha Pecaric. He is the man who translated the first post-war Torah into Polish along with the commentary.

About a year and a half ago I was invited by the Jewish Community Centre to some cooking classes and met very nice people there. Later a girl I met, an American, posted on her Facebook site that she needed an assistant to translate some documents from English to Polish. It was one of the very first documents of Makabi Warsaw which initially made me aware of Makabi. After I translated the documents, she invited me to a party at the football pitch. And now I can say that Makabi is the Jewish place for me in Warsaw because of the people there and its obvious Jewishness. However, there are many religious denominations involved – not only Jews. They are people who don't have any problem wearing the Star of David. You couldn't have imagined it 20 years ago; it would have been suicide. Makabi has become an important social outlet and I've met many people there.

As for anti-semitism, it isn't a huge problem but I had some issues with one of my best friends. When I began to explore my heritage, he found a translation of the Torah on my bookshelf and inquired about it. I told him I consider myself to be Jewish and it's something I've started to explore. He was taken aback. We were a bit drunk at that moment. Shortly after, he became very nervous and started to accuse me of many things. For example, he asked me what kind of Pole I am. If there was a war between Poland and Israel, who would I fight for. It was very hard for me because I've known him for fifteen years, since high school in Płock.

Yet I mostly have fine memories connected to my own Jewishness. However, for example, my wife told me that when we started dating each other (she is also from Płock) her father knew my family was Jewish and had problems with that.

My father is alive and very grateful for the research I've done. He is not a very emotional person, but he told me with tears in his eyes that he had the feeling his father would have been very grateful. This is something he couldn't do his entire life because of the time he lived in. But my father was also very grateful for finding the knowledge and preserving it. He is very pleased about the Jewish direction I have been moving in.

However, my mother isn't. She often discusses this with me. She has even encountered some anti-semitic incidents because people thought she must be Jewish as she is married to a Jewish man. She was called all kinds of names like 'Jewish whore' about 35 years ago. She told me about an incident in her local government building industry office; a few of her colleagues asked to see pictures of my wedding. They wanted to know why it was only a civil marriage, and insisted we have a proper church wedding in the future. She replied that it won't happen because her son has decided to be Jewish. I think it was a very important coming out for her. I'm very proud of her because she is from the generation that remembers very widespread anti-semitism in Poland. I know her concern about my Jewishness is only because she worries about possible repercussions. She is a moderately religious person who goes to church from time to time.

When I started to explore my roots, I was already too old to go on Taglit. But, in December 2010, my father proposed a family trip to Israel. It was completely at his initiative. At the time, I had started working and didn't earn much but he offered to pay for all of us. My father's sister joined us; we had a great time. I think that being at the Western Wall was a very emotional experience for my father and his sister. My father said he had done something his father would have wished to do.

We also had our honeymoon in Israel in 2014. My wife is very supportive. She is prepared to support my Jewishness as long as I don't become a religious extremist.

I recently organised a second Chanukah party in our home for friends – just to spread the word about tradition. It's a bit funny because it's not my home tradition but something I learned from books. And I was the only Jew at the table. I think Chanukah with friends is becoming our home tradition.

Regarding conversion, I'm not sure because the main thing about conversion is believing in God. My religious outlook is that I cannot exclude the possibility of the existence of God but I don't feel or believe at the moment. So conversion right now wouldn't be genuine and I don't feel the need to convert.

HANNA OLSZEWSKA

I'm 31 years old and have lived in Warsaw all my life. My mother is Jewish while my father is Polish. I graduated in social psychology at a private university in Warsaw and I now work in the Taube Centre for the Renewal of Jewish Life in Poland.

My mother kept her Jewishness a secret until I was sixteen. At the time I was sick at home for a month; one day she said: 'I need to tell you something.' She struggled to tell me, and showed me a newspaper with a big survey of Polish attitudes to racism. Having put me through this test, and being assured that I had a positive attitude, she then revealed that I was Jewish. She felt I was adult enough to keep the secret. I was so happy and thought: 'I'm a richer person in terms of my history.' I also became more self-confident as a result of this information.

My mother was always proud of being Jewish but nonetheless feared that bad times could return. It was not only due to the Holocaust, but also because of the terrible anti-semitic campaign of 1968. Even today the memory of the events of 1968 continues to stoke her fear. Her mother was traumatised by the Holocaust, and even her best friend in primary school didn't know she was Jewish. In fact, almost no one knows about my mother's Jewish background, apart from some people on my father's side of the family whom I told. But my mother would prefer that I kept it quiet.

Although she is a left-wing atheist, she actually married in a church. I was baptised; all Polish children tend to be raised as Catholics. But I only went to church when I had my first communion. One year later I decided I wanted to be exempt from religious classes. I didn't feel connected, and always knew I was different but didn't know the reason. My mother strongly influenced my outlook and so I always had anti-religious and left-wing political opinions, which set me apart from my peers.

My father didn't want my mother to divulge the truth about my Jewish origins; he believed this information would destroy my life. In his view it was so negative to be Jewish; the whole world disliked Jews. Two years ago I had a big fight with him while on a skiing holiday with a Polish group. An old man on the lift asked me if I was planning to get married. I replied that I'm not in a hurry; it's very important that my husband is Jewish. So my father said: 'But you are only one eighth Jewish.' I replied that every Jew would agree that I am Jewish. And he countered: 'Don't you want to have your Polish roots?' I explained that I wasn't denying them but that I felt more connected to my Jewish roots. He replied: 'You will be disappointed with all this Jewish stuff.'

When I was informed of my Jewish identity, I began to search for other people who had similar experiences and background. I know a Protestant minister who discovered he was Jewish, and conducts something like a Shabbat service in his church for people who were raised as Christians. Once they found out they were Jewish, they didn't know how to respond. I went to the church and encountered some neighbours from my apartment building. They had learned they were Jewish and because they had been very committed Christians in the past, they became messianic Jews for Jesus.

Around the time that I discovered my Jewishness, I found out that my best friend in high school was Jewish too. Her mother is a child of a Holocaust survivor and this girl knew about her Jewish roots from the age of seven because it wasn't kept as a family secret. However, she was very close to her father, who was a Catholic, and didn't feel the need to discover more about her Jewish identity. Having become involved in the Jewish community, I wanted her to participate in some activities. But her feeling was that she is a Pole with Jewish roots, and can't be fully Jewish because it wouldn't be authentic. I told her that genetically I have more Polish genes than Jewish ones; yet I have always felt more Jewish in my mentality. Of course, my identity has been evolving over the past fifteen years. At first I was a Pole with Jewish roots; then I became a Jewish Pole; and now I regard myself as a Polish Jew.

I went on Taglit in 2010 and wondered how I would respond when we landed in Israel. The previous year my mother had gone to Israel for the first time and, although she didn't regard herself as a Zionist, she started to cry when the plane touched down. In the first moments after landing, I didn't feel anything; but then I started to cry and continued crying for the next two hours. I simply didn't know what to do with my emotions. Since then I have made other trips to Israel.

For most people on Taglit, the end of the trip signifies their last contact with Jewish organisations. That's why post-Taglit I got involved in *Minyanim*, a Jewish Agency programme for young people in eastern and central Europe. It's designed to get potential leaders more engaged with their Jewish communities. Every year we aim to attract some post-Taglit people to teach them how to create a programme for their community and to understand the differences between our various communities. We meet three times each year, in various locations, with people from the other countries. My involvement in minyanim proved to be the best thing in my life because I hadn't been connected previously to the Jewish community. I couldn't see myself in a religious environment while other options, like the Jewish Community Centre, didn't yet exist.

The ability to create Jewish families is a challenge and intermarriage is a problem. I had a non-Jewish boyfriend for four years and even though he was very open-minded, he couldn't understand my Jewish interest and commitment. He regarded my involvement as religious although my activities were very secular.

So I started to look on the internet for Jewish guys and met my husband, Itay, through Jewishcafe.com, a dating site similar to JDate. He is an Israeli who was living in Brussels and was studying classical guitar and wants to do a Ph.D. Although he is a Jew with family origins in Iraq and Tunisia, we share the same attitudes. Despite the distance, we managed to meet once a month. He is also the first man in my life with whom I want to have children.

After one and a half years, Itay decided to move to Poland and one year later, we were married in Israel. Rabbi Schudrich even came to Israel to conduct the marriage ceremony. For me, a Jewish marriage represents a definitive return to my Jewish roots.

As for the future, we are not sure where we might settle eventually. But, for now, we have decided to live in Poland where we have more opportunities compared to living in Israel. Having been diagnosed with multiple sclerosis, I need to live where I have access to health coverage that will ensure that I receive the appropriate medical treatment. Itay also teaches Hebrew at the Lauder School in Warsaw. Meanwhile, there are increasing numbers of people here who are overcoming the problem of Jewish partners, and finding their partners in other countries.

ŁUKASZ GODLEWSKI

I was born in Warsaw in 1982 and regard myself as part of the Third Generation.

I come from a mixed marriage. My mother is Jewish, like her mother and her grandmother, who were also in mixed marriages. However my great-grandmother's story is different because she grew up in a Catholic orphanage after her parents died around 1914. She was about ten years old at the time, and remembered certain things about her Jewish past but always hid this information. As a result, my mother was never taught anything about her Jewish background.

All three women were baptised, and each married a Polish Catholic. I was also baptised but, at around the age of ten, my parents stopped pushing me to attend religious classes or church services.

When I was 23, my Jewish roots came to light. There had already been rumours in the family about our Jewish ancestry. I was very curious to learn more, and asked my mother to talk to my grandmother. She promised she would, but was not brave enough to approach her, probably because my Polish grandfather had negative views about Jews. However, my mother had always been interested in Jewish music and literature, having read Singer's books. Sometimes she and my father went to the Jewish theatre in Warsaw.

About ten years ago a key document proving our Jewish ancestry was discovered. My grandmother's brothers had decided to investigate, and undertook genealogical research. They found the marriage certificate of my great-great-grandparents, who were married in a synagogue near Warsaw. This exciting news made my mother and myself very happy. We now possessed knowledge of what we regarded as an interesting, different family history.

This information also cast a new light on my family background. Until then I knew that my great-grandmother had spent the entire war here in Warsaw. She came from an assimilated background and, with her Aryan papers, managed to avoid being sent to the ghetto. My grandmother used to say that when my great-grandmother got upset and emotional, she would utter strange words. Later the family realised those utterances were Yiddish. In 1967, just one year before the 1968 anti-semitic campaign, my great grandmother changed her surname from Lemberger. We're not sure why she took this decision, but the atmosphere in Poland must have already been quite bad.

The primary reason for my uncles' research efforts into our family history was their desire to move to Israel. Their motivation was largely economic as they had a difficult life in Poland, with no prospects for the future. About ten years ago they went on aliyah.

I discovered a new interest in my Jewish identity and started attending Hebrew classes at the Moses Schorr Foundation, next to the Nożyk synagogue. I also took Yiddish classes at the Shalom Foundation, but Yiddish was difficult because most people in the class spoke German, unlike myself.

I took the opportunity to go on Taglit and stayed in touch with the people on our trip. It also motivated me to return to Israel in recent years to visit relatives in Haifa. I have attended meetings at Moishe House, where a small group of young people live together. Although I'm not religious at all, I have taken a class on Judaism organised by the Polin Museum. As part of the course we visited all four congregations in Warsaw, and I was most curious about the progressive Judaism as practised at Beit Warszawa. In general I'm more attracted to the regular secular events, such as concerts, parties and Boker Tov on Sundays, at the Jewish Community Centre.

Has it become fashionable in some circles to be Jewish? Yes, I have noticed that; people start to look at you differently. Others would like to kick your ass. However, I don't think Poland is more anti-semitic than most countries, but probably more so in the countryside.

As for my sister, at the outset she disapproved of our enthusiasm. She thought our changed history was unimportant, or that we shouldn't tell anyone. Now she is fine, and calmer about it. She was supportive when I told her I would like to make *aliyah* and now has a strong desire to visit Israel herself.

As for confiding in my friends, old and new, about my identity – they are relaxed about it. But friends of my parents are not; that generation is different. They don't share our feelings, and don't understand why my mother is so happy to have learned the truth. One of my mother's friends said she would rather not discover that she had Jewish origins. My father asked her why; what if you found out you were French?, he said. Her reply was that being French is very different.

While I have considered going on *aliyah*, I'm still studying to complete my Master's degree at the Warsaw School of Social Psychology where they teach cross-cultural psychology. Although I originally intended to become a psychologist, my main job as a Warsaw city guide keeps growing. I often meet Israeli tourists and last week I spent three days with an Israeli couple in Warsaw and southern Poland to visit the *shtetl* where the woman's mother was born. Today I was at the Jewish museum with a group of Polish people from Lower Silesia.

If I got married, it wouldn't necessarily be important for my wife to be Jewish. Yet I would teach my children about their Jewish identity as well as their Polish one. They should know their Jewish culture. Jews and Poles have been together for so long; our culture has been influenced by both groups. I feel very attached to Polish culture and love the Polish language.

I believe that the situation for Jews in Poland will improve as more and more people discover their roots and are prepared to explore their meaning. Despite the election of a right-wing government last year, I don't feel that anti-semitism has increased. I'm a bit scared about various policies the government is trying to implement, but they don't relate to anti-semitism.

KAMIL MARCZAK

I was born in 1988 in Tychy, Lower Silesia, which had a small Jewish community. When I was twelve we moved to Warsaw, and I eventually studied at Warsaw University where I gained a Bachelor's degree in economics and a Master's degree in quantitative finance. I currently work for Polish investment funds, where I undertake internal auditing and financial reporting.

I come from a mixed family, with a Jewish mother and a Polish father. However, my parents were agnostics and never practised any religion in our home. When we lived in Tychy, my maternal grandmother had a lot of power over the household and virtually forced me, my younger brother, and twin sister to be baptised. My grandmother had actually converted and became a Christian Zionist fanatic. Yet once we left Silesia everything changed – and it changed even more when she died. As a result, the family was quite relieved.

We never discovered the true story of how my mother's parents survived the war. We know that my grandmother had been hidden, but she was so traumatised by the Holocaust that she forbade any discussion of that period. Whenever my mother tried to ask her, my grandmother would literally beat her. Unsurprisingly, my mother's wish to name me Abram so infuriated my grandmother that she threatened to legally terminate her relationship with our family. On the other hand, because my grandparents had worked so hard to hide their origins, they easily survived the anti-semitic campaign of 1968.

At the age of fourteen I began to realise what it meant to be Jewish. I had started asking my mother about certain things: the Hebrew Torah, which we had at home, and the meaning of Purim, when my mother gave me special cookies. These were typical things that had been passed on as family tradition but without any knowledge of their origin or content. So I can't say the realisation of my Jewish identity was positive or negative; it was something natural and neutral.

As I grew up, I met other people with a similar history. It wasn't a rapid process; it evolved as I grew more and more interested in everything related to being Jewish – the culture, history, religion. I was about seventeen when I became increasingly involved in Jewish organisations in Warsaw, such as ZOOM, the youth group. ZOOM provided a good point of entry, but if you wanted to go deeper into Judaism or pursue more serious activities, you had to find another organisation.

I skipped Taglit and got involved in *Minyanim* back in 2013. That's a true leadership programme as it also taught me to accept other people's opinions. You might not agree with them, but you need to support them because they have an equal right to their views.

The idea to re-establish the pre-war Jewish sports organisation, Makabi, occurred on a *Minyanim* trip. Makabi Warszawa was a very famous pre-war Jewish sports club, which also boasted one of the best football teams in Poland. Makabi was established during the First World War, when Germany occupied Poland. The German law demanded that the trainer must be a German, yet the participants spoke in Hebrew. The German, therefore, learned Hebrew in order to take on the role of trainer. That was the history: there were a bunch of Jews, and a non-Jewish trainer. Now we have an Israeli trainer, but he is not Jewish. He is a Christian Arab.

The core concept behind Makabi is that a sports organisation is a good vehicle for bringing people together since it doesn't touch on religion or politics. I would prefer we didn't insist that members had to be 100 per cent Jewish, but rather have them explain why they would like to join a Jewish sport club. Because of this approach, we have already attracted non-Jewish members and others who have discovered they are partly Jewish.

While I have largely chosen to go down the secular route in reclaiming my identity, I often participate in Shabbat services and attend one of the various synagogues on every major holiday. It's like the old Jewish joke about three synagogues: the one I go to on Shabbat, the one I attend on major holidays, and the one I never enter. So it could be either the Orthodox Nożyk synagogue or the Reform Eitz Chaim, but it wouldn't be the one run by Chabad.

Once I resolved my identity, I invited my non-Jewish friends to Shabbat at our home to impart some idea of Judaism. Furthermore my sister and I forced our parents to host a Chanukah party on two occasions; lots of non-Jews were invited. That's the easiest way to introduce Polish people to a Jewish holiday. My mother is happy that my sister and I are leading an active life in the Jewish community, but she also worries that our activities could expose us to anti-semitism. After a favourable article about Makabi was published in the leading daily paper, *Gazeta Wyborcza*, where our names were mentioned, some terrible comments appeared below the internet version of the article. They claimed we were creating a Zionist organisation in Poland and trying to take over the country, as we apparently had in the past. I was personally threatened a few times by anonymous idiots.

There is a serious problem with Jewish organisations in Poland due to their inability to manage their finances. We have become very used to receiving financial aid from foreign sources. However, in Makabi, we wanted to set a different example by implementing financial transparency. Moreover, we are aiming to ensure that half of our expenses are covered by members' fees.

I've never felt personally affected by anti-semitism. I believe that anti-semitic behaviour is not necessarily caused by an ideology; it's purely simple ignorance. People need to be taught what it means to hold these views. At music festivals, when I heard people shouting anti-semitic comments, I talked to them and they said they didn't intend to cause offence. Some even said they could easily switch to yelling 'stupid Gypsies' instead.

You must understand how traumatised my family is. My mother told us we have family in Israel, people who escaped from the train to Auschwitz. My family hid their Jewish identity so severely that they ignored the existence of the Israeli family.

I have visited Israel a number of times, and considered going on *aliyah*. But I don't want to be another guy who comes to Israel and asks the government for support. That's why I first want to gain a lot of experience that would be useful in Israel, and be able to finance myself through my work.

We are the third generation that is shaking off the trauma of the Holocaust that our grandparents – and even our parents – carried with them. We are far more comfortable than previous generations in expressing our Jewish identity. At the same time I don't believe in the Orthodox or Conservative approach, which insists that you must find a Jewish partner to maintain a Jewish life in Poland. We have a young community of people who have some kind of Jewish identity, as well as a lot of energy to develop something positive. We expect our community to grow.

OLGA LEWIŃSKA

I was born and raised in Kraków and I'm studying psychology at Jagiellonian University. My paternal grandfather was Jewish but not religious; he left the family to go to the United States when my father was only six or seven years old. My grandmother was not Jewish and didn't want to have anything to do with Jewishness. My own mother is Polish, which means I'm not a halachic Jew.

When I was a child we celebrated Christmas, although my parents were atheists. I didn't attend religious classes in school. Although I wasn't baptised, my mother insisted I should be christened. My father opposed the idea, and didn't attend the ceremony.

My father told me he has some knowledge of what happened to his father's family during the war, but feels very uncomfortable talking about it. When my father was around 40 years old, he tried to make contact with his father after a a gap of 25 years. After writing to him for a year, my grandfather finally replied. That connection triggered my father's interest in his Jewish roots. It was also around the time that the Jewish Community Centre (JCC) was set up in Kraków, which helped my father to engage with other Jewish people. He became more involved in Jewish matters, and this proved to be the most important part of his life.

Initially he started to attend the Izaak synagogue on Shabbat, and gradually became more observant. Two years later he went to Israel for three weeks with Shavei Israel. Upon his return to Poland, he became even more Orthodox. And yesterday, because it was Shavuot, he spent the night at the synagogue (studying the Torah). He also works as the manager of the Olive Tree kosher restaurant which provides catering for tourist groups from Israel. The restaurant's chef is a rabbi from Israel.

I don't fear anti-semitism but my father had some unpleasant encounters. Now that he is religious, he has a very big beard and wears a *kippah* under his hat because it's not a good idea to walk around openly with a *kippah* in Poland. Sometimes he gets unfriendly stares, but the atmosphere is increasingly growing more tolerant.

In 2012, I went on a Shavei Israel trip with other Polish Jews, most of whom were not halachically Jewish. Previously I was very interested in Jewish culture, but the religion seemed distant. However, after five minutes in Jerusalem, I really started to connect with the place. Those two weeks in Israel were quite amazing and encouraged me to think a little bit about religious aspects. Yet, because I grew up without God, I'm still not sure what that means exactly, although I feel He is somewhere. I now try to celebrate the holidays, and sometimes go to the Kupa or Izaak synagogues to do so. Occasionally I attend Shabbat dinner at the JCC.

On my second trip to Israel in 2013, I stayed on kibbutz Shefayim. I wanted to experience Israel in a way that was not necessarily religious. And that proved to be really worthwhile.

As my father's life has greatly changed, my parents are getting divorced – despite my father's attempts to reach a compromise with my mother.

My younger brother, who is seventeen, is interested in Judaism. He sometimes goes with my father to synagogue on Jewish holidays, and occasionally attends Sunday school at the JCC. He also wants to wear a *kippah* to school. I am opposed to this because kids in the gymnasium may not be very tolerant. When I was in high school my classmates knew I worked at the JCC, and were very curious about my Jewish interests. But they were older and more mature.

Since we started having public Jewish events, like the Kazimierz Jewish cultural festival, people are more knowledgeable about Jews and understand that being Jewish also has cultural dimensions.

A few years ago we held the first open synagogue night in Kraków. We were prepared for a small crowd, but around 6,000 people came from early evening to the small hours. At one synagogue about 1,000 people queued to enter for at least half an hour.

Because the Jewish community here is still relatively small, it remains difficult to find a Jewish partner. I used to live with my Polish boyfriend but, after my last trip to Israel, I broke up with him because he had a problem with Jewish people. For example, at Chanukah I wanted to light candles but he said he wouldn't allow it in our house. He couldn't explain why he objected to it, so I lit the candles anyhow. I'm now with a guy from Bielsko-Biała whose father probably has Jewish roots, but he doesn't know anything about his background. His brother wanted to confirm their Jewishness but couldn't find any documents proving their Jewish origins.

I feel Jewish but need more time to decide whether or not to go through the conversion process. At the same time I feel *really* Polish, and think it's normal to feel both Polish and Jewish. After all, my family has lived in Poland for centuries.

IZABELA (IZA) WOJNAROWICZ

I discovered I was Jewish when I was six or seven years old. Because I always had a dark complexion and hair, children would laugh at me and call me 'Gypsy'. In Poland this is a very pejorative word. I would run to my grandmother in tears. Finally she said: 'We are not Gypsies; we are Jews.' I asked what that meant and she explained that every Friday we sit together at the Shabbat table; and she described other Jewish customs and traditions.

I was not shocked by this news because my grandmother told me we were a special, chosen nation and ought to be proud of our traditions. I also learned Yiddish as a child because I often heard my grandparents speaking it if they didn't want me to understand their conversation. But, like many children, I very quickly picked up the language.

After learning about my Jewish identity, I told my best friend – but very confidentially. Yet within two days the whole school knew. It wasn't pleasant; they mocked me and tried to beat me. However, since I was very strong and tall, I fought back. In high school, I was too embarrassed to tell anyone. I met some twins there who were Jewish, and saw they had terrible problems with the other kids. I'm still ashamed that I didn't tell anyone I was Jewish.

I was raised by my grandparents, who were survivors of Auschwitz; my parents left me in 1974 when I was two weeks old. So although I belong to the third generation, I was brought up like a second generation child.

I grew up in Wieluń, in central Poland, where my grandfather lived before the war; he returned because of his very fond pre-war memories. My grandmother came from a very Orthodox family, while my grandfather rejected religion after losing so many family members and friends.

When I was six years old my parents returned and took me to live in Tychy, near Katowice, in Silesia. But I felt very distant from them, and was very rebellious; my grandparents had to come and live with us. When I was sixteen, my parents moved to Germany and I was left behind in Poland with my grandparents.

I graduated in Law and Economics from the University of Silesia in Katowice. I also won a fellowship to study at Queen Mary's College at the University of London, where I graduated in English Literature and History. Afterwards I returned to live in Tychy with my son and my Jewish husband, but he didn't want to pursue a Jewish life nor did he allow me to celebrate Shabbat or the holidays. He would say: 'Let's live like Polish people.' I told him I'm not only Polish but also a Polish Jew, and have to find an identity which combines both backgrounds. Due to my great love for my grandparents, I want to celebrate all our traditions because a nation without traditions will die.

As I didn't hide my Jewish identity in Tychy, many bad things happened to me. On several occasions someone daubed a swastika on my house and wrote: 'Juden Raus'. The situation was terrible because I was not only trying to run a substantial business, but also had cancer. My business partner cheated me out of my money; one day I found myself with nothing. When my car was burnt I decided to leave Tychy, move to Kraków, and start an internet business.

My current husband was raised as a Catholic although his paternal grandmother was Jewish. When we met, he became very interested in Jewish culture and the holidays. He was also very supportive because when I arrived in Kraków, following my traumatic experiences in Silesia, I was afraid to reveal I was Jewish to anyone outside our home. But he assured me: 'Don't worry. I love you and I will always protect you.'

Recently we met with close friends who are both well educated and have Ph.Ds in biology. When my husband mentioned that he was thinking of converting to Judaism, the friend started to scream: 'Are you crazy? You will be like a monkey in the tree. Besides, you know that Jews steal from the goyim according to the laws of the Torah.' I was in a state of shock, although they didn't know I was Jewish. My husband was absolutely furious, and we don't see those people any more.

Despite that unpleasant experience, living in Kraków after Silesia is like being in another country. Here I feel at home at last. The Jewish Community Centre has played a vital role, helping me to meet so many Jewish people. My little daughter goes to the kindergarten run by Chabad and attends Sunday School, *Unzere Kinder,* which is led by our Czulent Jewish Association. Things are also changing among young Polish people who are more open-minded and generally don't carry the same prejudices as older Polish people.

Today I regard myself as a Jew with Polish roots, but essentially more Jewish than Polish. I was in Israel on many occasions, and now sometimes feel like a stranger in Poland. Yet in Israel I also felt like a stranger. When people in Israel learn you are from Poland, they inevitably say: 'What are you doing there? Poles are anti-semites; it's in their blood.'

I've tried to raise my son as a Polish Jew. That means he knows about all the Polish traditions – even though we don't have a Christmas tree nor Easter eggs. He doesn't want to be a Catholic, but is still exploring whether he wants to be Jewish or neutral. I'm really happy today, however, because he told me he wants to come to Shabbat dinner. That means I brought him up well.

JUSTYNA SZPANOWSKA

Although my mother is herself not Jewish, she told me the truth about my Jewish relatives when I was twelve or thirteen years old. I had not known until then that my paternal grandmother was a child survivor of the Holocaust. These disclosures coincided with the time when I moved from primary school to gymnasium (secondary school). There we were taught about various religions and some basic sociology. This encouraged me to ask questions about the Jews and what happened to them. That discussion persuaded my mother it was the right time to speak.

I wasn't really shocked at this revelation about my background, probably because I didn't grasp the full importance at the time. I had no idea that someone could hate me simply because of my Jewish origins; furthermore I felt one hundred per cent Polish. Yet many people, when told you have Jewish roots, will insist you cannot call yourself Polish.

Yet I was very happy, and felt it was special to belong to the chosen people. I became more curious about Judaism and Jewish culture. When I announced the news to a few of my classmates, some thought it was very cool, while others responded in a very mean way. In Polish the word 'Jew' can sound like a curse or a bad word. But I fought back, while my mother told me not to worry about those comments of prejudice. Ironically, my maternal grandmother often uttered remarks that could easily be regarded as anti-semitic, but I would attribute her words more to a lack of education than racism.

My mother believes everyone should be aware of their origins; I think she slightly regrets she isn't Jewish herself. That's why she contacted you to arrange this interview when she saw the notice about your book. For her, being Jewish revolves mostly around culture and history. She feels that the Holocaust is something we should all remember, and therefore strive to make the world a better place.

My paternal grandmother was a teenager when she discovered her Jewishness. Her adoptive mother, who was dying, felt compelled to reveal that she had been a child rescued during the Holocaust. My grandmother suffered greatly because of the Holocaust; unfortunately, I never managed to get close to her. She was not religious at all and only marginally connected to the Jewish community. At around the age of 50, she applied to Yad Vashem to have her adoptive parents acknowledged with a Righteous Gentile award. Yet when she died two years ago, we still didn't have many details about her past. She never acquired much knowledge about her Jewish family history.

Prior to going on Taglit, I went to a few meetings at both the Jewish Community Centre and ZOOM as well as attending Jewish summer and winter camps. At one summer camp in Hungary, run by the American Jewish Joint Distribution Committee, I experienced my first *Shabbes* during which I cried a lot. The singing touched something very profound in me. I realised that Judaism is so full of emotions and being together with other Jews is very important.

My father was aware of his mother's Jewish past since he was a teenager, but hadn't felt strongly connected to it. He has attended a few meetings of the Second Generation and occasionally went to gatherings of Holocaust survivors when his mother was still alive.

Despite his Jewish lineage, he agreed to have my sister and myself baptised. In Poland it is as natural as washing your baby at birth. My baptism was partly influenced by my maternal grandmother who was ill in the hospital when I was born, but had requested that a baptism take place. Fortunately, that attitude towards baptism is changing in Poland. There is a growing number of children whose parents have chosen not to baptise them.

I went on Taglit a few years ago and loved it. Although I was aware of the strong message they were trying to get across, my only regret is that we didn't have an opportunity to talk to any Palestinians. The other participants on the trip were a varied group of young Poles. Some were afraid to tell their Polish friends they were going to Israel, and claimed it only involved a trip to Egypt. For example two sisters from Kielce, a traditionally anti-semitic city, didn't tell their friends about their Israeli trip because they knew they would encounter disapproval.

Last year I spent two months working as a nanny for a British family in Herzlia and Tel Aviv. It proved to be a wonderful experience and I'm convinced I would be happier living in Israel. The political situation in Poland is very worrying, reflected by a rise in anti-semitism. In the last election, I became very involved with Razem ('Together'), a new left-wing political party. But this nationalist government scares me and I often feel that I want to move abroad.

After a period of illness, I'm now making plans with my fiancé for the future. He is a non-practising Catholic but, like many Poles, cannot be sure whether he has any Jewish family roots. Although he visited me in Israel and liked the country, he still wants to have a church wedding. While I'm very angry with the Polish church, I may agree so long as I could choose the wording of the wedding ceremony.

ANDRZEJ JANKOWSKI

I was born in Warsaw in 1985 and belong to the Third Generation.

Somehow my grandfather was not forced to leave the country in 1968. He began to speak a few years before his death, so we managed to record many of his testimonies. But this issue is still mysterious to us. Most likely he had some powerful friends. Previously he worked as a clerk at the Communist Party headquarters. He wasn't anyone important, but he was close to important people. In 1968 they moved him to the National Bank, which means he was pushed sideways.

Before the war he was a communist sympathiser in Łódź. He was of bourgeois origins from a family that was quite wealthy. As often happens in such cases all three sons were leftists. His oldest brother, who inspired him, was also a kind of Trotskyist. The older brother had escaped from the Germans and was in the Soviet Union. He found shelter in Lwów but he wasn't in the Gulag.

My grandfather, who was much younger, was not involved but those were his sympathies. When the war broke out, he was mobilised by the Polish army to defend Warsaw. He spent a year in Poland, and then followed his brother to Lwów, where they tried to bring the rest of the family. Łódź was part of the Reich, so it was more difficult to escape. Then the war with Germany broke out. My grandfather joined the Komsomol and probably owes his life to that decision. As a member of the Komsomol he was evacuated to the Urals in the Soviet Union. The two other brothers were killed in Lwów.

My grandfather made friends with a lady who happened to be the sister of my grandmother. Once the front line started to move west, he was able to visit her family in Kiev and met his future wife (my grandmother).

He returned to Poland with his wife, who was Jewish. They were *shtetl* people. They first settled in Lower Silesia in the town of Wałbrzych. He worked there for the trade unions; they lived there for a few years. Later he got a party job in Warsaw and lived there until his death. My mother was born in 1953.

The children were not told about their Jewishness. They knew about the family in the Soviet Union but thought of them as Russians. I think they knew something, but in a vague, intuitive way. They knew they were different in some way, but didn't consciously acknowledge this.

The prominent Jewish Communists often moved in their circles. Their friends were Jewish, even though they didn't care about their Jewish backgrounds or identities. So my grandfather was surrounded by Polish Jewish Communists. They lived in Mokotów.

They had a Christmas tree in the house but without a star on top. It wasn't a Catholic upbringing. My grandfather developed his own identity as a Polish Communist. Perhaps he had already developed this identity during the war because the Russians saved his life.

My mother felt Polish, but at the same time she represented a minority. Bear in mind that the committed Communists were a minority in this country. She was baptised in order to have a Catholic marriage with my father. She needed to collect the three sacraments in a Catholic church. She needed to get baptised, to have a holy communion.

We, the children, were raised as Catholics and we were baptised. The Jewish issue appeared in the family at the time of my parents' divorce in 1993. I also have an older sister who was born in 1977. She was a teenager when my parents divorced, and was the one who asked questions and went on the first Polish-Israeli student exchange which was arranged with her school.

My parents divorced when I was nine years old. The first time I heard about being Jewish was when my sister provoked my mother into having a discussion. And my mother admitted she was Jewish. It was an accident that my sister went to Israel in 1993; it wasn't at her initiative but it opened up the subject.

My mother reluctantly admitted the truth. It was very bad news for me. I knew from the courtyard what the word Jew means in Polish society. Jew means someone who is weak or greedy or not trustworthy. I didn't know it was a nationality, more like a label. I used the word to offend someone when I was a little kid. Then my mother told me I am Jewish and I thought: 'What the hell is going on?' It was a horrible shock.

My parents lived in Wola, a working class district in Warsaw. When they divorced, my father started a relationship with another lady and didn't keep in touch. My mother, sister and I started to make contact with the community and to attend Jewish events. It was the beginning of the Lauder Foundation in Poland, with Jewish camps and so on. We jumped into this stream of Jewish revival.

My mother became involved possibly because she was emotionally wrecked after the divorce. She met a group of people, many of whom had a complex identity and didn't know how to ask questions. So she met similar people of her kind, and also many people who were helpful.

The Jewish organisational approach works very well. When the Lauder Foundation came into Poland to organise Jewish life, they did it effectively; they helped to organise life for people in circumstances like my mother who had suffered unemployment. She did have some jobs before she started to work as a librarian in the Jewish school, but those were on much worse terms and conditions. At the same time that she began working within the Jewish community, I became a student at Lauder Morasha school. I started there when I was eleven years old. At the time it taught students until the end of high school. However, my class was the last one in the old system. I spent four years at Lauder and it changed my attitude towards my Jewishness completely.

As for the truth about my Jewishness, I remember I shared this information in secret with my close friends. I understood I was walking on very unsteady ground because it was a very different time – it was the start of the 1990s when there was a very different social atmosphere in Poland. I was in a regular Polish school where few people knew about Jews. My attitude changed completely when I changed schools; I decided to leave my primary school for the Lauder school.

After high school I studied sociology and then worked for many years. Now I'm studying history at weekends, but in the external system of Warsaw University.

As for my sister, she was the most courageous and committed among us. She was in her late teens when her family fell apart and she wanted to establish her life on a rock, not on sand dunes. At the beginning she was just very curious – it was something that interested her. She had this feeling of mystery.

Things moved very rapidly after she found out because she moved to Israel after passing her high school matriculation. In the two years following her discovery of her Jewish roots, she made a radical decision to live a Jewish life. It's also a question of age and of life's baggage. I was a little kid, about nine years old. My sister was very unhappy with our family life and became a rebellious teenager. She then received this information about us; and she had nothing to lose. She didn't feel there was a strong, stable foundation in our family life because our parents got divorced. So she was looking for something more solid and greater. And the Jews provided that.

She lived in Israel for five years. Originally she planned to stay there forever, but then came the second intifada and she wanted more security. She went to London to study Biblical Hebrew and Jewish theology at UCL where she got her B.A.

She then returned to Poland; about three years ago she met her husband and had a son. She is working at the Jewish Historical Institute but spends more time with the Taube Centre for Jewish research and genealogy. They are offering the programme Mi Dor Le Dor (From Generation to Generation). She is running a year's programme; each programme has its leader who organises the schedule and discussions and meets people. That's her role there.

My mother had more of a secular Polish identity in the way she was brought up. She knew many Jewish people and she visited her Jewish family in the Soviet Union because my grandmother was from the Ukraine. Those people were Jewish and she had this feeling that she had a special connection with these people and belonged to a distinctive group. But I think an awareness of being Jewish was more in the subconscious layer; she never developed a strong Jewish identity.

At the moment I'm also working for the Jewish community of Warsaw. I'm an assistant to the board and do various tasks to make other people's life easier.

Being Jewish in Poland is quite relaxed now, but there are times when I feel uncomfortable. For example, I went on a trip recently with students from my school about the history of architecture. We visited churches and palaces, and several times I had to reproach someone who spoke badly about Jews. I had to tell them I felt uncomfortable. It was not a situation I had confronted for a long time. I have been living within a circle of people with whom I was never afraid. So I had to leave my comfort zone. As it turned out, it was a case of someone repeating some stereotype; it wasn't very anti-Jewish. Once in a while it's very uncomfortable and makes me ask questions about how much I know the country I live in; how much I live in an isolated bubble.

As for being involved in religious congregations, I am not. I'm becoming increasingly interested in the spiritual life but don't feel affiliated with any religion. From time to time I go to synagogue for Shabbat or Purim or Yom Kippur. At Purim there is a ball; it's more like a community event. Although I go to synagogue sometimes, I'm a secular person; but it doesn't mean I don't have religious questions. I'm a seeker, I would like to learn much more because I have a feeling that I don't have a deep knowledge.

I went on Taglit in 2005 and it was both a good and bad experience. It was certainly an intense experience. You encounter strong propaganda. For people of the first post-Communist generation in Poland the narrative sold to us was not very convincing, like making the desert bloom and all those slogans, the lack of criticism. Later I discovered Israelis are often much more critical of their country and its policies. Taglit offered us a very simple message and we don't like simple messages or propaganda.

As for Polish Jewry having a positive future, although there is a feeling that it's flourishing, there is a lack of numbers. But changing my life completely just for the privilege of finding a Jewish partner and maintaining Jewishness in my family sounds absurd to me. I feel very Polish. At the same time, I have a feeling that if I fell in love with a non-Jewish person, then there is a possibility that the Jewish line in my family will disappear.

However, there are few Jewish girls around. When you live in Israel or New York this question is not so sharp; it's not a question of life or death for your community. But here it is.

PAULA TONDER

I was born in Wrocław in 1996 and raised here. My half brother and I share the same father, whose mother was Jewish. So we both have Jewish roots. As my father was baptised and my mother is Polish Catholic, I was also baptised and grew up in a Christian household.

My grandmother was born in Lwów to a Polish father and Jewish mother. The family was sent to the ghetto in Tarnopol, apart from her father. He realised he must rescue as many members of the family as he could. In 1942 he managed to get my grandmother and her mother out of the ghetto, and found them shelter with a Polish woman, Urszula Pakuła, in Stanisławów. There his wife, my great grandmother, was shot by the Gestapo. My grandmother, who was still a baby, was hidden by the Polish woman until 1945. She took care of her, and then married her father. My grandmother was about two years old. She did not recall her early life, but occasionally had flashes of memory which she tried to ignore. She was baptised in Stanisławów in August 1944, and brought up Catholic. For many years she was unaware that the woman raising her was not her real mother.

My great-grandfather forbade his wife to tell the truth to the child. When he died, the Polish woman, Urszula Pakuła, felt the need to divulge the family story. She thought my grandmother had to know about her real mother. You were in the ghetto, she said, I rescued you. My grandmother was 45 years old at the time. She was shocked. But she had nursed suspicions for some time, and was not convinced that the woman who raised her was her real mother. She'd also had flashes of memory from the past, which she couldn't grasp. When she discovered the truth, she began to search for family survivors during the 1980s, but didn't find any.

Before I was born, my grandmother and her Polish husband made *aliyah* (to Israel). I don't know the reason for this. They spent up to five years in Israel.

By the time I was born, my grandmother was back in Poland and I knew nothing about the period in Israel.

After the death of my grandparents, my father decided to throw out a lot of possessions they had accumulated. Although I was only eight years old, I opposed his decision. I decided I would sift through my grandmother's belongings, and keep what I wanted. And that was how I found an Israeli passport with strange letters that was issued in October 1994.

I asked my father why my grandmother had a passport different to mine. But he didn't know many details; my grandmother hadn't talked about it very much. Over the years I nagged my father to explain more about the family background, but he didn't want to talk about his Jewish origins. In part this was because his parents never told him the details of her history. Nevertheless, the discovery of the passport and some of my grandmother's letters was a key moment. I felt there was another dimension apart from our Christian identity. While the realisation was exciting, I was disappointed that my grandmother hadn't told me about it, and that everyone had hid it from me. I was angry that I did not have the opportunity to talk about it with my grandmother. She was the best source, and she was gone. They didn't tell my father the details; even her husband knew only a little bit. She knew a lot, and that's it. I have had to search and think about the meaning of this. It's not so simple.

In high school, we were assigned a project to create our family tree. So I dug out all the documents and managed to trace the lineage as far back as my great-great-grandparents. I also went to the Jewish Historical Institute in Warsaw where I received help from a girl from Wrocław who was working on the JHI's genealogical project.

Ten years after the discovery of the passport, I went to speak with a social worker who had cared for my grandmother under the auspices of the Jewish social care services. If she had been eligible to be looked after by this care system, she probably had to prove that she was Jewish. The social worker confirmed this by showing me some relevant documents, including my grandmother's life story and another document confirming that she and her family had been in the ghetto.

At that point, I developed a strong interest in Judaism. Since I also wanted to go to the synagogue, a friend of my father's, who had converted to Judaism, offered to take me for my first service when I was about eighteen. He made the experience easier as he explained the appropriate behaviour during the prayers. After that occasion I began attending synagogue regularly. I also discovered that my grandmother would go to Jewish community events. Once, when I was at the synagogue on Rosh Hashanah, an old woman told me: 'Alicia Tonder, I knew her!' It was fantastic to learn that people in the community had known her.

As for my family, it's very complicated. My father is curious and would like to come for Shabbat services. But he doesn't want to abandon the faith he was brought up in. My mother, and my grandmother in particular, don't want to hear about all this. In previous years, my mother yelled that I shouldn't go to synagogue; that I had been baptised. I haven't even spoken to my grandfather for half a year because of this dispute. I think they are mostly worried that I might convert to Judaism. Fortunately, my mother is starting to get used to the idea that I am increasingly attached to the Jewish community and has become less hostile.

I've become involved with the community in various ways. Despite the demands from my work and social life, I try to join Shabbat services as much as possible. Two years ago I went to Israel with Taglit, which proved to be a very good experience. There are also Shabbatons every couple of months for Taglit alumni in Wrocław. When you start coming to the various events, it can be intimidating. But, over time, I've become more confident.

If I should plan to raise a Jewish family, I will need to undergo a conversion. But even if I don't convert, I don't want to neglect my Jewish identity. After all, you don't have to be halachically Jewish if you just want to participate in the community.

Esther Fuerster

I was born in Lublin, where my mother was studying medicine, but raised in Rzeszów. I am 30 years old. My maternal grandmother was Jewish, which means my mother is also halachically Jewish. My father is a Nigerian who came to Poland on a government-sponsored student exchange programme to study agrarian economics. He met and married my mother, and although he was forced to return for some time to Nigeria as his student visa had expired, he eventually moved to Poland permanently and became a citizen.

My grandmother survived the war, helped largely by the fact that she was very assimilated into Polish society. After the war she decided against raising my mother with a Jewish identity.

I was baptised in the Catholic church; my mother felt it was generally safer to baptise all children. As we were quite a secular family which didn't attend church, the baptism occurred at night – almost so that no one would witness it. Although my father later objected to my taking communion, my mother insisted – once again – that it would be the better option.

When I was aged seventeen my mother, during a conversation about the family, disclosed our Jewish background. On this occasion, in the midst of an argument, she grew very agitated and said: 'This problem is all because your grandmother was Jewish.' I was surprised and didn't really know what she meant. At the time, I wasn't aware you were Jewish as a result of your maternal lineage. Following her outburst, my mother told me to forget what she had revealed. 'It only causes problems and we don't need that', she said.

In retrospect, I'm really grateful that my Jewish identity was hidden at that time. If I knew everything about my identity, I don't think I could have coped very well with both the race issue as well as the Jewish background. Although

I thought I didn't experience much racism as a youngster in Rzeszów, my mother told me it was only because she continually protected me. Apparently racist incidents occurred on almost a weekly basis. So if I had known I was also Jewish, it would have been quite a load to carry. I was also known by my Nigerian name, Ese, when I lived in Poland.

I wasn't aware of any other Jewish people in Rzeszów when I lived there. The synagogue has been restored and part of the building was converted into an art gallery. In the park, which used to be a Jewish mass grave, a memorial stone was erected around eight years ago. There is also a Jewish cemetery that survived the war. There was a ghetto in Rzeszów during the war, but I only learned about this six years ago as a result of my own research. To this day nothing has been taught in the school curriculum in Rzeszów about the Holocaust.

When I was nineteen my parents sent me to Britain to attend university. I graduated with a B.A. and an M.A. in London as well as a diploma in Public Service Interpreting. In the meantime, I became acquainted with various individuals who helped me to gradually become more and more religious.

I got to know people at Chabad and also started attending shul regularly or going to the Jewish Learning Exchange in Golders Green. I began to meet amazing people with whom I became friendly. But since I couldn't find any family documents to prove that I was halachically Jewish, I went to the Beth Din in London and, after meeting with the Dayan, decided I would have to undergo the whole conversion process. I'm really surprised at how many Polish people are in a similar situation. Often they were born to Jewish parents, or to a Jewish father and a non-Jewish mother, and have the same problem producing family documents.

As I grew increasingly religious, my mother became less secretive about her own identity. She also became more comfortable about the path I have chosen, and once proudly announced: 'My daughter even goes to an orthodox shul.' While my mother grew increasingly open about our heritage and my spiritual journey, my father initially felt quite uneasy because, I assume, this is not what he imagined would happen in our family. On a return visit home about three years ago, everyone behaved awkwardly around me. I realised there was no one to speak to. I certainly didn't wear my Magen David while moving around town.

I came to the decision that I didn't want to build my life either in Poland or England. I went to Israel on the government-sponsored Masa programme, which brings young Jewish people to Israel for volunteering work. I spent ten months in Beersheba, where I taught English in a primary religious school. I immediately felt at home in Israel although life can be quite difficult, particularly the bureaucracy. So I started my own blog as a means of addressing the challenges I face in Israel. It has proven to be quite successful. It's funny that in Poland I'm regarded as a mixed-race Polish Jewess, but in Israel people seem to be confused by my looks, my origin and my accent.

I've attended a Chabad seminary in Jerusalem and have recently completed the conversion process with the Beth Din in London. Meanwhile my parents have visited me here, and my mother now loves Israel. Even my father, who was very much against my decision at the outset, is interested to understand what I am learning and and why I am enthusiastic about Israel. Having finally appreciated what it means to live as an Israeli, I have taken the opportunity to officially make *aliyah* and I'm now working for the Ministry of Justice.

ERYK KOWALSKI

I have two citizenships, Polish and German, but I didn't live in Germany. My paternal grandfather came from there; he was forced to return to Poland when Polish Jews were evicted from Germany in the 1930s. They had their citizenships removed as well. It was like a one-way passport.

The family survived the war in Russia. They returned to Poland after the war and encountered some issues with former neighbours in the place they came from, a small town in southern Poland. The Polish people were very unhappy to see former Jewish residents return. The Poles said they weren't going to give them back their property. There was no governmental structure at that time or security forces to enforce order. So my family decided to move on.

Why did they stay in Poland? That's a good question. However, I know some members of my family were already involved here as Communists. There were empty cities in the west of Poland which were formerly German lands. People could obtain fine unoccupied houses. There was a huge incentive to go there. So my family moved into a German house in Szczecin. I was born outside Szczecin in August 1990 and spent the first years of my life there. My family stayed in north-west Poland, partly in Szczecin and others in small places outside the city. It was easier to assume a new identity.

I moved to Warsaw because I like big cities. I will finish my university studies in about a year; I already work and combine the two. I'm studying law at the University of Warsaw, and also quantitative economics at the Warsaw School of Economics. I already have a BA and have finished my MA studies as well; I just have to defend my thesis.

My economics studies are designed to allow me to support myself. I have some experience in the world of consulting, and I'm currently working for Procter & Gamble in a department called in-house consultancy.

My parents were not Communists at all although my grandparents were sympathetic. My father, however, was involved in the anti-Communist movement.

My father is very ambitious. He is both an engineer and a lawyer and works in both areas. He has developed some patents. He runs an engineering company and is also doing some legal consulting. My mother is a history teacher and used to teach at a private university in Bydgoszcz where my parents now live. Bydgoszcz is a centre for the kind of economic activity that my father is involved in. Some global players are based there.

I come from a very secular background. As for being Jewish, I always knew, it wasn't a secret. My father is not Jewish, but Catholic. He has a Jewish background – his father was Jewish – but not his mother. My mother is fully Jewish. It's good to have some balance; I'm immersed in both the Jewish and non-Jewish worlds.

My mother is secular but my father had me baptised. Most Jews are baptised. Do some regard it as a kind of insurance policy? Exactly. But I grew up in a very secular background. Being baptised as well may sound very contradictory. It was never a problem to combine both aspects of my background. So being Jewish was always like being part of my family's history.

Nevertheless, I preferred not to reveal that my family was Jewish. I didn't want to be identified with Jews. There is a scepticism toward Jews among Polish people, and I think it's on a subconscious level. Polish people are not exposed to Jewish culture at all. So there are statements embedded in the language like: 'Don't be a Jew' or 'Don't Jew me out of the money'. It's something we should get rid of but I wouldn't regard it as full-scale anti-semitism.

In my last year of high school, I revealed my background to a few friends. At this time, I was already involved in rediscovering this past. As a young person, I was looking for some intellectual room for development and the whole Jewish scene seemed a nice place to do so.

My friends were interested, curious. I sort of lived in a bubble in the sense that I attended an elite high school, the best high school in a city of half a million people: children of the intelligentsia. So I didn't experience any hostile reactions.

The constructive period began when I moved to Warsaw for my studies. I was nineteen years old.

I had to find new friends and was open to new experiences. It was like a *carte blanche*. Going to the Polish Jewish youth organisation, like ZOOM, you are welcome by the mere fact that you are Jewish.

In Poland, Jews often come from more privileged families with some more interesting backgrounds and professions and there is an atmosphere of intellectual sophistication. Those aspects drew me into this world and these were the kinds of experiences I was seeking.

I had a kind of Jewish hunger. There was a sort of Jewish spirit that drove me to perhaps grow in terms of Jewish knowledge. It was intellectually compelling and offered spiritual improvement as well. There is a form of intellectual engagement which makes you see beyond what meets the eye. I went on Taglit to Israel as well as participating in other programmes.

At a certain moment, I realised this whole world revolves around religion. I come from a Jewish house with some Communist background, so to me it was obvious that we can be fine as Jews without religion. But now that I've been exposed to the Jewish world, I've realised that it all boils down to the religion which is the backbone of the whole system.

I've also taken part in a few lectures delivered by different rabbis. I felt it was intellectually attractive. Not only some story, but in every generation you have a layer of commentaries and disputes and discussions and each generation has contributed their own interpretation.

So I realised it is my heritage which I can profit from. This is the heritage we are entitled to - like our heritage from our parents. It's like a collective ownership. So let's investigate what it actually is – what can help one grow, what can give a certain set of skills which would be helpful in all areas of life, whether personal or professional. That's how I became closer to religion.

It reached its peak when I went to a yeshiva in Vienna, because I speak fluent German. We don't have this kind of infrastructure in Poland. All our yeshivas ceased to function in 1939. It's a shame because we were one of the most important centres for yeshiva study in the world.

I went to Vienna in July 2013 for eight months after applying for an exchange with an economics university in Vienna. I lived at the yeshiva and most of the time was dedicated to Torah and Talmud studies. But one a half days a week I attended some lectures at the university. It was a Litvak yeshiva, very Orthodox. I kept all the rules and I still have my funny hat. It was a really nice part of my life.

Did I find it very constricting? It was my choice, so I could leave at any time. I therefore didn't feel constrained. I always perceived it as a phase, as an interesting journey into the Orthodox world, to taste it and then come back. It was like a journey abroad into a a brave new world. I was happy with my decision because most people of my background will never have this kind of experience. This religious life resembles a trance in which you become very peaceful and very quiet and start seeing the world in a different perspective.

As for my parents' reaction, they trust me. They know I am resistant to propaganda, and said: whatever makes you happy. When visiting my parents I conform to their lifestyle. I'm not fully Orthodox. I'm traditional and cherish Jewish traditions and I try to keep *Shabbes*. I'm somewhere on the way. My parents perceive it as an interesting hobby. I'm still not sure where I'm heading, but I'm happy with this set of values.

Regarding synagogue, I go almost every day to *daven*. I come here at 7:00 AM for Shacharit. Then I go to work. Sometimes we don't have a minyan but 80 per cent of the time it's not a problem. It's an important part of my life.

Unfortunately, this is a very small community, and not just for the Orthodox. In the Warsaw *kehilla* we have 600 members. My realistic assessment is that we have 3,000 Jews in Warsaw who at least have some halachic background. We all come from assimilated families; so it's all reconstruction, there is no continuity. Therefore, it's a very weak community. We're ethnically mixed.

I'm thinking of moving abroad, particularly as I speak fluent English and fluent German and French as well. I agree it's a shame that people like myself feel they have to move abroad. But I fall into a pattern that started in 1945. The more Jewish or Zionist you are, the more you are prone to live abroad. So we have negative selection.

Regarding the issue of finding a Jewish partner, that's my problem too. I'm 24 years old, healthy, and have two degrees, and yet I'm not capable of finding a person with whom I could share this kind of life. I don't think it's going to happen here – I'm not even waiting for it. It makes me feel all the more that I should probably emigrate.

I'm actually pessimistic about the future of this community. This whole narrative about the Jewish revival is sort of our internal propaganda which helps us to be more optimistic regardless of all our problems. We're already mixed. I have non-Jews in my family while many others have it even worse. Most of the people are only one-quarter Jews who just want to cherish their grandparents' tradition. So one more step and they will not even be eligible to go on Taglit because you must be at least one-quarter Jewish. So I think it will become more watered down. I'm sceptical but I hope I'm wrong.

As for the hidden Jews, many are not even conscious of their backgrounds. Now there are grandchildren of these post-war Jews who have assimilated and one generation onwards they will only be one-eighth Jews. The children of the Third Generation will be mostly one-eighth Jews. So even if we have thousands of hidden Jews, in the coming years, that will become irrelevant.

Regarding Taglit, I'm a Taglit patriot. I was a *madrich* and went on Taglit twice. I'm involved with post-Taglit activities. Besides I'm a Zionist, and very happy there is this option on the table for Polish Jews. They can build up their Jewish identity in an authentic way which is connected with the land of Israel.

There is an issue with documents. Many people say they have a Jewish background but they cannot prove it. That's a huge problem here because people can abuse this situation and I'm sure many do. But the nice thing about Taglit is that you have to prove your birthright. So people who have been on Taglit surely have some Jewish lineage.

Since Taglit was started in 2001-2002, we already have a pool of 600 Taglit alumni in Poland and the number keeps growing. They have proven their background with documents and are therefore eligible to become Israeli citizens and are encouraged to convert.

So, if we are looking for any hope, then a post-Taglit alumni network is like a beacon. All kinds of people go to Taglit – the whole spectrum of society – rich, poor, big cities, small cities. And I would not usually meet these people because I live in a Warsaw bubble. So it helps build up the unity of the Polish-Jewish community. I'm also very much into the activities of the Jewish Agency.

Taglit-Birthright in our very secular post-Communist community plays the role of an entrance ritual – something like a secular Bar Mitzvah for Polish Jews. Everyone is welcome to all kinds of programs like *Minyanim*. Most Taglit participants know nothing. But going to Taglit encourages and empowers them to become involved in activities.

ACKNOWLEDGEMENTS

I owe an immense debt to all the interviewees who agreed to be profiled in this book. In many cases it was a challenging experience for them, and quite often proved to be painful as deep-seated memories and emotions were brought to the surface. Their stories will undoubtedly shed more light on their country's history as well as that of contemporary Polish Jewry.

My journey began with initial conversations with outstanding scholars of Polish Jewry as well as public figures in Poland. Dr Francois Guesnet, Professor Antony Polonsky, Stanisław Krajewski, Konstanty Gebert, Helena Datner and Poland's Chief Rabbi Michael Schudrich convinced me that a work exploring the hidden identities of Polish Jews was both feasible and worthy. I am grateful for their encouragement and insights.

The Polin Museum of the History of Polish Jews, which has quickly emerged as one of Poland's leading cultural institutions, provided a supportive base in Warsaw to conduct interviews. Joanna Król and Albert Stankowski suggested contacts and assisted my work with the museum's letter of recommendation.

In Warsaw, Aleksandra (Ola) Kopystyńska and Zofia Kamionowska of the Association of Children of the Holocaust enabled me to work in their offices while interviewing members of the Association. Rabbi Gil Nativ of Beit Warszawa welcomed me to his congregation while Monika Elliott, Karina Sokołowska and Agata Rakowiecka of the Jewish Community Centre helped me to connect with various interviewees from their growing membership network.

Jonathan Ornstein, the director of the Jewish Community Centre in Kraków, along with Anna Gulińska, the programming director, played an invaluable role in offering facilities and contacts in Kraków. They confirmed the widespread view that the JCC has been a key catalyst behind the impressive revival of the Kraków Jewish community.

The assistance provided by two individuals in Wrocław transformed a difficult start into a productive visit. Irena Gaweł, head of the Wrocław branch of the Association of Children of the Holocaust, and Jan Kirschenbaum, a local community activist, ensured that excellent interviews took place with members of the three generations. Jan also played a crucial role as an interpreter.

Without skilled Polish interpreters, this work would have been impossible to carry out. I am therefore indebted to Anna Geller, Marzena Szymańska-Błotnicka and Zuzanna Kołodziejska-Smagała in Warsaw. Zuzanna went beyond the bounds of interpreting by doubling up as a translator – whenever necessary. In London, Marta Dziurosz was always available to assist me with translation and interpretation of the highest professional standards.

Over the years, I have often enjoyed the warm hospitality and stimulating conversation of the Gutkowski family in Warsaw. Ania, Piotr and Krzysztof have ensured that my Warsaw trips were not only productive, but also memorable. Their knowledge and contacts in the Jewish community of Warsaw opened doors that might otherwise have remained closed.

In a variety of ways, I was fortunate to have the generous assistance of people based in London, Sweden, the United States, Portugal, Israel and throughout Poland. They include Marta Ansilewska, Rabbi David Basok, Rabbi Haim Beliak, Rabbi Jonah Bookstein, Lena Bergman, Ora Dresner, Rabbi Yehoshua Ellis, Katie Forrester, Michał Galas, Edyta Gawron, Jan Gebert, Michael Geller, Mariana Katzarova, Jerzy Kichler, Kamil Kijek, Jan Lorenz, Željka Marošević, Dr Joanna Nalewajko-Kulik, Elena Piatok, Anat Plocker, Moshe Rosman, Leo (Poldek) Sobel, Aleksander Sołtysik and Malwina Tuchendler.

My friend and colleague in London, Judah Passow, shared the extensive technical and practical knowledge he has acquired as the author of several photographic books on Jewish and Israeli themes. He also helped to demystify the mechanics of book publishing.

Lisa Hyde, my editor at Vallentine Mitchell, played a key role in shepherding this work to its publication. Her patience and guidance throughout the production process were invaluable.

Many thanks to my son, Daniel Cohen, for the encouraging chats, his helpfulness and, as ever, his extraordinary knowledge.

Working closely over a lengthy period with my photographer, Witold (Witek) Krassowski, proved to be a tremendous education in the art and practice of photography. Witek was always prepared to travel great distances to ensure that excellent photographs would accompany the profiles. He is a gifted artist and I will be eternally grateful for his early faith and readiness to collaborate on this project.

And finally, much credit must go to Rivkie Fried, my wife and co-pilot. This work has benefited greatly from her excellent editorial skills and thoughtful advice.